LOGOS AND POWER IN
ISOCRATES AND ARISTOTLE

Studies in Rhetoric/Communication
Thomas W. Benson, Series Editor

LOGOS AND POWER IN ISOCRATES AND ARISTOTLE

EKATERINA V. HASKINS

© 2004 University of South Carolina

Cloth edition published by the University of South Carolina Press, 2004
Paperback edition published in Columbia, South Carolina,
by the University of South Carolina Press, 2009

www.sc.edu/uscpress

Manufactured in the United States of America

19 18 17 16 15 14 13 12 11 10   10 9 8 7 6 5 4 3 2 1

Library of Congress Cataloging-in-Publication Data

Haskins, Ekaterina V., 1969–
  Logos and power in Isocrates and Aristotle / Ekaterina V. Haskins.
    p. cm. — (Studies in rhetoric/communication)
  Includes bibliographical references and index.
    ISBN 1-57003-526-1 (cloth : alk. paper)
  1. Isocrates—Criticism and interpretation. 2. Speeches, addresses, etc., Greek—History and criticism. 3. Aristotle. Rhetoric. 4. Rhetoric, Ancient. 5. Oratory, Ancient. I. Title. II. Series.
  PA4218.H37 2004
  885'.01—dc22

2003021065

Chapter one is a revision of the author's article "Rhetoric between Orality and Literacy: Cultural Memory and Performance in Isocrates and Aristotle," *Quarterly Journal of Speech* 87 (2001): 158–78, and is included here courtesy of the National Communication Association. An earlier version of chapter two appeared as "*Mimesis* between Poetics and Rhetoric: Performance Culture and Civic Education in Plato, Isocrates, and Aristotle," *Rhetoric Society Quarterly* 30 (2000): 7–33, and is adapted here by permission of the Rhetoric Society of America. Parts of chapter five originally appeared in "Orality, Literacy, and Isocrates' Political Aesthetics," in *Rhetoric, the Polis, and the Global Village: Selected Papers from the 1998 Thirtieth Anniversary Rhetoric Society of America Conference,* ed. C. Jan Swearingen and Dave Pruett. They are included here courtesy of Lawrence Erlbaum Associates.

ISBN: 978-1-57003-873-0 (pbk)

In memory of Michael Calvin McGee

CONTENTS

Series Editor's Preface | ix
Acknowledgments | xi
Editions, Translations, and Citation Conventions | xiii

Introduction | 1

One
Between Orality and Literacy | 10

Two
Between Poetics and Rhetoric | 31

Three
Between *Kairos* and Genre | 57

Four
Between Identification and Persuasion | 80

Five
Between Social Permanence and Social Change | 108

Six
Classical Rhetorics and the Future of Democratic Education | 130

Notes | 137
Bibliography | 149
Index | 163

SERIES EDITOR'S PREFACE

In *Logos and Power in Isocrates and Aristotle,* Ekaterina V. Haskins compares and contrasts the rhetorical theories of Isocrates and Aristotle. In rejecting some earlier readings of Isocrates that depicted him as a mere practitioner and, worse, read his work through the lens of Aristotelian rhetorical theory, Haskins treats both writers as rhetorical theorists. In the process she illuminates both authors in fresh and interesting readings that seek to promote a "performatively grounded notion of human agency" and a "socially productive approach to rhetoric." Haskins challenges Aristotelian notions of discursive agency, the role of ethics in deliberation, the scope of traditional rhetorical genres, and the nature of the audience. Haskins asserts that rhetorical theory and rhetorical education are necessarily political, and she aligns her own project with those who ask not "what is rhetoric?" but "what can a rhetoric be?"

Haskins develops her consideration of Isocrates and Aristotle in chapters on orality/literacy, poetic/rhetoric, *kairos*/genre, identification/persuasion, and social change/social permanence. These frames, with Isocrates typically more on the left and Aristotle more on the right of each pairing, create the ground for analysis that is both historically informative and theoretically provocative.

THOMAS W. BENSON

ACKNOWLEDGMENTS

I would like to thank the College of Arts and Sciences at Boston College for its generous support of this project through research incentive grants, undergraduate research assistantships, and a faculty fellowship in the fall semester of 2002. This book began as a doctoral dissertation written at the University of Iowa in 1998–99. As I was writing the early version of the thesis, the university housed an interdisciplinary symposium on Isocrates and civic education. I am grateful to my teachers David Depew and Takis Poulakos, the organizers of the symposium, for inviting me to participate. The experience of seeing the same topics debated in real time by scholars from across the humanities inspired this book's interdisciplinary approach. Although my treatment of Isocrates and Aristotle bears an imprint of the disciplines of rhetoric and communication, many of the issues explored in this book were also raised and illuminated by philosophers, ancient historians, and classical philologists.

In the process of revising this book, I have benefited from encouragement and constructive feedback from Barry Blose, my editor at the University of South Carolina Press, and from two reviewers, whose vigilance and criticisms have been most valuable.

Last but not least, I owe a hefty debt of gratitude to my graduate mentor, Michael Calvin McGee, whose intellectual and pedagogical commitment to rhetoric as a critical practice inspired me to pursue this project in the first place. Sadly, Michael died not long before the book was completed. I have dedicated it to his memory.

EDITIONS, TRANSLATIONS, AND CITATION CONVENTIONS

I rely primarily on the Loeb Classics Series for Greek citations of Isocrates, Aristotle, and Plato. For Greek citations of Gorgias, I am using the edition of *Die Fragmente der Vorsokratiker,* by Diels and Kranz (1952). Translations of Isocrates are by David C. Mirhady and Yun Lee Too (with the exception of *On the Peace, Panathenaicus,* and *Panegyricus,* for which I use the Loeb edition's translations). I use George A. Kennedy's (1991) translation of Aristotle's *Rhetoric.* Translation of Gorgias's "Encomium of Helen" is taken from Rosamund Kent Sprague's *Older Sophists.* In citing Isocrates, I use the paragraph numbering employed by current editions and translations. In quoting Aristotle, I use Bekker line numbers.

In most cases requiring the use of third-person personal and possessive pronouns, I have avoided gender-specific pronouns. However, when describing matters pertaining to ancient Greek culture and oratory, I have used the masculine pronoun to reflect the historical conditions of public speechmaking in the fifth and fourth centuries B.C.E. On the issue of women's voices in ancient Greek literature and society, see André Lardinois and Laura McClure 2001.

LOGOS AND POWER IN
ISOCRATES AND ARISTOTLE

INTRODUCTION

To devote equal attention to Isocrates and Aristotle in a book-length study may strike some as an odd enterprise. As one of the premier philosophers of the Western tradition, Aristotle articulated many of the issues that still animate scholarly debates in a variety of humanistic disciplines. Despite his considerable repute in antiquity and the Renaissance, Isocrates, by contrast, became a marginal figure in the intellectual history of classical Athens. In disciplinary histories of philosophy and rhetoric, too, Isocrates occupies a much less illustrious place than Aristotle. Indeed, our understanding of the very terms "philosophy" and "rhetoric" is largely beholden to the legacy of Plato's Academy and Aristotle's Lyceum.[1]

To probe the connection between Isocrates and Aristotle, then, is to invite a reconsideration of Isocrates within intellectual history in general and the history of rhetoric in particular. There are good reasons to do so. Doxographic tradition and textual evidence suggest that Isocrates and his younger contemporary were intellectual rivals. Ancient biographies indicate that Aristotle probably received a well-rounded "liberal education" from the school of Isocrates before joining Plato's Academy. Anton-Hermann Chroust proposes that it was thanks to his sojourn at Isocrates' school that Aristotle's "first literary effort was concerned with rhetoric, and that at a relatively early stage of his 'academic career,' he was considered fully qualified to take issue with Isocrates' particular brand of rhetoric and, hence, was entrusted with offering in the Academy a full-fledged independent 'course of lectures' on rhetoric" (1973, 102).

In Cicero's portrayal, however, Aristotle's lectures on rhetoric reduced his rival to a self-indulgent stylist: "When Aristotle observed that Isocrates succeeded in obtaining a distinguished set of pupils by means of abandoning legal and political subjects and devoting his discourses to empty elegance of style, he himself suddenly altered almost the whole of his system of training, and quoted a line from *Philoctetes* with a slight modification: the hero in the tragedy said that it was a disgrace for him to keep silent and suffer barbarians to speak, but Aristotle put it 'suffer Isocrates to speak'" (*De Oratore* 3:141). Although Cicero's report may be inaccurate, from the perspective of the history of rhetorical theory, Aristotle appears to have had the last word. Not only was Isocrates' contribution to the theory of persuasive discourse overshadowed by Aristotle's

Art of Rhetoric, but the very "foundational" story, and hence the *telos* of the art of rhetoric (the discovery of available means of persuasion), has been codified, it seems, exclusively by means of Aristotle's pronouncements about it.[2] Judged against Aristotle's systematic analysis of the means of persuasion, rhetorical genres, and stylistic devices, Isocrates emerges merely as a teacher of oratory, and his record reveals a mixed bag of display speeches, political pamphlets, and addresses to and on behalf of powerful patrons.

The goal of this book, in part, is to reassert Isocrates' rhetorical practice and the vision of discourse it promotes as a worthy rival, rather than a mere precursor, of Aristotle's *Rhetoric*. Instead of assimilating Isocrates' pedagogical and political writings to an ostensibly unified Aristotelian theory of rhetoric, I emphasize the discontinuity between these two classical paradigms.[3] Isocrates' resistance to codification of rhetorical knowledge had been often taken as a sign of a theoretically feeble, albeit vastly successful, educational program. For example, Friedrich Solmsen's landmark essay "The Aristotelian Tradition in Ancient Rhetoric" (1941) bemoans the fact that in regard to Isocrates, "we lack a starting point of the same solidity and authenticity as Aristotle's three books on rhetoric" (36). Isocrates was thus cast as a discursive practitioner whose advice on speechmaking and writing was absorbed, corrected, and systematized by Aristotle's *technē* (productive art). As Aristotle remarked on professing eloquence by example (*Sophistical Refutations* 183b36–184a8), it was similar to teaching shoe making by displaying specimens of various kinds of shoes.

On the other hand, scholars have attempted to reconstruct Isocrates' own theory of discourse by extracting from his writings a set of principles or criteria that can qualify as an implicit theory of rhetoric (e.g., Gaines 1990, Papillon 1995, Rummel 1979). These efforts are a welcome change from a dichotomy of theory and practice, according to which only formal treatises such as Aristotle's *Rhetoric* can qualify as theory.[4] The history of rhetorical theory indeed would be little more but a long footnote to Aristotle if scholars disregarded those compositions that lie "between the non-theoretical texts of Homer and the formal rhetorical theory of Plato and Aristotle" (Schiappa 1999, 110).

Isocrates' textual record displays enough self-reflexivity and attention to the rules of composition and audience adaptation to warrant the label of rhetorical theory, the latter understood as a combination of both preceptive and paradigmatic elements (see Leff 1986, Papillon 1995). This study, however, seeks not only to reconstruct such a theory but also to highlight the manner in which Isocrates ensures the pedagogical and political relevance of his prose. I argue that Isocrates accents his role as an agent of knowledge to oppose precisely the sort of theoretical detachment one finds in the intellectual projects of Plato's Academy and Aristotle's Lyceum.[5]

My purpose, therefore, is not simply to reevaluate Isocrates' contribution to the history of rhetoric. I provide a reading that compares and contrasts the texts of Isocrates and Aristotle in order to describe a more performatively grounded notion of human agency and a more socially productive approach to rhetoric than can be supported by Aristotle's writings alone. My argument, then, promotes a historically grounded yet noncanonical conception of human agency and rhetorical performance more associated with Isocrates than Aristotle.

The words "logos" and "power" in the title of this book designate the twin forces at the nexus of which human agency is articulated and exercised. I argue that despite Aristotle's interest in rhetoric as *technē,* his understanding of language and performance places rhetoric and its power outside the domain of ethical and political deliberation, thus asserting an extralinguistic nature of human agency. Isocrates, on the other hand, promotes rhetoric as a discourse that constitutes both culture and human agency. Isocratean prose underscores the performative—that is, active and continually born anew—quality of human agency.

This orientation toward the performative conception of discourse resonates with a rising scholarly attention to critical social aspects of a broad range of aesthetic texts, ranging from artistic prose to film to mass spectacle. Isocrates' aesthetically influential political rhetoric, his *logos politikos,* offers a compelling classical paradigm for contemporary scholars of public discourse who wish to theorize performances that flourish beyond the scope of traditional genres of political address. Whereas Aristotle provides a convenient triumvirate of rhetorical genres and a fixed vision of the rhetorical audience, Isocrates articulates a more expansive and fertile understanding of the roles of the author, the audience, and the occasion. Isocratean performance aestheticizes public address in a way that draws upon and resonates with other discourses of Greek culture, while Aristotle divorces rhetoric from the cultural influence of Greek poetry and drama.

Indeed, I would like to argue that Isocrates shuns the term *rhētorikē* and instead chooses the word *philosophia* to describe what he professes to defend: a broad conception of discursive education over and against a narrow Platonic-Aristotelian notion of rhetoric. Contemporary audiences outside the academic circle of rhetorical studies and composition should sympathize with the impulse to eschew the label "rhetoric," for even today the word is often invoked to describe manipulation and empty verbiage. The telltale scarcity of *rhētorikē* in Isocrates' vocabulary can be therefore read as a tactical maneuver in a polemic between rival intellectual movements in Athens of the fourth century B.C.E. By refusing to identify the object of his pedagogy and writing as rhetoric, Isocrates declines to play the game of status and marginality on Plato's terms (see Hariman 1995).⁶

In the intellectual discourse of the twentieth century, the term "rhetoric" underwent substantive revision. No longer universally identified as a mere productive art in the service of "higher" disciplines (such as political science and philosophy), it now refers both to social practices that shape individuals into collectivities and critical-theoretical reflection about these social practices. Rather than answer the "foundationalist" question, What is rhetoric? contemporary rhetorical theory responds to the question, What can a rhetoric be? In so doing, rhetorical theorists not only recognize the cultural specificity of rhetoric as a form of social practice but also acknowledge the political character of theorizing itself.⁷

Besides its participation in the contemporary theoretical debate over the function and scope of rhetoric, this study also addresses enduring pedagogical issues facing the modern university. Isocrates and Aristotle were both highly influential educators in fourth-century B.C.E. Athens, one as the founder and head of a successful school of *logōn paideia,* the other as the founder of the Lyceum, a more theoretically oriented institution. Isocrates could be viewed as the first advocate of what we now call "liberal education"; his educational program presented rhetoric as a way of training students to be active citizens. By making artful discourse integral to culture and politics, Isocrates promoted an idea that education and civic life are inseparable. Aristotle, on the other hand, developed a sophisticated conceptual apparatus to describe various fields of knowledge, thus removing intellectual pursuits from the affairs of the state. Within this conceptual apparatus, rhetoric as a detailed account of persuasive means was allotted a minor part.

Today, in spite of efforts to provide students with a comprehensive liberal education, modern university curricula continue to operate under the Aristotelian assumption of disinterested knowledge. Such an orientation is most apparent in the field of rhetoric and composition instruction, in which "rhetoric," understood in Aristotelian terms as lacking a subject matter, plays a merely instrumental, technical role. This book, then, is partly an inquiry into Aristotle's motives for the separation of education of a citizen from rhetorical performance. This separation becomes more intelligible if we take into account Isocrates' intense advocacy of political discourse as a vehicle and model of citizen education (*paideia*).

Theories, whether ancient or modern, are not produced in a vacuum, nor do they find their way into the educational and political practices by sheer chance. When casting Isocrates and Aristotle as opponents in a debate over what arts of discourse can and should be, I am also pulling into the orbit of my argument their predecessors and contemporaries as well as conflicting modern interpretations of classical texts. The terms I employ (e.g., "rhetoric," "philosophy," "performance," "agency," "identity") are of interdisciplinary derivation and bring with them a set of unresolved historical and theoretical issues. Classical philologists, philosophers, historians of rhetoric, and scholars of communication have different disciplinary histories and assumptions as well as distinct agendas within the modern university. But it is precisely the critical momentum generated by overlapping controversies in different humanistic disciplines that may propel the present state of knowledge about classical antiquity. Such an approach, I believe, enables us to go beyond the narrowness of the purely content-based method displayed by traditional histories of rhetoric and much philosophical and literary commentary. It also aids in making classical rhetorics relevant to today's social and educational practices.

It is not my purpose, however, to produce an exhaustive account of all the cultural influences on and the historical ramifications of the statements made by or on behalf of Isocrates and Aristotle. In the spirit of the "hermeneutics of suspicion," I do not hold that there is, or can be, only one grand narrative—in this case about the history of rhetoric and philosophy—waiting to be told. On examining the writings of Isocrates and Aristotle, I do not seek to set the historical record straight once and for all; rather, my goal is to theorize the conditions of possibility for civic performance and human agency that emerge from a self-reflective reading of classical texts.

Instead of constructing a chronologically arranged narrative of progress or degeneration, my argument follows a thematic pattern. Accordingly, Isocrates and Aristotle (and to some extent Plato) are positioned as opponents within five different yet overlapping interpretive frames:

Orality	Literacy
Poetic	Rhetoric
Kairos	Genre
Identification	Persuasion
Social change	Social permanence

The matrix of the five dialectical pairs above designates not a set of logical opposites but poles of a continuum. The right-hand categories represent a vision of a highly disciplined rhetoric in the sense of both academic disciplinarity and the social role played by discourse. Such rhetoric is more like a neutral tool than an identity-shaping performance. The left-hand column encapsulates a vision of rhetoric as an ever-evolving social performance, rife with ambivalent ethical and political tendencies. My argument is, roughly, that Aristotle displays both possibilities but gravitates toward the stability implicit in the right-hand categories. He thus drastically limits the constitutive potential of rhetoric by making it subordinate to putatively extrarhetorical knowledge (*epistēmē*) and practical wisdom (*phronēsis*). Isocrates, on the other hand, though avoiding disclosure of the negative side of rhetoric's constitutive power, nevertheless develops a strong version of the performative vision.

Each of the five dialectical pairs provides a separate terministic lens for individual chapters. Thanks to the work of Eric Havelock and Walter Ong, the first pair, orality and literacy, is now recognized by both classical philologists and historians of rhetoric as a productive site for questioning the presumptions underlying traditional principles of rhetoric. So-called secondary orality, augmented by mass media, embodies a tension between the oral and the literate rationalities operating in social discourse. We can no longer view rhetoric (written, spoken, or visual) as implementation of discursive rules inscribed in canonical textbooks. Reflecting on the role of radio in "rediscovery of rhetoric," Havelock notes the "myth-making" quality of the oral discourse backed up by written message (1986, 30–31). The contemporary situation can be seen, in fact, as somewhat similar to that of the late fifth century B.C.E. in Greece, where oral composition and performance of the epic were being replaced by a combination of writing and recitation while orality survived in most forms of public life, especially drama and oratory.

The emergence of rhetoric as a discipline, as distinct from an everyday practice, in the fourth century B.C.E. is typically associated with the rise of literacy and with the "rationalization" of discourse that attended literacy. However, after Eric Havelock's *Preface to Plato, The Literate Revolution in Greece,* and "The Linguistic Task of the Presocratics" had made this point, many studies examining the surprising tenacity of oral practices in a "literate" culture began to appear. This newer approach avoids the determinism of earlier theories of orality and instead investigates the gray area between orality and literacy.

Abiding by this situated approach, I intend to show how Isocrates and Aristotle, both of whom were literate and composed for reading audiences, employ literacy to different ends. Isocrates uses prose writing to construct an identity for himself while preserving the performative orientation of the oral tradition. Like Isocrates, Aristotle draws upon the resources of the oral culture, especially in his use of *endoxa* (common or received opinions), in his arguments. But he subverts performativity in order to extract from poetic and rhetorical discourse its propositional content.

The second chapter, framed by the terms "poetics" and "rhetoric," continues to inquire into the divergent ways Isocrates and Aristotle appropriate the mythopoetic tradition. In this chapter, however, the focus shifts from the contextual issue of orality and literacy to the question of *mimēsis* (imitation, representation). I argue that Isocratean civic education pivots on a performative understanding of *mimēsis* that emphasizes the continuity between *paideia* of the poetic tradition and civic training. Building on the longstanding cultural association between speech and conduct, Isocrates insists that training in eloquence is also training in moral action. In this light, *mimēsis* is conceived as both the means and the end of education, which for Isocrates continues throughout one's life.

In this way, Isocrates counters Platonic efforts to denigrate poetic *paideia* as a form of mass hypnosis. Plato's attack on poetry and poets is addressed at length in this chapter in order to set in sharper relief Isocratean and Aristotelian approaches to the role of *mimēsis*. As distinct from Isocrates, Aristotle responds to Plato's indictments of poetry by separating the imitative *mimēsis* typical of performance-based culture from *mimēsis* as representation. He assigns a higher value to the latter type because it is more conducive to intellectual learning and the life of contemplative leisure. Consequently, Aristotle produces a hierarchy of *mimēsis* in which the performative type figures as either a primitive stage in the development of poetic craft or as a stylistic embellishment that is parasitic upon the representational function of plots and rhetorical proofs. By stressing the centrality of the plot and discounting the performative components of tragic drama, Aristotle is able to claim poetry as a more philosophical discourse than history. As distinct from drama as an instrument of philosophical illumination, rhetorical performance exposes the philosophical orator to exigencies of audience and occasion, which makes rhetoric a lesser of the two verbal *technai*. Whereas Isocrates sought to strengthen the bond between poetic performance and political discourse, Aristotle's systematic treatment not only separated them into two distinct spheres but also imposed formal and substantive restrictions on poetry and rhetoric.

Chapter 3 argues that the splitting of rhetoric into three genres in Aristotle's *Rhetoric* is a strategy to restrict political invention made possible by the practice of oratory in Athenian democracy. Although Aristotle's notion of genre is rich enough to imply not only a complex of thematic and stylistic elements but also a situation (*kairos*) in which they are deployed, the focus on propriety of linguistic expression assumes an extrarhetorical nature of rhetorical situations. Specifically, I address how Aristotle's essentializing of subject matter appropriate for each genre downplays the politically inventive capacity of performance. In this generic scheme, any improvisation is thus an "excess" added to the foundation of required elements.

In the prose of Isocrates, on the other hand, one finds a heterogeneous mix of "generic" features precisely because Isocrates does not bind his performance to any fixed occasion. Instead, he defines *kairos* as the right moment to deploy one's discursive skills and cultural knowledge. This does not mean that a speech or a written address is conjured ex nihilo, for the response to a situation is crafted out of fragments of other discourses with which the speaker gains familiarity through extensive training and political practice. It is this "intertextual" stitching of previously uttered speech that marks Isocrates' strategy as similar to that of the oral rhapsodes of the Greek poetic tradition. His method of composition is also congenial to Bakhtin's idea of continuity between ordinary and literary discourse as expressed by his notion of "speech genres." Speech genres, unlike the ritualistic and ostensibly timeless notion of rhetorical genre, presuppose social heterogeneity of stylistic and thematic features as well as their subordination to the author's distinct position in the chain of communication. Instead of simply occupying a subject position in a thematically and stylistically determined utterance, the author reaccentuates others' discourses to answer the challenge of a *kairos*.

The issue of generic propriety versus strategic response to a situation leads me to a corresponding problem of the rhetorical audience. In chapter 4, accordingly, I argue that Isocrates articulates an expansive, as opposed to a generically constrained, notion of audience both explicitly and implicitly. He does so explicitly in his "Hymn to Logos." But his pamphlets and epistles also manifest a grasp of what contemporary rhetorical scholarship, following Kenneth Burke, calls *identification*. Rather than matching persuasive strategies to an a priori given audience, as Aristotle recommends in the *Rhetoric,* Isocrates hails his audience into existence.

Isocrates' lifelong rhetorical pursuit of Panhellenic unity through the sharing of culture (*paideia*) is a striking counterpart of Aristotle's own Panhellenism. Whereas Isocrates conceives of culture discursively, as the effect of many persuasive *logoi,* Aristotle considers cultural traits simply innate. Although Isocrates and Aristotle share a commitment to an expansionist foreign policy, Isocrates' prose seems a better guide if we wish to grasp a rhetorically crafted unity, whether this unity is being created for benign or malevolent political purposes.

Aristotle's view of the audience as given also poses a problem for contemporary scholars of public discourse who wish to give "rhetorical knowledge" and "rhetorical audience" important parts in our conception of the political. However, by transforming the public opinion (*doxa*) of his day into the means of persuasion, Aristotle reifies rhetorical knowledge, makes it natural. The functions of the rhetor and the audience are thus reduced, respectively, to repetition and recognition of rhetorical knowledge embedded in enthymemes. I propose that this model of rhetorical transaction allows Aristotle to justify a restricted participation in politics by the *demos* and thereby to overcome the confusion of political roles peculiar to democracy and other "deviant" political regimes. Aristotle's flattening out of performative context of rhetorical utterance eliminates contingencies of identification, disengaging the constitutive power of logos from the domain of rhetoric.

My interpretation of theories of discourse in Isocrates and Aristotle brings me to a final question embedded in the title of chapter 5, "social change" and "social permanence": how do these theories illuminate or facilitate today's academic disputes over the goals and function of rhetoric in education and culture? The argument proceeds by way of discussing the terms for speech and power in their classical contexts as well as their contemporary appropriations. Instead of seeking a perfect match between ancient discourses and modern theories, I argue, in the spirit of Richard Rorty, for an "ironic" perspective as a self-critical alternative to the transcendental strategies of philosophical rhetoricians and social theorists.

I conclude by pondering the ramifications of applying "classical" theories of rhetoric to contemporary discursive education. Considering a vastly different context of the technologized public culture and the difficult position of the university as an institution responsible for democratic education, I offer a sketch of what Isocratean *paideia* for the future might look like. Rather than advocating a particular content of this education, this sketch presents a general approach to the roles that teachers, students, and texts play in a cultivation of cultural knowledge and political identity.

One

BETWEEN ORALITY AND LITERACY

In the story of rhetoric's origins and blossoming, the transition from oral modes of communication to writing is assigned one of the leading parts. "Disciplinary" accounts of the emergence of rhetoric are virtually unanimous in the claim that rhetoric as an art becomes possible only with systematic description of its principles.[1] In particular, it is only thanks to writing, especially prose writing of the late fourth century B.C.E., that rhetoric seems to achieve its full potential as a "self-conscious manipulation" of the author's medium (Cole 1991, ix) by means of which "one can ultimately view alternative forms of expression as tactical options in seeking to communicate effectively" (Johnstone 1996a, 6). These formulations suggest that the evolution of reflection about speech was destined, thanks to the onset of "literacy" in the fourth century B.C.E., to culminate in Aristotle's explicit theory of rhetoric.[2] On this reading, pronouncements about the power of logos before Aristotle are but a series of incompletely articulated claims that awaited a systematic treatment one finds in Aristotle's treatise.[3]

I suggest instead that the consequences of the "literate revolution" for reflection about language and its power must be reconsidered in light of the surprising survival of "oral" tradition within the literary practices of philosophers and rhetoricians. The respective approaches of Isocrates and Aristotle to discourse, performance, and pedagogy are very much influenced by their different reactions to the emerging technology of writing. With a plethora of scholarship spanning the last twenty-five years at their disposal, classical rhetoricians and philologists now recognize orality and literacy not as mutually exclusive poles but as complementary forces. Many studies have sought to amend Eric Havelock's overly deterministic position, according to which the shift from oral to literate modes of communication in ancient Greece caused a drastic transformation in mental habits leading to the phenomenon of the Greek Enlightenment. As summarized by John Halverson (1992), Havelock's theory holds that "the creation of the Greek alphabet (and it alone) was able to bring about widespread literacy, which in turn radically and permanently transformed human consciousness. Alphabetic literacy enabled thought to transcend the limitations of 'oral mind,' represented by Homer, to become the instrument of logic, philosophy and science" (148). Scholars now examine the persistence of orality in what previously had been considered a uniformly "literate" culture and emphasize the *uses* of literacy in a concrete historical cultural context.[4] Accordingly, I stress the gray area between orality and literacy in order to show how Isocrates and Aristotle chart two divergent ways of textualizing rhetorical practice in a "literate" age that remains in many ways oral.

When perceived through Aristotle's conceptual lens, rhetoric is akin to an instrument. It is an arsenal of persuasive means that are external to rhetors and their historical situations. Isocrates' extant writings do not methodically specify the governing rules of rhetoric, but in his self-reflexive and politically charged prose, he assigns discourse a socially constitutive, not merely instrumental, function. To appreciate the difference between Isocratean and Aristotelian understandings of logos and human agency, we must first reconsider the traditional opposition between "mythopoetic" and "rational" notions of speech, the former typically attributed to oral cultures and the latter to literate. The Isocratean use of literacy transforms the mythopoetic logos into a discourse that engenders, rather than merely serves, the rhetor's political identity. Aristotle, on the other hand, subverts oral aspects of his linguistic resources in order to emphasize the logos that at once reflects purpose and stability of the ordered cosmos and serves as a conduit of extralinguistic content.

Between Mythopoetic and Rational Reflection

The history of classical rhetoric has been scripted as a tale of cultural and technological progress. Transition from a mythical to rational worldview as a result of increased literacy appears no less significant to the birth of rhetoric than to the emergence of abstract thought itself. As the story goes, the world of Greek gods—personified arbitrary forces of nature—gave way to abstract modes of thinking, thus allowing an individual to make judgments about causes and effects without the crutches of myth.[5] This trajectory, however, presents too crude a picture of "rationality" and too simplistic an account of the cultural and social function of myth. Rationality does not necessarily go hand in hand with the categorical slicing of the phenomenal world, and myth is not mere poeticized fiction. A different approach to mythical and rational consciousness calls for viewing *muthos* and logos not as polarized states of culture but as complementary linguistic resources of collective memory and critical reflection (Jarratt 1991; Buxton 1999). With this approach in mind, then, we may reevaluate the mythical heritage of the fourth-century theories of Isocrates and Aristotle.

Archaic Greek culture did not distinguish between the "mythical" and the "real" in a religious ritual, prophetic utterance, or poetic performance. Indeed, the value of these types of speech stemmed from their claim to truthfulness. In archaic usage, however, the word for "truth," *alētheia,* did not designate the unassailable verity of an idea separated from its material symbol. It signified the power of memory over forgetting. As Egbert Bakker (1993) explains,

> It is the Muse, an external personification of mental faculties like memory and imagination in the psychology and poetics of archaic Greece, who stands at the basis of activation and remembrance in the poet's mind and who in that capacity is a safeguard against forgetfulness, and eventually absence and death. What is activated is saved from *Lēthē* (Forgetting) and is thus *a-lēthēs* (free from *Lēthē*), an adjective that in later Greek comes to mean "true." The truth of epic tradition, however, is very far removed from the philosopher's notion of true and false statements: what is true in the epic tradition is what is active and thereby "present" or easily activated and thereby "near." (14–15)

In an oral setting, epic and religious poetry served as chief vehicles of propagation of cultural beliefs and norms of conduct. The absence of our traditional split between fictional and real resulted from another seeming lack of differentiation: speech was viewed not in terms of its thematic substance and a corresponding style of expression but in terms of its efficacy. For example, Marcel Detienne (1996) points to several mythical characters whose power to "realize" or "accomplish" is celebrated by the tragedians of the fifth century: "When Hermes plays the part of an inspired poet who, with skill and knowledge, can draw harmonious sounds from the lyre, far from pronouncing 'vain, useless' words, he 'realizes' the immortal gods and the dark earth" (71). By contrast, Cassandra, a truthful prophetess who does not wish to deceive, "seems capable of producing only 'vain' (*akranta*) or even 'untrustworthy' words" (77).

The opposition between powerful and weak words obtains in the realm of mortals as well (at least those who make up the human cast of the Homeric epics). As Richard Martin's (1989) study of implicit speech typology in the *Iliad* suggests, the effect of the spoken word was measured according to its power to influence action and collective memory. For example, the Homeric hero Achilles, admitting that his boasting had little effect, says, "A vain epos I tossed forth that day" (qtd. in Martin 1989, 28). Conversely, the speech that commands recognition and brings about a desired action becomes "winged"; such "winged words" contrast with "vain" utterances both in their immediate effect and lasting quality (ibid., 36–37).

Still, the question remains: what, in addition to its perceived power, enables poetic speech to achieve the quality of *alētheia*? Because of poetry's ties to religious ritual, the answer seems simple enough. For Detienne (1996), it is "an act of faith that authenticates the power speech holds over others" (76). "The poet's speech," he claims, "never solicits agreement from its listeners or assent from a social group. . . . It is the attribute and privilege of a social function" (75). Yet however sanctioned or ritualistic poetic speech may be, its impact is still contingent upon the audience's response. Though his conclusions bolster Detienne's observations of the repetitive and sanctioned character of poetic performance in archaic Greece, Bakker (1993) points out that the efficacy of each performance depended on the skill of the rhapsode and the audience's direct involvement in "the performance event" (15). *Alētheia* escapes forgetting thanks to the capacity of a performance to "realize" the mythopoetic life world. At the same time, *alētheia* is closely followed by *lēthē*, since any performance, like Cassandra, is in danger of failing to persuade the listeners.[6]

The culture of poets and prophets conceived of speech as an aesthetically potent, almost magical, social event that activated in the listeners commonly held truths. Even naturalistic cosmology, which marks the emergence of Western rationality, depends greatly on the mythopoetic tradition for its themes and language.[7] Although the written fragments of the Presocratics tend to disengage their thinking about the world from the arbitrariness of Hesiod's "Theogony," their appeal to contemporary audiences is beholden to poetic diction. As Havelock (1983) observed in his analysis of the Presocratics, criticism of the old world of myth, with its anthropomorphic deities and their deeds, does not try to break with the "thought-world of the oral period"; instead, this type of discourse "seeks to alter the direction of a tradition" (236). The linguistic shape of much Presocratic writing is driven by what Kevin Robb (1983) terms an "oralistic" impulse. Robb points to the fragments of Heraclitus to illustrate how "the philosopher's thought . . . was distilled into the form of the traditional saying or aphorism" (198). Among the oralistic devices inherited from the preliterate era, Heraclitus's "persuasive euphony" is essential, however inessential it may seem in the eyes of today's objectivist rationality:

> The inclusion of persuasive euphony as a great philosopher's conscious motive, and the goal to no small part of his professional labor, will be distasteful to some because today it is remote from professional philosopher's training and goals. Truth and clarity are thought to be better served when uncluttered by attention to prose style, and mathematical notation is the purest truth of all. But the philosopher's own complaint is unambiguous; he was forced to compete for an audience with street singers and rhapsodes, masters of aural appeal—no less than the poets of Greece in the persons of their reciters and performers, master artists—and to that competitive end he forged a rare verbal artistry. (199)

Given that philosophers, regardless of the peculiarities of their worldview, had to compete for the audience's minds by appealing to their ears, one might ask if "oralistic" clothing of the utterance is only conveying a "deeper" truth it intended to communicate. Can we speak of a new, nonmythical "content" that is surreptitiously lodged in the familiar and memorable "form"? I suggest that we cannot. To be sure, the cosmic forces that are more inscrutable are replacing anthropomorphic deities of myths and epics. Such is the trajectory of change carried out by thinkers like Xenophanes, Anaxagoras, Heraclitus, and Parmenides (Havelock 1983). However, the "truth" of philosophical statements is wedded to their linguistic expression, with all of its aesthetic and cultural resonance. In this sense, the mythopoetic truth, *alētheia,* which has to do with remembrance through repetitive reenaction, is not opposed to the truth of the cosmic order contemplated and performed by the philosopher.

Oral tradition had not waned by the time the older Sophists arrived on the scene, though the use of writing had increased. Like the Presocratics, the Sophists make good use of culturally embedded attitudes toward speech.[8] In contrast with philosophers, rhetoricians are concerned not so much with the relationship between words and things as with the social function of language.[9] This bifurcation of rational thought about language develops, as Detienne (1996) puts it, "along two major lines: as an instrument of social relations and as a means of knowing reality" (106). Detienne's claim is correct only insofar as "rhetoricians" *emphasize* the former and "philosophers" the latter. The line between the two paths remains blurred, for language as an instrument of thought about reality is derived from its social function.[10] Even as Isocrates follows the former route by adapting the resources of mythopoetic tradition to his rhetorical and political project, his *philosophia* relies on a secularized and practical conception of knowing, and even as Aristotle subordinates his discourse on rhetoric to a distinct epistemology, his own philosophical prose functions rhetorically and politically.

Gorgias, whose reflection on language represents a crucial juncture in the development of so-called rational thought, gives us an image of logos as both a social force and a way, however deficient, of making sense of our world. Though traditionally Gorgias has been classified in opposition to the philosophers, his extant fragments portray him as someone who navigated freely among discursive types now separated into philosophy and sophistry. Positioned on the cusp between orality and literacy, he shares with his philosophical predecessors and the tragedians of the fifth century an ambivalent attitude toward myth and poetry. On the one hand, he distances himself from the oral culture of mythmakers and poets; on the other hand, he strives to harness the sensual and social forcefulness of this past.

This attitude is most apparent in Gorgias's *Encomium of Helen,* which embodies the tension between oralistic culture's nonrational persuasion and the self-reflexive distance aided by the onset of literacy. In the *Helen,* Gorgias at once acknowledges the efficacy of performance of the myth and breaks its spell by revealing the chemistry of oral persuasion. Indeed, he pronounces speech (logos) "a powerful lord (*dunastēs*), which by means of the finest and most invisible body effects the divinest works: it can stop fear and banish grief and create joy and nurture pity" (1972, 8). The personification of the logos as an arbitrary ruler bears resemblance to the mythical narrative casting used by several Presocratics and by the poets of the archaic age. The power of the logos is akin to brute force (*bia,* 12) that moves the hearer in an almost physical way. Yet unlike the Presocratics, Gorgias is not concerned with the cosmic logos. Rather, he employs poetic technique to expose the mechanism of *alētheia* in its sense of un-forgetting. Because "memory of things past and awareness of things present and foreknowledge of the future" are unreliable (11), he contends, it is easy for people to come under the influence of speech.

However, besides reactivating culturally embedded truths, speech in Gorgias appears as a potent force that can be deployed by human agents to different ends. In addition to exposing the linguistic mechanism of enculturation, Gorgias sheds light on its new rationalistic uses aided by the onset of writing. Speech, as it is practiced by the new "masters of truth," to use Detienne's expression, is now seen as a vehicle of social control. As exemplars of these new linguistic practices, Gorgias presents a motley crowd of experts:

> To understand that persuasion, when added to speech, is wont also to impress the soul as it wishes, one must study: first, the words of astronomers who, substituting opinion for opinion (*doxa*), taking away one but creating another, make what is incredible and unclear seem true to the eyes of opinion; then, second, logically necessary debates in which a single speech, written with art but not spoken with truth (*alētheia*), bends a great crowd and persuades; and third, the verbal disputes of philosophers in which the swiftness of thought is also shown making the belief in an opinion subject to easy change. (13)

Doxa (opinion) is juxtaposed with *alētheia,* the latter having been interpreted, even by such an authority as Charles Segal, as "objective factuality" and the truth of the "phenomenal world" (1962, 112–14). I contend, however, that Gorgias is not contrasting *doxa,* the opinions crafted by speakers and accepted by the audience, with empirical facts. Instead, he is pointing out a shift from orally reinforced, univocal cultural knowledge to a multiplicity of truths spawned by the emergence of literate practitioners of persuasion in the second part of the fifth century. Gorgias's promise to remove blame from Helen by displaying the truth (*deixas talēthes,* 2) is a claim not of fact but of value, since he proposes to beat the inspired poets at their own game. Likewise, the expression "written with art but not spoken with truth," applied to "logically necessary debates" (13), refers to a desire to take advantage of the audience rather than to misrepresent reality. Gorgias thus continues to view speech as action rather than as a reflection of extralinguistic content. The myth of Helen's abduction becomes objectified; it is used as a *paignion,* a plaything (21).

Yet the logos, the vehicle of myth's survival, retains a semiautonomous status, even while it is being molded by the verbal artist. The new possibilities of the logos are predicated on the secular understanding of persuasion and human agency, but they are compatible with the transcendental quality of myth, if we take myth to be the mechanism of storage and activation of culturally valuable knowledge. What Gorgias bequeathed to fourth-century rhetoric is precisely this critical appreciation of the ambivalent potential of nonrational discourse. In his own performance he defies the separation between the rational and nonrational. He is an artist whose rationality is manifested by linguistic self-reflexivity rather than by a commitment to an "objective" way of thinking.

Literacy, Alētheia, *and Discursive Identity*

Unlike Gorgias and the other oral performers, Isocrates is a prose writer whose self-declared difference from the Sophists seems to put him in the same intellectual camp with Plato. Isocrates explicitly shuns and even attacks the oral culture of his contemporaries and often casts himself in the role of a truth seeker. At the same time, he promotes the type of discourse that co-opts, thematically and stylistically, mythopoetic elements of composition and address associated with orality. Isocrates' use of literacy does not demand a separation between the linguistic apparatus of performance and extralinguistic content in order to improve on contemporary oratory. On the contrary, Isocrates retains the oralistic emphasis on the act of speech and its social impact. But literacy permits him to strengthen the link between the linguistic act and the rhetor's political identity. These claims can be supported by the examination of his "quietist" literary strategy, his appeals to truth (*alētheia*), and the oral resources of his literary political discourse (*logos politikos*).

Ancient biographers and some contemporary critics tend to explain Isocrates' preference for writing by his physical ineptitude as an orator. However, as Yun Lee Too (1995) convincingly argues, Isocrates' *ipsissima verba,* on which traditional accounts are based (e.g., Jaeger 1971), constitutes a deliberate strategy of self-depiction as part of a carefully crafted public persona. Isocrates engaged in writing not only to compensate for his bodily weakness or lack of courage; he pursued writing with a dual goal of shifting the focus of contemporary rhetorical practices from their traditional sites to a broader political forum and crafting his own distinct civic identity. At the same time, his avoidance of the courts and the assembly—the places where citizens could influence the affairs of the polis through the power of their oral performance—marks Isocrates for his fellow Athenians as one of the "quietists," or *apragmones*. According to Deborah Steiner (1994), in the context of the Athenian public culture, these individuals' choice of reading and writing as well as their absence from public spaces of the polis signal "disenchantment with democracy and the desire for different social and political discourse" (187). Gunter Heilbrunn (1975) corroborates this interpretation when he reads Isocrates' quasi-biographical statement about the lack of "voice and daring" in *To Philip* as an "accusation of the Athenian democracy" (175). Yet unlike other literary *apragmones* of his generation, especially Plato and other Socratics, Isocrates adopts the quietist stance in order to reinvent democratic rhetoric, not to disavow its legitimacy altogether.

Isocrates' criticisms of contemporary rhetoricians are well known: he seldom misses the opportunity to expose demagogues in the assembly, sycophants in law courts, logographers, and teachers of eristic disputation. Demagogic orators, who have undermined the civic potential of Periclean democracy, exemplify the excesses of oral powers of logos. In the pamphlet *On the Peace,* Isocrates puts his outrage at the abuse of public performance in the mouth of a pacifist speaker who faces a hostile audience:[11]

> I observe that you do not hear with equal favor the speakers who address you, but that, while you give your attention to some, in the case of others you do not even suffer their voice to be heard. And it is not surprising that you do this; for in the past you have formed the habit of driving all the orators from the platform except those who support your desires. . . . Indeed, you have caused the orators to practice and study, not what will be advantageous to the state, but how they may discourse in a manner pleasing to you. (3–5)

One might conclude from this passage that Isocrates objects to aesthetically pleasing oral performance, just as Plato does in his *Gorgias,* when he chastises loudmouthed politicians who pander to their audiences in order to achieve selfish ends or when he banishes poets from the city in the *Republic*. Plato's animosity, however, targets rhetorical instruction and poetic performance because they fail to measure up to the philosophical ideals of justice and truth. Unlike Plato, Isocrates does not condemn the aesthetic dimension of rhetoric. It is not the power of the spoken word that he questions, but the unrestrained pursuit of individual gain to the detriment of the political power of the demos, which has become the dominant type of rhetoric in the courts and the assembly. Isocrates' concern is echoed by prominent fourth-century Athenian orators Demosthenes and Aeschines, who fault their audiences for becoming "prisoners" of the crowd pleasers and as a result weakening the democracy (see Ober 1989, 321–22). Those whom Isocrates casts as his rivals, opponents, and detractors are guilty of not telling the truth. But what does he mean by "truth" (*alētheia*)? And how does his usage of the word position him among rhetoricians and philosophers?

It is difficult to discern what Isocrates means by *alētheia* by reading English translations only. The Loeb translation by George Norlin often renders phrases like *alēthē legein* as "to state the facts," whereas a more idiomatic translation is "to speak truthfully, in a truthful manner."[12] More than philological niceties are at stake here. The former translation proposes that a distinction be drawn between objectively reported facts and fictitious account, the latter between honorable and shameful conduct. For Isocrates, honorable conduct depends on the exigency. For instance, the speaker of *On the Peace,* overwhelmed by the Athenians' bullylike actions toward their allies, exclaims, "I am at a loss what I should do—whether I should speak the truth (*tais alētheiais*) as on all other occasions or be silent out of fear of making myself odious to you. . . . Nevertheless I should be ashamed if I showed that I am more concerned about my own reputation than about our common safety" (38–39). The honorable, and hence the true, thing to do is to act in the interest of the city and the alliance, however unpopular one's advice may sound at the moment.

The opening of the pamphlet *Against the Sophists* adds another dimension to the contrast between honorable and dishonorable action. Isocrates criticizes other educators for offering empty promises to their prospective students. "If all those who undertook to teach were willing to speak the truth," he begins, "and not to make greater promises than they plan to fulfill, they would not have such a bad reputation among the general public" (1). The truthfulness Isocrates invokes here is linked to the mythopoetic tradition's perception of speech as either efficacious or vain. To Isocrates, the philosophical and educational doctrines of these experts, like false oracles, do not yield the expected results. They promise to the young men that through their expert kind of knowledge they will attain a happy life (3). On the grounds that it is beyond human capacity to divine the future, Isocrates contends that claims to such knowledge are a false advertisement. To drive home this point, he appeals to Homer: "We fall so short of this intelligence that Homer, who enjoys the highest reputation for wisdom, has written that the gods sometimes debate about the future—not because he knows their thoughts but because he wants to show us that this one thing (i.e., knowledge of the future) is impossible for human beings" (4). The attitude presented here is the one Isocrates will reiterate throughout his pedagogical and political career. It summarizes to a large degree his relationship with the Socratics, whom by virtue of the common label he lumps together with the sprawling cottage industry of the science of speech, *tōn logōn epistēmē*. Isocrates objects to the practices of speech instructors because they profess to teach success through a *tetagmenē technē,* undertaking "to pass on the science of discourse in the same fashion as they would teach the letters of the alphabet" (10).

Isocrates, then, uses *alētheia* as a goading term in order to praise or blame political action or, in other cases, to point out fruitless promises of contemporary educators. The two senses of truth remain closely connected, because for

Isocrates proper rhetorical education is a training ground for citizenly conduct. This is why, I believe, he resists the *technai* of literate teachers of eloquence and chooses to pursue prose writing as a primary vehicle of his education and politics.

By abandoning the traditional venues of public performance for writing, Isocrates attempts to foster a different type of democratic rhetoric, which he terms *logos politikos*. Such a rhetoric, observes Takis Poulakos (1997), "was an indistinguishably ethical and political art," for it combined both *eu legein* (the art of speaking well) and *phronein* (prudential thinking) for the benefit of the polis (68). The difficulty in articulating the difference and value of this educational project had to do not only with the lack of the immediacy and power of oral address but also with the suspect status of writing in the fourth century B.C.E.[13] Despite the use of writing by historians Herodotus and Thucydides, as well as by fifth-century dramatists, Athens was still primarily an oral culture in which writing functioned either as a supplement to oral communication or, among the elites, as a diversion (*paignion*) (Harris 1989, 65–92).

To distinguish his art from both of these functions, Isocrates attacks logography (ghosted speechwriting) and the intellectual exercises of the literate elites. To Isocrates, the former is contemptible because it is an instrument of the new politician and the litigious sycophant. The latter, though it does not promote unscrupulous quest for political power or material gain at the expense of others, is self-indulgent and often inconsequential. But it is precisely the novelty and elite flavor of such writing that may cast doubt upon Isocrates' own project. To set himself apart, in a famous passage in *Antidosis,* Isocrates explicitly contrasts his version of rhetoric—"speeches addressed to Hellas and the polis"—with other types of prose writing: "genealogies of the demigods," "studies in the poets," "histories of war," "dialogues," and "private disputes" (45–46).

What, then, should be the model of *logos politikos,* the discourse that is at once aesthetically pleasurable and beneficial to the state? Isocrates looks to the mythopoetic tradition as his resource. In *To Nicocles,* he instructs a rhetorician seeking the audience's consent to follow the example of Homer. "Clearly those who wish to do or write something to please the masses do not seek the most useful speeches but those that are full of fictions (*mythōdestatoi*)," he writes, "for people delight when they hear such narratives or watch contests and competitions. Thus, one should admire Homer's poetry and the first inventors of tragedy for perceiving human nature for what it is and for using both these forms of pleasure in their poetry" (48). Isocrates sees his prose writing as a labor more challenging than that of poets. In the *Evagoras,* he lists the advantages of poetic craft. To the poets have been granted "many decorations (*kosmoi*)"; they are free to address epic subjects; they can go beyond "conventional language" by using "borrowings, new terms, and metaphors"; above all, poetic compositions "persuade their audiences by their fine rhythms and proportions" (11). Isocrates enumerates these advantages as an implicit promise to surpass the poets, a gesture that is reminiscent of Gorgias's boast in the *Helen*.

In an oral setting, the appeal of mythopoetic discourse is not purely thematic (in the sense of the audience's recognition of familiar characters and stories); it relies on the reactivation of emotions attached to shared cultural knowledge (such as the Greek expedition against the Trojans or the Greek victory in the Persian Wars) through a rhapsodic performance.[14] But Isocrates is not a rhapsode who captivates the hearers by his mimesis of Homeric verses. He is a prose writer who adapts mythopoetic discourse for his educational and political project. He appreciates the potential of oral performance even as he disdains the uses to which demagogic orators put it. As Too (1995) points out, Isocrates repeatedly draws attention to the lack of his bodily presence in his writings; on several occasions he describes his prose as "bereft." However, Too also suggests that repeated references to the apparent weakness of discourse stripped of the speaker's voice and the immediacy of the occasion "anticipate and defuse the criticisms that may be brought against the written text, above all the *logos politikos* which he produces" (120). While Isocrates loses the advantages of oral performance (such as improvisation and immediate audience feedback), he gains something that only writing can grant: time. Removed from traditional sites of public deliberation with their pressures to pass judgment soon after a speech was over, written rhetoric benefited from a slower pace of reading and a possibility of rereading. According to Poulakos (1997), "With time on its side, eloquence would have a chance to develop its intrinsic qualities even as it continued to cater to an external situation, and to become a self-sufficient art even as it continued to be shaped by a purpose outside its form" (70).[15] In addition, written discourse enjoys the dissemination that is not guaranteed to oral performances. As Isocrates himself states in the *Evagoras*, speeches are more enduring than statues, since they may be published throughout Hellas (73–74).

The question arises, however, how would the writer's discourse, which now is "more closely tied now to the cultural and the thematic" (Poulakos 1997, 70), exercise its influence on the audience? In the absence of the author's body and voice, what features of the written text would secure the delight and wisdom embedded in common cultural references? Though a critic of contemporary uses of orality, Isocrates presents himself as an inheritor of the mythopoetic tradition nonetheless. Unlike Plato, who defends orality but denigrates the mythopoetic tradition, he takes upon himself the rhapsodic labor of reactivating familiar cultural themes. Yet his mimesis is at once akin to and radically different from that of an oral rhapsode. The similarity between Isocrates and his poetic predecessors (referred to as *aiodoi* or *rhapsōdoi*) rests on the mode of composition and address. As *rhapsōdoi,* whose name derives from *rhaptō* (sew together) and *aoidē* (song), Isocrates weaves his texts with a poet's attention to the rhythm of his utterance (Lentz 1989, 131). This link to the poetic tradition is not confined to the phonetic and syntactical levels of discourse. Like *rhapsōdoi,* who often stitched together "many and various fabrics of a song, each one already made" (Nagy 1996, 66), Isocrates inserts into his compositions fragments of already completed writings. Thus, intertextuality becomes a form of rhapsodizing. In *Antidosis,* a piece dramatized as a courtroom defense speech, "Isocrates" asks the clerk to read from previously published speeches—*Panegyricus, On the Peace, To Nicocles*—and quotes his "Hymn to Logos" from the *Nicocles* to display "what other kinds of speech I have been concerned with that have given me such a great reputation" (43).

It is certainly possible to conceive of the *Antidosis* as a panoply of examples of eloquence intended primarily as instructional showpieces. However, a reading attuned to the performative aspect of this unusually lengthy "court speech" shows Isocrates' writing as a genuine response to challenges against his character and his educational agenda rather than a mere epideictic exercise. It would not be too large of a leap to compare Isocratean self-defense in the *Antidosis* and other writings to the *muthoi* of epic heroes.

Martin (1989) distinguishes between the effect of speech, rendered by the term *epos,* and the status-linked performance, marked by the term *muthos.* In Homer, *muthos* is "a speech-act indicating authority, performed at length, usually in public, with a focus on full attention to every detail"; it usually occurs when someone is boasting or defending his reputation (12). In *Antidosis,* too, the reputation (*doxa*) of the speaker is contested and speech performs an authoritative function. Isocrates himself draws a parallel between his discourse and "musical and rhythmical compositions" (47). In addition, he urges the audience to "pay greater attention to what will be said than to what came before" and "not attempt to go through it all the first time" (12). Significantly, written discourse is presented as an answer to previously uttered speech and as a composition to be heard (or read aloud) by "those present" rather than by a solitary reader. Despite the written mode of composition, Isocrates emphasizes the act performed by the speech rather than presenting it as a mere expression of his thoughts. His logos, in other words, is not an autonomous medium that guarantees transmission of the message; the author portrays himself in a constant agonistic dialogue with the audience (see Too 1995, 113–50).

The main distinction between rhapsodic and Isocratean performance resides in the identity of the performer. Whereas the fabric of Homeric epics is held together by recurring performances of the *Iliad* and *Odyssey* at the Feast of the Panathenaia in Athens (Nagy 1996, 69), textual integrity in Isocratean writing is secured by the author's constructed identity. Rhapsodic *mimēsis* brought to life the characters of an Achilles or an Agamemnon or even Homer himself, while the rhapsode's persona remained in the shadow despite considerable inventiveness and variation that he could bring to the performance. Gregory Nagy (1996) argues that when "the rhapsode is re-enacting Homer by performing Homer, . . . he *is* Homer so long as the mimesis stays in effect, so long as the performance lasts" (61). In Isocrates, on the other hand, the author's "I" refers most of the time to himself, and mythopoetic material is often employed to highlight his own constructed identity as a citizen-rhetor and educator. *Panathenaicus,* a speech composed to celebrate Athenian leadership among the Hellenes, illustrates the construction of the author's identity by its association with mythical personae. Here Isocrates invokes the memory of Agamemnon not simply to underscore the common heritage of the Greeks but also to draw an analogy between the Homeric hero's *doxa* and his own lifelong literary labors of promoting *homonoia,* or unity, among the Greek states. "Although he took command of the Hellenes when they were in a state of mutual warfare and confusion and many troubles," he writes, "[Agamemnon] delivered them from these. Having established concord among them and despising deeds which were superfluous, prodigious and without benefit to others, he assembled the army and led it against the barbarians. None of those with a good reputation at that time or coming later will be found to have engaged in an expedition finer or more useful to the Greeks than this individual" (*Panathenaicus* 77–78). Not a military leader but a retiring citizen, Isocrates sees his *doxa* resting on his being a leader of words, *tōn logōn hēgemōn* (*Panathenaicus* 13), who through his logos has worked to foster concord and goodwill between the Athenians and other Greeks. And thanks to the literary medium, he can summon the textual record of his statements as a proof of his identity as a citizen-rhetor.

Isocrates appeals to the mythopoetic tradition—the cultural capital of the Greeks—in a way that both illuminates contemporary oral rhetorical culture and produces a serious critique of its political and ethical shortcomings. Weary of other intellectuals' attempts to forge a scientific blueprint for virtuous conduct and effective speechmaking, Isocrates fosters a performance-oriented conception of eloquence. He does so not through the laundry list of technical advice on speechmaking but through his own performance. Drawing on oral tradition's perception of speech as conduct rather than a reflection of thoughts or reality, Isocrates carefully crafts his own image as a political agent. Though lacking bodily presence and the aural impact of speaking, his oppositional persona gains its power through the record of deeds done in writing.

Endoxa, *Literate Categorization, and the "Available Means of Persuasion"*

Aristotle opens his *Metaphysics* with praise of the natural human desire to know. A sign of this desire, he says, "is our liking for the senses" (980a21–22). From among the senses the philosopher selects sight: "We choose seeing above practically all the others, not only as an aid to action, but also when we have no intention of acting. The reason is that sight, more than any of the other senses, gives us knowledge of things and clarifies many differences between them" (980a23–26). This statement may be read as symptomatic of the liberation of the mind from the shackles of myth, for the world has now been laid in front of an eager and discriminating gaze. A few lines further, Aristotle explains the development of crafts and sciences and sets up their hierarchy, in which purely theoretical sciences, pursued for their own sake, tower over the so-called useful crafts. In this context, the privileging of seeing acquires a new layer of significance. It asserts the ocularcentric rationality over the phonocentric. The critical eye now dominates the easily seduced ear.[16]

A problem with this account emerges, however, if we take into consideration Aristotle's expressed commitment to *phainomena* and *endoxa,* appearances and received opinions, which he seems to integrate into investigation of any subject matter, including the art of rhetoric. Indeed, many scholars make so much of his method of inquiry that Aristotle might not seem too different from Isocrates.[17] In spite of his attention to appearances and opinions, however, Aristotle atomizes and reassembles bits of "popular wisdom" contained in *endoxa* to shape a system that is intended to minimize, if not exclude, contradiction or conflict. Yet in rhetoric Aristotle confronts a formidably unstable object of inquiry from his point of view, and he therefore strives to neutralize it by forging a protective membrane between propositional content and the performative force of rhetorical utterances.

At first sight, Aristotle's attention to *endoxa* makes him seem more receptive to his cultural milieu than his familiar portrait of a logician and empiricist would present. Available through what people say, *ta legomena, endoxa* come from the philosopher's linguistic and political community—in short, from the mixed heritage of poetry, rhetoric, and philosophical reflection. In the *Topics,* Aristotle defines *endoxa* as "the things believed by everyone or by most people or by the wise (and among the wise by all or by most or by those most known and commonly recognized)" (100b20). Notice how received opinion is stratified a priori between the multitude and the wise. It is interesting to see how this distinction bears on Aristotle's method of selecting the most serviceable beliefs. In the *Metaphysics,* for instance, he faults dialecticians (the "wise" in his hierarchy of opinion-carriers) for relying on popular opinion (*endoxon*) (995b20–25). This seemingly innocuous aside should be kept in mind as we continue to observe Aristotle's handling of *endoxa* in various contexts.

Still, Aristotle welcomes *endoxa,* even though he painstakingly qualifies what is acceptable. His most famous passage on the endoxical method is in the *Nicomachean Ethics:*

> Our proper course with this subject as with others will be to present the various views (*phainomena*) about it, and then, after first reviewing the difficulties they involve, finally to establish if possible all or, if not all, the greater part and the most important of the opinions (*ta endoxa*) generally held with respect to these states of mind; since if the discrepancies can be solved, and a residuum of current opinion left standing, the true view will have been sufficiently established. (1145b1–6)

Having assembled all available opinions on a subject, Aristotle then tries to limit the multitude of the possible viewpoints to a neat, consistent definition. Martha Nussbaum (1986) describes the direction of Aristotle's intellectual exercise: "This profound natural desire to bring the matter of life into a perspicuous order will not be satisfied, he believes, as long as there is contradiction. Our deepest commitment . . . is to the Principle of Non-Contradiction, the most basic of our shared beliefs. The method of appearance-saving therefore demands that we press for consistency" (247). Nussbaum aims to show that Aristotle subscribes, thanks to his friendliness to appearances, to a kind of philosophical, and hence ethical, pluralism, which sets him strikingly apart from Plato's ethical austerity.[18] What Nussbaum does not question is Aristotle's response to cultural and situational contexts out of which *endoxa* arise.[19]

If Aristotle strives to iron out contradictions among the many fragments of discourse he deems relevant to his subject matter, he must reconstitute the things said in terms of agreements and oppositions. In consequence, views that seem to cancel each other are usually left behind, and ones that appear unanimous are saved. This procedure, especially if its goal is to arrive at the most general definition, will by necessity flatten out the context of the utterances. A philosopher may rely on judgments about X pronounced by members of his or her linguistic community, but their motives and biases will be obscured in a propositional statement like "X is Y." In other words, the "residuum" of opinion will be exactly that: a referential statement devoid of markers of situation, purpose, and audience. Philosophical writing, then, will tend toward maximum abstraction. Indeed, in contrast with the Presocratics, Plato and Isocrates, Aristotle's sifting through the *endoxa* is not couched in a language meant to attract attention to itself, least of all to compete for acceptance with others. When references to myth and poetry do occur in Aristotle's prose, they are almost invariably stripped of their performative context. It is as if what has been said before is now placed on the flat surface to be examined as an object. This strategy is particularly evident in cases in which a phrase from a poet is quoted to offer an illustration of a theoretical point. Reviewing the claims of the "first philosophers" in the *Metaphysics,* for example, Aristotle turns to Empedocles to point out that "if we follow Empedocles' argument, and do not confine ourselves to his mumbling way of expressing it, but attend to what he has in mind, we will find that love is the cause of good things, and strife of bad" (985a3–5). The desire to get to the propositional content of the argument eliminates other potential questions Aristotle might have asked.

The amputation of text from context is the product of a tendency toward abstraction abetted by literacy. Yet while in some cases Aristotle's tackling of *endoxa* is relatively innocuous, other examples may strike most modern readers as curiously reactionary. I am thinking, in particular, of a passage from book 1 of the *Politics* in which Aristotle distinguishes between the functions of female and slave in a household:

> By nature, of course, female and slave are distinct. . . . Among the barbarians, however, the female is in the same position as the slave. But that is because there is nothing among the barbarians with the natural capacity to rule, and their community is that of male and female slave. Therefore "it is reasonable for Greeks to rule barbarians," say the poets supposing that to be barbarian and to be a slave are by nature the same thing. (1252b1–9)

The problem here is not with the *endoxon* itself, since the poets and tragedians of the classical period have thoroughly mythologized "the barbarian" as the Greeks' "Other" (Hall 1989). Rather, it stems from the manner, at once serious and casual, in which the utterance is incorporated into the exposition of the origins of the polis. Aristotle accepts this opinion as given, indeed, as a backing for his own claim, and so precludes the opportunity of questioning the situation of its original performance (Euripides' *Iphigenia in Aulis*) as well as its cultural value. A politically loaded statement has turned into a fixed assertion. As Havelock puts it, the "narrativized usage has turned into a logical one" (1986, 105). Havelock sees in Aristotle's *Politics* the expression of the same sentiments about the nature of humans as political animals as are present in Hesiod and Sophocles, only conveyed through a different syntax: "By the time the Aristotelian passage was written, it had become possible to describe this 'man' not by narrating what he does, but by linking 'him' as a 'subject' to a series of predicates connoting something fixed, something that is an object of thought: the predicate describes a class, or property, not an action" (105).

Havelock's account of literate categorization is typical of a generalized theory of literacy. It is also unsettling, for it not only shows the *possibility* of turning a narrative into a proposition but also describes this transformation as a politically neutral, almost natural, process. Aristotle's literate usage sanctifies, so to speak, the relationship between the subject and the predicate by rendering it timeless and immutable. Note that his subject in the *Politics* is not celestial bodies or even animals, things that are beyond the realm of human affairs, but discussion of the most appropriate form of government.[20] In this context, Aristotle mentions the *doxa* of those who view slavery as a culturally created institution. But perhaps since their view is at variance with a series of "natural" correlations he has laid down already (husband-wife, master-slave, parent-child), Aristotle addresses it as a way of showing the "extremes" of *endoxa* concerning slavery. Indeed, the correspondence between master and slave to Aristotle is both natural and logical. In the *Categories,* the text explicating the logical function of predication, Aristotle uses "master" and "slave" to demonstrate the proper application of reciprocal terms: "Take the attribute 'master' from a 'man': then, indeed, the correlation subsisting between 'man' and 'slave' will have vanished. No master, in short, no slave" (7b4–7). What begins as a richly ambivalent poetic utterance achieves its logical end as a severely circumscribed residue of opinion.

In assimilating *endoxa* to his discourse about the first philosophy (metaphysics) and politics, Aristotle not only removes utterances from their original contexts but also discards those statements that do not meet his philosophical criteria. Arguably, when he approaches rhetoric, Aristotle changes his method of cataloging the received opinions (see Most 1994). Still, as in other cases, he presents a "literature review" of previous (incorrect or incomplete to his mind) statements about the art. Not content with the existing *technai* that instruct students of oratory how to rouse the audience's emotions, he sets out to produce a *technē* more attuned to the theoretical tenets of the Lyceum. But precise definition of the subject eludes him: in an effort to pin down what rhetoric is, Aristotle reaches for its association with other, considerably more stable, areas of inquiry: "Rhetoric is a certain kind of offshoot [*paraphues*] of dialectic and of ethical studies (which it is just to call politics)" (*Rhetoric* 1356a25).[21] By choosing the term *dunamis* (faculty), he implies that it is not an activity (*energeia*) but a capacity that can be grasped by a student of dialectic and politics. What happens to *endoxa* in the service of an art that, to Aristotle, is itself an offshoot of dialectic?

Endoxa in the *Rhetoric* furnish raw material for enthymemes, or rhetorical syllogisms. One must use them in place of complicated logical demonstrations, for addressing popular audiences differs greatly from scientific or ethical teaching. Thus enters into Aristotle's plan the need to persuade the hoi polloi:

> Rhetoric is useful [first] because the true and the just are by nature stronger than their opposites, so that if judgments are not made in the right way [the true and the just] are necessarily defeated [by their opposites]. And this is worthy of censure. Further, even of we were to have the most exact knowledge, it

would not be very easy for us in speaking to use it to persuade some audiences. Speech based on knowledge is teaching, but teaching is impossible [with some audiences]; rather, it is necessary for *pisteis* and speeches [as a whole] to be formed on the basis of common beliefs (*endoxa*). (*Rhetoric* 1355a22–29)

This passage demonstrates Aristotle's vision of rhetoric as something external and inferior to both scientific and ethical deliberation.[22] It also indicates an intention to straighten up the heretofore frivolously applied *technē* by focusing on proofs (*pisteis*) and arguments (*logoi*). Indeed, anything outside proof Aristotle considers merely an appendage (1354a14). Still, he must concede some power to *endoxa,* since the multitude are likely to respond to what harmonizes with their collective perceptions. In the case of rhetoric, then, *endoxa* seem to take on an even greater significance than in other treatises of Aristotle.

Here, one may expect that the aural echoes will flow back into the desiccated grooves of logical propositions. For in spite of the literary abstractness of Aristotle's overall project, he is spelling out the rules of a spoken, rather than written, art. Could it be, then, that Aristotle's "truth," at least in this particular context, is a harkening back to the mythopoetic *alētheia,* the truth reactivated in the (popular) audience's minds? Indeed, following William Grimaldi's (1980) commentary on the *Rhetoric,* scholars have defended the audience's active role in Aristotle's construction of rhetorical proofs (e.g., Farrell 1993, 95–97). Others have insisted that orality, no matter how much Aristotle squeezes it out of *ta endoxa* in the rest of his inquiries, makes a comeback in the form of "an unspoken oral premise" in the enthymeme. By turning to the opinions in the audience's minds as a source of persuasion, Aristotle seems to retain "ties to the common wisdom and concrete particulars that are a staple of the oral culture" (Lentz 1989, 172).

However, the equation of Aristotle's "truth" with the mythopoetic unforgetting is offset by the fact that "the common wisdom and concrete particulars" have already been neutralized by virtue of their classification into commonplaces.[23] Aristotle devotes his *Topics* precisely to that task. Furthermore, in the *Rhetoric* he insists that one's capacity to discern the true (*alēthēs*) from that which resembles it belongs to the same capacity, so that "an ability to aim at commonly held opinions [*endoxa*] is characteristic of one who has a similar ability to regard the truth" (1355a15). The truth he refers to is opposed to appearances rather than to oblivion. Consequently, it is the propositional content of *endoxa,* not their performative forcefulness, in which Aristotle invests most effort. Thomas K. Johansen (1999) explains that Aristotle transcends the cultural context of *endoxa* because of his belief in the cyclical view of history and immutability of true opinions: "The reason why Aristotle thinks that man can repeatedly come up with the right theories is that he believes that man by nature is a potential knower and that natural potentialities generally are realized. Truths grasped by our predecessors have been preserved for us in the form of *endoxa*. That is why we can grasp the truth adequately if we attend correctly to the *endoxa*" (288).[24] In the *Rhetoric,* as Jacques Brunschwig (1996) has pointed out, Aristotle "often uses the vocabulary of vision, as if the relevant object were already here, existing (*huparchon*), and just waiting to be brought into view" (44). Epistemologically, rational agents' capacity to discern the truth is extrarhetorical, for it precedes their participation in civic rituals that activate communal memory. *Endoxa* are to be sifted through only to reveal what is common about human behavior in general.

Even when emotions (*pathai*) come into play as sources of proof (*pistis*) in the second book of the *Rhetoric,* their treatment manifests an instrumental attitude characterized by "'surgical' detachment and description" (Dubois 1993, 125):

> The philosopher observes emotion without sharing it and proceeds like Socrates in the Platonic dialogues, like the Stranger in the *Sophist,* to hunt down the emotions, to pursue them relentlessly through division until the quarry is driven to earth. . . . Emotions are to be evoked and visited upon his audience as part of the orator's performance. The self-control of the orator and philosopher requires that he survey the field of emotions, assess the value of a particular emotional simulacrum, display it for the audience, produce and destroy it in his audience. (Dubois 1993, 125–26)

For Aristotle, the principles that govern emotional excitation can be examined apart from the contexts in which specific passions had been produced by real orators. The individual verbal style and oral delivery become superfluous once the general mechanism of persuasion is laid down. In a particularly revealing passage of book 3, Aristotle states:

> But since the whole business of rhetoric is with opinion, one should pay attention to delivery, not because it is right but because it is necessary, since true justice seeks nothing more in a speech than neither to offend nor to entertain; for to contend by means of the facts themselves is just, with the result that everything except demonstration is incidental; but, nevertheless, [delivery] has great power, as has been said, because of the corruption of the audience. The subject of expression (*lexis*), however, has some small necessary place in all teaching; for to speak in one way rather than another does make some difference in regard to clarity, though not a great difference; but all these things are forms of outward show and intended to affect the audience. As a result, nobody teaches geometry this way. (*Rhetoric* 1404a1–12)

Several crucial points about the oral aspects of rhetoric are articulated here. First, rhetoric (unlike scientific instruction) cannot influence opinion without ingratiating the hearer. The rhetorician's speech reaches its goal by exciting the senses of a diverse public, while the geometrician's terse instruction addresses a select group of like-minded students. Second, this wandering into the territory of emotions is a risky enterprise and should be constrained. In this context, it appears that speeches concerned with civic matters should not emulate the dramatic style reserved for poetic performances—one should not divert the audience's intellect from the "facts."[25] Finally, the manner of discourse is actually external to the matter at hand. The linguistic form is separated from its extralinguistic content. We get a set of conflicting statements: Aristotle concedes that persuasion is a blend of emotional and intellectual exhortation but demands discursive discipline as an antidote for speeches that flatter and gratify the listener's fancy. On the other hand, these statements do not sound so contradictory; rather, they display an attempt to put a fence around a certain acceptable range of performative power. Poetic speech, predictably, is not the standard by which this acceptable range is determined.

Aristotle points to Gorgias as the one who invented the poetic style of oratory, which he considers inappropriate for rhetoric though "even the majority of uneducated think that such persons express themselves most beautifully." From Aristotle's point of view, poets achieved their reputation by "uttering silliness" (*legontes euēthē*) (1404a25). The new nonpoetic style that he offers as a replacement of poetic diction possesses "clarity" (*saphēneia*) as one of its chief merits: "speech is a kind of sign, so if it does not make clear it will not perform its function" (1404b1). Aristotle seems to be at pains to sever the force of the spoken word from its function of signification. For him, language allows the expression of relationships among things, and hence clarity becomes the standard against which all expression must be judged.

In contrast with Isocrates, whose view of language is inseparable from his understanding of political agency, Aristotle sees language primarily as a rational representation of natural relationships that exist outside the tumultuous wrangle of the Athenian culture. While Isocrates adopts an adversarial identity by leaving the sites of contemporary rhetorical practice, Aristotle puts himself above the fray to construct a consistent hierarchy of knowledge appropriate to theoretical sciences and pragmatic arts. His *Rhetoric* functions as both a guide for statesmen with training in philosophy and codification of the commonplaces upon which rhetorical arguments are to be built.

Aristotle approaches rhetoric with the conceptual apparatus of his logical treatises ready at hand and reluctantly concedes some importance to the elements that are "external" to the rhetorical demonstration. Though ostensibly arising out of the rhetorical culture, Aristotle's scheme furthers an understanding of language as a system of rules that dictates performance, not the other way around. Consequently, the power of speech is circumvented in order to give way to a distinctly transparent literate conception of the logos as reflection of the cosmos, not a creative force that shapes thought, action, and identity of human agents.

The Logic of Literacy and Literate Logics

The assumption that rhetoric emerged as an "art" in the fourth century B.C.E., and that the disciplined *technē rhētorikē* of Aristotle crowns the evolution from the oral mythopoesis to literate rationality, appears excessively deterministic, since it pictures a uniform trajectory of linguistic and cultural change from orality to literacy.

Isocrates and Aristotle epitomize two divergent *literate* logics and two dissimilar visions of discourse, though both rely on oral culture's mythopoetic elements. Aristotle renders the oral utterances of contemporary Greek culture abstract and timeless by focusing on propositional content rather than social forcefulness. He catalogues culturally particular elements of public discourse as instantiations of supposedly universal principles of eloquence. As a result, he presents us with a picture of the rhetorical art that transcends historical specificity of received opinions and veils the political motivation behind this act of transcendence. The Isocratean use of literacy, on the other hand, does not remove him from the political and cultural life of the community. Nor does it reduce narrative elements to logical propositions. Offering his compositions as proof of his unwavering commitment to discursive education, Isocrates transforms the "mythical" logos with its sensual impact and cultural resonance into a discursive site of critical reflection and political intervention.

Why should it matter that Isocrates and Aristotle differ in methods and goals of their appropriation and critique of the performance-centered Greek culture? Can we not simply settle for a view that Isocrates was a teacher and practitioner of rhetoric and Aristotle a theorist? To assimilate Isocrates' oeuvre into Aristotle's account of rhetoric, however, would be to impose Aristotle's epistemological and political perspective upon an articulation of logos that goes against the very presumptions of Aristotle's worldview. Whereas Isocrates preserves and amplifies the culture's emphasis on the act of speech, Aristotle approaches language as a reflection of extralinguistic reality. If Isocrates views rhetorical performance as constitutive of one's political agency, Aristotle relegates performance to an external stylistic function. In other words, Isocrates and Aristotle constitute two distinct, even antagonistic, paradigms of reflection about discourse and human agency.

Two

BETWEEN POETICS AND RHETORIC

The uses of literacy by Isocrates and Aristotle resulted in two antagonistic modes of conceptualizing discourse and human agency. Contrasting Isocrates' and Aristotle's views on traditional performance culture and civic education will contextualize this antagonism further. Although historians of rhetoric have begun to reevaluate the extent of Aristotle's divergence from Plato on the subject of rhetoric, few would disagree that Aristotle's positive treatment of poetry and drama is a decisive break from the Platonic distaste for the poetic tradition.[1] Whereas Plato severely criticizes both poets and rhetors for their deceptive and immoral influence on the young, Aristotle approaches rhetoric with grudging acceptance and treats poetry with respect. I propose, however, that Aristotle's privileging of poetry over rhetoric as an intrinsically noble and not merely useful subject completes, rather than opposes, Plato's utopian political project. Aristotle shares with Plato a distrust of the performance-centered culture and its effects on the training of citizens. It is, by contrast, Isocrates' view of performance (*mimēsis*) as a source of civic education that Aristotle counters with his separation of performance into poetics and rhetoric.

Isocrates defends a program of civic education in which the traditional Greek association between speaking and acting (*legein kai prattein*) is upheld. Isocrates thereby promotes a performative view of the rhetorical training as a *mimēsis* of civic excellence. In calling this educational program *philosophia* and aligning it with the poetic tradition, he challenges Plato's Academy. Plato discounts poetic *mimēsis* on the grounds of its alleged epistemological poverty and immorality. Plato's indictment of poetry, however, is accomplished by way of analytic separation of *mimēsis* as representation from *mimēsis* as performative imitation and audience identification. Isocrates, on the contrary, insists on keeping these aspects of *mimēsis* inseparable as conditions of activating and sustaining civic identity.

Whereas Isocrates gives us a vision of performance as a lifelong pursuit of political honor and recognition, Aristotle considers it but a stepping stone toward the life of leisured pursuits and contemplation unburdened by exigencies of public performance. This presumption of Aristotle, articulated in his *Politics,* can in turn shed light on the hierarchy of *mimēsis* we find in the *Poetics* and *Rhetoric*. Aristotle assigns a higher value to representational *mimēsis* of the tragic plot, thereby elevating poetry to a quasi-philosophical status. Performative *mimēsis,* by contrast, appears either as a primitive stage in the genesis of poetic craft or as a stylistic ornament added to the representational function of plots and rhetorical proofs.

Before proceeding to Isocrates and Aristotle, it is necessary first to consider how Plato dethrones poetry as a traditional method of enculturation and, in so doing, sets up the conditions for fragmenting *mimēsis* and anticipates the schism between poetics and rhetoric.

Plato and the Heritage of Mimēsis

It is almost as difficult to translate accurately the term *mimēsis* as it is to define the word *logos*. The uncertainties of translation are, in fact, traces of a complex relationship between classical literate theorists and the oral Greek culture on whose grounds they were staking out the claims of new disciplines.

Of Plato, Eric Havelock (1963) writes that *mimēsis* is the "most baffling of all words in his philosophical vocabulary" (20). Although Havelock's immediate concern is not with the ambiguous relationship between poetry and rhetoric, his attempt to reconstruct Plato's "cultural situation" offers some useful clues regarding the points of departure for both Isocrates and Aristotle. Havelock reads the *Republic* as Plato's manifesto against the mimetic heritage of Greek poetry and drama rather than as a theoretical treatise on political philosophy. His polemic with the advocates of Plato as an appreciator of art is instructive in its own right, but his observations concerning Plato's ambiguous description of *mimēsis* are particularly germane to our discussion.

In the *Republic,* Plato uses the term *mimēsis* in three different though related contexts. The first mention of the term is seemingly mystifying, for Plato initially defines it as a method of dramatic impersonation as it was employed by reciters of Homeric epics and fifth-century dramatists. *Mimēsis* here is the opposite of simple narration in the poet's own voice (*Republic* 392d–393d). At the same time, Plato inserts a suggestion that anyone who speaks in the voice of another imitates that person: "And is not likening one's self to another in speech or bodily bearing an imitation (*mimeisthai*) of him to whom one likens one's self?" (393d). Havelock senses in these two overlapping meanings of imitation Plato's responsiveness to his "cultural situation," in which the creative artist and the performer are indeed not as separate as they may be for the modern reader (1963, 23).

Havelock's observation has since become a useful starting point for a whole generation of classical scholars who have endeavored to reappraise the performative culture in antiquity.[2] The polysemy of *mimēsis* also suggests a reason for Plato's uneasiness about the term: he fears that mimicking someone's verbal medium (*lexis*) may in fact lead one to adopt that person's identity (we shall return to this aspect of imitation later). Almost imperceptibly, in this early analysis of poetry, Plato sneaks into his account of *lexis* a remark that foreshadows the expulsion of poets from the polis in the final book of the *Republic*.

From *mimēsis* as the mode of dramatic impersonation, Plato moves to *mimēsis* as *learning* by imitation of behavior. This aspect comes up during the discussion of proper schooling for the guardians of the state (*Republic* 394e–397b). As Havelock comments: "Mimesis now becomes a term applied to the situation of a student apprentice, who absorbs lessons, and repeats and hence 'imitates' what he is told to master" (1963, 24). The transition from the situation of the poet and the performer to the situation of a citizen-soldier in training may befuddle a modern reader, says Havelock. The confusion is due to a continuous slippage: from the dramatic enactment to the mimicry of speech style to the imitation of model behavior. However, this sort of imitation, typical of a student reciting and memorizing poetic verses in the course of a traditional training in *mousikē,* was no doubt embraced by Plato himself (see Solmsen 1966).

The slippage of the meaning of *mimēsis* is carried over into book 10 to include both the total act of poetic representation and the audience's emotional identification with the performance. The former goes beyond the dramatic style to account for the *content* of poetic communication, which in Plato's time was akin to "a sort of encyclopedia of ethics, politics, history and technology which the effective citizen was required to learn as the core of his educational equipment" (Havelock 1963, 27). The latter, in Havelock's phrase, is "the name of our submission to the spell" of a performance (26).

In the interest of the proper education of the citizenry, Plato condemns poetic education on two grounds: its woeful inadequacy and incompleteness with respect to the subject matter and its corrupting effect on the listener. Plato cannot control the audience's response to the verbal magic of the poets. But he can expose poetry's failure qua representation of subject matter by appealing to his theory of forms. Because poets imitate not even the object in nature but its mere appearance, Socrates and his young companion Glaucon reason, the product of imitation will be far removed from the truth (596a–598c). Hence Plato justifies the banning of poets from the ideal city by reducing poetic craft to the manufacturing of appearances. Poets are ignorant of the subject they depict and use "words and phrases to paint colored pictures" that are charming but worthless. They speak "with meter, rhythm, and harmony," but if you "strip a poet's works of their musical coloring and take them by themselves," they will be like "the faces of young boys who are neither fine nor beautiful after the bloom of youth has left them" (*Republic* 601a–b). In short, poetic artistry consists of imitating and producing simulacra in the absence of true knowledge.[3] Here we see at once an expansion of *mimēsis* from dramatic imitation to the entire spectrum of artistic depiction and a simultaneous reduction of poetic craft to style as an outward show.

Aristotle's pronouncements about style (*lexis*) in the *Rhetoric* bear a strong resemblance to this Platonic reduction. Style is conceived as the outer layer of a properly conceptualized *technē*. In his exposition of the origins of *lexis,* Aristotle mentions rhapsodists, actors, and Sophists as individuals engaged in superficial mimicking of ornate phrasing. He literally says that "poets while uttering silliness (*legontes euēthe*) appear to have gained their reputation thanks to style (*dia tēn lexin*)" (*Rhetoric* 1404a25). Both Plato and Aristotle declare poetic style senseless and pleasing only to the "children and foolish people" (*Republic* 598c) and the "majority of uneducated" (*Rhetoric* 1404a25).

But *mimēsis* as audience identification, "our submission to the spell," does not lend itself to an epistemological critique. Plato cannot explain it away by pointing out how poorly artists and poets do the job of representing reality. On the contrary, in the course of the conversation between Socrates and Glaucon in book 10 of the *Republic,* we find out that poets may be doing their job all too well—and not by simply splashing paints or pouring out ornate phrases. They tug on our heartstrings by impersonating people in various and often conflicting emotional states. Moved by our sympathy for the characters, we allow ourselves to identify with their emotions and actions, even if such identification goes against the twin Platonic commitment to "reason and law." To Socrates, this is plainly unacceptable. But this mimetic situation is loathsome not only because the poets lack expert knowledge of the subject. Rather, it is because their models of imitation are not what they ought to be. The poet, says Socrates, is "related to the excitable and multicolored (*poikilos*) character, since it is easy to imitate." By contrast, "a rational and quiet character, which always remains pretty well the same, is neither easy to imitate nor easy to understand when imitated, especially by a crowd consisting of all sorts of people gathered together at a theater festival" (*Republic* 604e–605a). It is not a mere stylistic variety but the variety of actions and emotive responses experienced by actors and spectators together that threatens Plato's rational city.

Plato does carve out an intellectual and political space from which he can launch an assault on the oral culture from a literate point of view. Havelock himself takes great pains to explain just how radical was Plato's assault on the Homeric heritage. Oddly, however, Havelock situates the oral culture within the matrix of Plato's critique. Havelock expatiates on the encyclopedic quality of Homeric epics and on the oral resources of Hellenic intelligence in order to elevate their function of preservation of vital cultural information. But because he is defending the "content" of Homeric education, Havelock focuses on representational *mimēsis* as an epistemological issue in order to contextualize

Platonic objections to the illusionism purveyed by the poets. In sum, Havelock stresses the "what" over the "how."

Mimēsis as identification, however, hinted at by Plato in book 3 and presented as a full-blown (self-)deception in book 10, is no less important to the "cultural situation" of which Havelock so assiduously reminds us. In fact, in his polemic over the pre-Platonic attributions of the term, Havelock points out that the earlier usage "refers to 'sympathetic behavior,' not to abstract copying or imitation, and in great many cases this behavior is physical, a matter of speech, gesture, gait, pose, dress and the like." He further states that "the inferior status" of a bad copy is indeed required by the Platonic analysis, where it was suitable to "the Platonic epistemology" while even such sophisticated sources as Democritus still define "miming" as "a pattern of behavior, whether good or bad, by its correspondence to some 'live' standard" (Havelock 1963, 58 n. 22; see also Else 1958).

It appears that Plato invented the pejorative sense of *mimēsis* as bad representation in order to condemn style to a cosmetic role. But *mimēsis* as an education enacted together by the performer and the audience does not recede into the shadows even in Plato, so to speak. It crops up in Platonic dialogues with the haunting persistence of a phantom, often turning "Socrates" himself into a mime, making him speak in voices other than his own. In the *Phaedrus* and the *Menexenus*, for example, the character Socrates dramatically marks his imitations as alien discourse. But there is a larger issue of the mimetic quality of Plato's dialogues in general, especially given their educational role within in the Academy. With a certain degree of stretching, Plato can be said to mime Socrates in the same way rhapsodes were imitating a Homer or an Achilles.

Let us return to the function of *mimēsis* that loops around the actor, the verbal-imagistic apparatus, and the audience's response to the performance—the "how" of Homeric education. I have suggested that in Havelock's study, this aspect is underdeveloped in comparison with the question of oral preservation of "the Homeric encyclopedia"—the "what" of Homeric discourse. The remainder of this section, then, amends Havelock's otherwise astute exposition of poetic *paideia* with respect to its performative aspects.

Havelock reconstructs the mimetic situation of an epic performance from a psychological point of view, speculating on how rhythmical repetition, melody, and dance produced nonrational "memorization" in the performer and the audience:

> The learning process . . . was not learning in our sense but a continual act of memorization, repetition and recall. This was made effective by practising a drastic economy of possible linguistic statements, an economy enforced by rhythmic patterns both verbal and musical. In performance the co-operation

of a whole series of motor reflexes throughout the entire body was enlisted to make memorization and future recall and repetition more effective. These reflexes in turn provided an emotional release for the unconscious layers of personality which could then take over and supply the conscious mind a great deal of relief from tension and anxiety, fear and the like. The last constituted the hypnotic pleasure of the performance, which placed the audience under the minstrel's control, but was itself the ready servant of the paideutic process. (*Preface* 157)

Havelock's description of the spell effected by verse and melody reflects some of the most famous classical statements about the power of logos, such as Gorgias's *Encomium of Helen,* which ascribes to words accompanied by music a wondrous capacity to "stop fear and banish grief and create joy and nurture pity" (8). Most important, this analytical "reconstruction" of the psychology of the oral *paideia* allows Havelock to pinpoint the yet unbroken union between the manner of learning and the object of learning. Recalling Plato's objections to poetry as a bad copy, Havelock is finally able to ascertain the "raison d'être of his attack": "in the poetic performance as practised hitherto in Greece there was no 'original'" (1963, 159). There was only "the tradition" that "the minstrel recited," explains Havelock. But the "content" of the tradition comprised "the doings and sayings of heroes," which the minstrel and his audience "reenacted" and made "their own" (1963, 159–60). It is therefore the repetitive and often ecstatic reenactment of the poetic lore that authorizes noble deeds and condemns disgraceful behavior in a culture, rather than the knowledge of the just and the beautiful "in itself."

However, the emphasis on repetitive "automatism" of poetic performance leads Havelock to conclude that the range of meaning afforded by such means of communication was limited. He postulates, in a strikingly deterministic fashion, "The requirements of memory are met in a fundamental fashion through practising a strict economy of possible combination of reflexes. There are a million things you cannot say at all in metrical speech and it will follow that you will not think them either" (1963, 149). Havelock connects the ease of memorization abetted by rhythm and melody with a restricted range of experience encapsulated by a poetic statement. Yet in light of Plato's own misgivings about the diversity of poetic *lexis* and the corresponding variety of characters "imitated" by a poet (*Republic* 604e–605a), Havelock's analysis appears unjustifiably reductive. The problem, at least in Plato's eyes, is too much vicarious experience, not too little. In fact, the experience conjured by Homeric discourse is astounding in its vividness and richness of detail. As Eric Auerbach's (1953) study of the *Odyssey* confirms, all events and psychological processes in the epic are fully externalized, "nothing must remain hidden and unexpressed" (4). Recourse to metric formula does not entail poverty of depiction.

Havelock also overpresses the "pathology" of identification induced by the poetic performance. "The pattern of behavior in artist and audience," he summarizes, "can be described mechanically as a continual repeating of rhythmic doings." As the show unfolded, the rhapsode "sank his personality in his performance" and the audience "entered effectively and sympathetically into what he was saying and this in turn meant that they became his servants and submitted to the spell" (1963, 160). Havelock implicitly relies on an assumption of an autonomous "personality" that is ecstatically surrendered to the aural spell. I believe that such an assumption is more congenial to Plato's agenda, since one cannot assume there is such an identity in the first place.

To begin with, rhapsodes did not possess a "personality" outside the performance. Rather, their personality comprised all the roles they enacted—a circumstance that irritates Plato's Socrates in the *Ion,* as the philosopher struggles to pin down what it is exactly that identifies a rhapsode. For Plato, who you are is determined by the knowledge you possess. However, Ion's knowledge, unlike the expertise of the doctor, the fisherman, or the charioteer, does not attach itself to a particular group of objects. More than that, it is not attached to objects at all: the rhapsode knows "the kind of thing . . . that a man would say, and a woman would say, and a slave and a free man, a subject and a ruler—the suitable thing for each" (540b). The dialogue closes with frustrated Socrates accusing Ion of acting "just like Proteus": "you twist and turn, this way and that, assuming every shape, until you elude my grasp" (541e). Socrates offers Ion two options: admit your artistry as a deceiver (and then you are at fault) or admit divine possession (and then you do no wrong). Plato's Ion vainly chooses the second alternative. Socrates wins: now he can equate poetry with a divine madness that temporarily possesses an artist and bestows upon him a different personality and a gift to subdue others with words.

As for the listeners, their identification with gods, heroes, and common humans, however pleasurable, is even more deleterious to Plato. As he indicates in the *Republic,* the diversity of experience will lead to confusion about one's proper role in the polis. This is why, in the earlier "reform passages" of the *Republic,* Socrates initially proposes to allow only those recitations that promote citizens' understanding of their place in the social hierarchy (386c–389d). *Mimēsis* as pathology of submission is, by extension, the name of the Platonic fear of social chaos. However, in the *Ion,* Plato explains away the threat of rhapsodic effect on the audience by discounting it as inspired hysteria, a condition of being *enthousiastikos:* "They are seized with the Bacchic transport, and are possessed—as the bacchants, when possessed, draw milk and honey from the rivers, but not when in their senses" (533e). If the performer's threat is defused by the attribution of a divine inspiration, the audience's "madness" is but a reverberation of "enthusiasm" set into motion by the Muse. Identification in this sense is thoroughly irrational and as such cannot serve a didactic purpose.

Havelock simply cannot grant oral poetic *mimēsis* the reflective capacity he assigns to a fully literate culture of reading. For him, only literacy, in the sense of physical and emotional separation of the individual from the written record, allows us to stand outside the roles with which we fuse in the moment of performance. Yet the mutually enriching relationship between nonrational identification and self-conscious reflection is the most likely reason for the persistence of oral recitation into the literate era. Archeological evidence from the fifth century B.C.E. suggests that the written composition was meant to be read aloud rather than studied quietly and independently.[4] In the previous chapter, I argued that Isocrates, a wholly literate wordsmith, still conceives of his writings as pieces to be performed and heard. Finally, though the status of oral performance in Plato's Academy is uncertain, the dramatic evidence of such dialogues as the *Phaedrus* and the *Symposium* indicates that the great enemy of oral culture himself was still hanging on to oral instruction.[5] It follows that, however vigorously Plato downplays its epistemological and moral value, oral *mimēsis* is nonetheless a potent and persistent medium of indoctrination.

Havelock contributes to our understanding of *mimēsis* only by showing how the philosopher pries apart the mimetic process in order to redirect its awesome powers to the ends of true knowledge. Depicting poetry as divine rapture, Plato preserves one part of what Homeric *mimēsis* offered—its ability to enthuse the learner in the same way the Muse entered the body of Homeric reciters. On the other hand, he cuts off the identity-shaping part of *mimēsis* by further dividing it into style (*lexis*) and the object of representation. As we saw, in Plato's *Ion* the rhapsode claims to know and convey the proper way to speak for all social groups of a society (rather than to teach his listeners technical skills Plato ascribes to Homeric *paideia* in his sarcastic argument in the *Republic*). Ion's didactic claim is remarkable in that it does not split proper social action from acts of speech—a union Plato is at pains to dissolve. In a textually based education, in which the knower is separated from the known, such function of poetic instruction seemingly recedes into the low stratum of culture. For Havelock, Plato's literate revolution changes Greek *paideia* forever. This may be true if the line were traced directly from Plato to Aristotle. But the alliance between pleasure and instruction, between speech and moral action, between poetic and political discourse survives and grows even more prominent in Isocrates' version of literate *paideia*.

Mimēsis *in Isocrates*

If the *Republic* is a demonstration of the underpinnings of Plato's educational reform, *Antidosis* is a manifesto of Isocratean *paideia*. The following section, then, interprets *Antidosis* as an affirmation and defense of the cultural sources and performative nature of political identity. Isocrates strives to revive the old cultural assumption that eloquence and virtue go hand in hand (which Plato is so adamant to obliterate). Because Isocrates displays the "what" of his "philosophy" precisely by showing the "how," my reading will focus on the performative and agonistic (not merely propositional) functions of this text.

Antidosis is mimetic in itself: Isocrates sets up the account of his career and his pedagogical views as a speech of self-defense in the Athenian court. Although the title and the procedure of this fictional "trial" give an impression that litigation is over a property exchange, Isocrates deliberately resorts to the language of another well-publicized self-defense—Socratic *Apology*.[6] *Antidosis* is punctuated with statements that bring to mind the trial of Socrates as Plato related it. The most evocative allusions are the indictment of corrupting the young men (*Antidosis* 30), Isocrates' claim of unfamiliarity with law courts and public offices (38, 144–45), and the marshaling of the names of his famous students to debunk the charge of corruption (92–96).

Why, then, does Isocrates choose to "quote," sometimes very closely, Plato's *Apology*? Given the late date of the *Antidosis*—Isocrates was eighty-two—the pamphlet was most likely written for a literate audience familiar with both Plato's and Isocrates' "publications" and knowledgeable about the rivalry between the two schools. If this conjecture is accurate, the first impulse is to conclude that Isocrates was explicitly comparing himself and his achievements to Socrates, the philosophical martyr par excellence, and claiming Socrates for himself against Academy's intended monopoly. It is plausible that the intellectual pedigree gained by the use of an analogy with Socrates could be a boost to Isocrates' ethos. We may recall that Isocrates is fond of comparing himself to Homeric heroes, so why not wrap himself in Socrates' mantle as well?

I believe, however, that Isocrates does not wish to be seen as another Socrates, overtones of martyrdom notwithstanding. Rather, I think that Isocrates engages in this mimetic act to amplify the intensity of the attack on his educational program. The defensive posture also allows Isocrates to sharpen the contrast between himself and those for whom Socrates epitomized "wisdom" and "philosophy."

One does not have to look far to discover the gap between Isocrates and his "model." In the *Apology,* Socrates describes his wisdom as a gift bestowed on him by divine powers and his calling, philosophy, as a perpetual questioning and discrediting of all those who profess to be wise. Socrates declares: "God has specially appointed me to this city, as though it were a large thoroughbred horse which because of its great size is inclined to be lazy and needs the stimulation of some stinging fly. It seems to me that God has attached me to this city to perform the office of such a fly" (*Apology* 30e). Although a critic of popular democracy, Isocrates nonetheless holds a view of *philosophia* diametrically opposite that of Socrates. He gives the name *philosophia* to the educational practice that in the fifth and even early fourth centuries had been called *mousikē,* which involved memorization and recitation of the poetic tradition. The passage, in which Isocrates makes this radically anti-Platonic move, deserves to be cited at length:

> Some of our ancestors long ago saw that although many arts existed for other matters, none had been established for the body and soul, and when they had invented two disciplines, they handed them down to us: physical training for the body, of which gymnastic is a part, and philosophy for the soul, which I shall be discussing. These two disciplines are complementary, interconnected, and consistent with each other, and through them those who have mastered them make the soul more intelligent and the body more useful. They do not separate these two kinds of education but use similar methods of instruction, exercise, and other kinds of practice.
>
> When they take on pupils, physical trainers instruct their students in the positions that have been discovered for competitions, and those whose concern is philosophy pass on to their pupils all the structures which speech (logos) employs. When they have given them experience and detailed knowledge of these, they again exercise the students and make them accustomed to hard work, and then force them to synthesize everything they have learned in order that they may have a more secure understanding and their views (*doxai*) may be better adapted to the right moments (*kairoi*). It is not possible to learn this through study, since in all activities, these opportune moments elude exact knowledge (*epistēmē*), but in general those who are particularly attentive and can understand the consequences most often apprehend them. (*Antidosis* 181–84)

Every sentence in this description is weighed strategically to enhance the agon between Isocrates and his intellectual competitors. First of all, the name *philosophia,* attached to the old art of training the psuche, flies in the face of Plato's lifelong attack on the traditional poetic education. Isocrates not only asserts the legitimacy of the old *paideia* but also gives it a status higher than that of Plato's dialogues by his use of the term *doxa.* Next, the arts for nurturing the body and the mind are said to be "homologous" (*homologoumenas*). This is an implicit reference to the infamous analogy constructed by Plato in the *Gorgias.* According to this analogy, poetry and rhetoric are to the soul what cosmetics or cookery are to the body. Thus, poetry and rhetoric cannot promote justice and temperance in the soul just as cosmetics and lavish meals corrupt the body's health (*Gorgias* 502a–504e). Elsewhere in the *Antidosis*, Isocrates reiterates his objection to the Platonic search for an art that will "implant justice in the souls of the citizens" (*Gorgias* 504d), using nearly the same phraseology as Plato: "I think that an art that can produce self-control (*sōphrosynē*) and justice (*dikaiosynē*) in those who are by nature badly disposed to virtue (*aretē*) has never existed and does not now exist" (274).[7]

Wisdom (*sophia*) for Isocrates is neither a divine gift nor a scientifically precise art. Rather, it is an intelligence acquired through habituation and trial by concrete circumstances. "I think that the wise (*sophoi*)," he says later in the *Antidosis*, "are those who have the ability to reach best opinions (*doxai*) most of the time, and philosophers are those who spend time acquiring such an intelligence as quickly as possible" (271). Isocrates' statement is not a mere exhortation that practice makes perfect, even though he admits that his view of the issue happens to be "simple" (*haplōs*) (271). A great deal more is at stake here.[8] Isocrates advocates discursive education (*logōn paideia*) as a training in social conduct. A student coming to Isocrates for instruction should expect not only to memorize poetry and prose for the sake of gaining facility in speech but also to gradually become a public person whose actions are worthy of being praised in similar discourses.

In putting *eu prattein* and *eu legein*—acting well and speaking well—on the same level, Isocrates affirms the continuity between the traditional poetic education (*mousikē*) and the "philosophical" program of his school. If he were to assert the claim of a marriage between moral action and eloquent speech in the fifth century, his proposal would need little, if any, justification. But Isocrates is writing in a cultural environment in which the professionalization of speech education on the one hand, and the separation of "philosophy" from the day's business in the Academy on the other, make any such claim instantly controversial. Whereas in the earlier years of his career he distanced himself from the professional teachers of speech to defend his occupation (as is evident in *Against the Sophists*), at the time of the *Antidosis* the threat emanates from elsewhere.

Who is the attacker, then? The ignoble sycophant Lysimachus, though he is posited as the one who had brought on the suit, hardly fits the bill. He is but a vehicle for setting up the fiction of the trial. The most likely detractor, I think, is Isocrates' primary intellectual competitor—Plato's Academy.[9] For it is Plato's intellectual progeny who apparently lent credence to Lysimachus's accusations: "Why should we be surprised at him, when even some of those who are experts in argumentation bring similar charges against beneficial public speeches as those brought by the basest men? They are not ignorant of the speeches' power, or of the speed with which they benefit those who employ them, but they expect that by slandering their discourse they will increase the honor of their own profession" (*Antidosis* 258).

Plato and his disciples are not named, but the between-the-lines character of this rebuke, as well as the subdued quality of other criticisms of the "experts in argumentation" point to a rival well known among contemporary readers, rather than to run-of-the-mill logographers and sycophants. Isocrates' exposition of *philosophia* and zealous defense of cultural sources of *paideia* should be read as part of his objections to "the leaders in eristic and those who teach astrology, geometry, and other branches of learning" (261).

Isocrates cannot ignore his powerful opponent, and in his subtle attack, he adopts a middling position between the view of the commoner and the intellectual. Isocrates mentions that in the eyes of popular opinion, such studies are "babbling and hairsplitting" (262) and that "students do not remember them for very long because they do no have a bearing on our lives" (262), but quickly interjects that his own stance is different. Instead of calling them useless, Isocrates maintains that the utility of the theoretical *mathemata* is of a different kind: "When we spend time in the detail and precision of astrology and geometry, we are forced to put our minds to matters that are hard to learn, and moreover, we get used to working persistently hard at what has been said and demonstrated to us, and we cannot let our minds wander. When we are exercised and sharpened in those matters, we are able to receive and learn more important and significant material more quickly and easily" (*Antidosis* 265).

Theoretical studies of this sort, declares Isocrates, are not "philosophy." Rather, they serve well as "a mental gymnastics" and "a preparation for philosophy" (266). With this seemingly benign maneuver, Isocrates turns the hierarchy of knowledge espoused by Plato and Aristotle completely on its head, depicting the subjects that are pursued for their own sake as accessory to a more important and worthier education—*philosophy* in the true sense of the term.[10] What, then, is the end of Isocrates' *philosophia*? Moreover, does the Isocratean view of speech lend itself to the distinction between external and internal ends?

According to Isocrates' hierarchy, what the eristics offer in the course of mastering the art of disputation—namely, the taxonomy of probabilities, necessary signs, and proofs—is secondary to the suasory power of an honorable reputation: "The reputation of being a gentleman (*kalos kagathos*) not only makes the speech more persuasive but also makes the actions of one who has such reputation more honorable" (280). It appears that "the reputation of being a gentleman," in this picture, designates *both* external (instrumental) and internal (autotelic) ends. As a speech manifesting the quality of *kalokagathia*, it bolsters the impact of discourse upon the audience—a technical proof that Aristotle calls *ēthos* in his *Rhetoric*. At the same time, *kalokagathia* is a kind of mimetic magnet for those who embark on the study of philosophy in Isocrates' sense: these persons fashion their conduct in accordance with lofty ethical examples set up in poetry and prose.[11]

Importantly, Isocrates does not differentiate between these apparently distinct senses of *kalokagathia*. In his mind, like points on a turning wheel, they form a mimetic continuum of action-thought-speech. Isocrates explains his vision in great detail as he addresses a controversial notion of "advantage" (*pleonexia*). Again, the word's true meaning, he claims, like the meaning of many crucial terms he invokes, had been misconstrued by "foolish people" (*Antidosis* 275). If "philosophy" had been unfairly usurped by theoretically oriented institutions like the Academy, "advantage" has become attached to individualistic pursuits by the likes of Plato's character Callicles, who is featured in the *Gorgias* as an unprincipled beneficiary of a rhetorical education. For Isocrates, on the contrary, advantage is inseparable from the good repute earned by the speaker from members of the speech community. Therefore, his triple condition for becoming such a person balances the desire for personal distinction with the responsibility to the hearers. "People improve and become worthier," proposes Isocrates, "if they are interested in speaking well, have a passion for being able to persuade their audience, and also desire advantage (*pleonexia*)" (*Antidosis* 275).

Showing how his *philosophia* can set the student on the path of amelioration, Isocrates highlights the correspondence between the types of discourses and the quality of thought and action:

> Someone who chooses to speak and write speeches worthy of praise and honor will not possibly select topics that are unjust or insignificant or that deal with private arguments but those public issues that are important and noble and promote human welfare. If he does not discover any such topics, he will accomplish nothing. Then from the evidence relevant to the topic, he will select the most appropriate and advantageous. Someone who is accustomed to examine and evaluate such topics will have this same facility not only for speech at hand but also for other affairs. As a result, those who are philosophical and ambitious in their devotion to speaking (*logoi*) will at the same time speak well and think intelligently. (276–77)

Two points require explanation, given the claim that Isocrates' *philosophia* is an extension of the traditional poetic education, devised, as he says, "long ago" (181). First, we need to review the discourses that Isocrates presents as an alternative to the contemporary training in litigation. Second, we must address the manner of *mimēsis*, which instills and reinforces the union between *eu legein* and *phronein*.

What are these discourses, the ones that "promote human welfare" and that Isocrates contrasts with the petty and private quarrels, the label he gives to the often messy business of the Athenian courts? As we can gather from the "evidence" Isocrates presents in his defense in the *Antidosis,* they are "of a political character pertaining to Hellas, to be delivered in panegyric assemblies" (46). Such speeches surpass "private disputes" not only in the loftiness of their theme. They are also aesthetically superior in that they "are more like musical and rhythmical compositions," they "set out events with a more poetic and complex style," they "seek to employ grander and more original enthymemes," and "dress up the whole speech with many eye-catching figures of speech (*ideai*)" (47).

Again, Isocrates' word choice is replete with polemic overtones. The terms "colorful" (*poikilos*) and "dignified" (*onkōdēs*), which in Isocrates pertain to the stylistic and thematic range of superior political discourse (*logos politikos*), in Plato have a resolutely negative connotation. In the *Meno,* the adjective *onkōdēs* is aligned with another derogatory term, *epachthēs,* to describe an arrogant and annoying character (90b). *Poikilos* (colorful, variegated, mottled) is a catch-all term singled out to attack poetry and its dangerous political influence in the *Republic.* It characterizes now a style (*lexis*), now a personality type (*ēthos*), now a democratic form of government (*politeia*). The different connotations of *poikilos* are no doubt linked: for Plato, a style rich in figurative language is congenial to multifaceted and shifty persons who form a motley, disorganized democratic polity.[12] Aristotle also reminds us of this affinity of poetic style and the corrupted audience in book 3 of the *Rhetoric,* though his comment refers not to education but to the deployment of excitable speech in the law court (1404a5–6).

Isocrates extols the virtues of poetic style because of its difference from the language of oratory as it was practiced in contemporary Athenian courts. Shouldn't one be skeptical, then, of a claim about the continuity between poetry and oratory in Isocrates? Shouldn't we take his exalted praise of logos as a political fiction, no less utopian than Plato's ideal city?

To be sure, Isocrates shares with Plato a certain reformist tenor. But his reform is directed not at purging linguistic and cultural resources of the Greek *paideia,* as is Plato's program, but at integrating them more fully into the rhetorical practice and education of democratic Athens. Isocrates gives an indication of this integration in a passage that contrasts the skill of forensic pleaders with the advantage gained by pursuing *philosophia:* "Those who appear to be skilled in juridical speech are tolerated only on the day they happen to be pleading, whereas the others are well regarded and highly respected in all public gatherings at all time. In addition, if the former are seen twice or three times in the lawcourts, they are hated or criticized, whereas the latter are more admired the more often they appear and the more people hear them. Finally, those who are skilled (*deinoi*) in legal speeches have no ability for those other speeches, while the others, if they wished, could quickly pick up forensic pleading" (48–49). Rather than deny legitimacy to agonistic rhetorical practices, Isocrates issues a plea to uphold the principles for which Athens is famous among the rest of the Greeks. His is a call for consistency: "It is shameful that although in other matters we are agreed to be the most merciful and gentle of all the Greeks, our behavior in court cases here patently contradicts this reputation" (20–23).

Through his dramatization of self-defense in the *Antidosis,* Isocrates affirms the viability of oratory strengthened by its association with discourses that are more akin to publicly performed poetry. Because his alleged "offense" stems from his words, Isocrates presents portions of his compositions, which display both his style and his wisdom, as *pragmata,* facts of the case to be judged by the audience. Isocrates also stresses the aesthetic power of his texts by using a vivid analogy: "Like fruits, I shall try to offer a sample of each. When you have heard a small portion of them, you will easily recognize my character (*ēthos*) and you will learn the power (*dunamis*) of all my speeches" (54). The Greek word for "fruit," *karpos,* can also mean "result" or "product" of one's actions; in archaic poetry, it often refers to the "fulfillment" of oracles. All three meanings resonate with Isocrates' faith in the mimetic magnetism of political prose that imitates poetry.

We are still to consider the didactic process by which one becomes *sophos* in the Isocratean meaning of the word. Recall the story Isocrates tells about the invention of the arts for the training of the body and the soul, one called *gumnastikē,* the other *philosophia.* The counterpart of gymnastics, however, has always been *mousikē,* to which the schooling in writing, *grammatikē,* was later added. What does Isocrates mean by such radical a renaming of *mousikē*? A possible answer lies in the polemical character of the pamphlet itself. If it is indeed an extended argument against the "eristics," the renaming acts as a challenge to a philosophical program that considers the art of discourse peripheral to inquiries of a theoretical nature.

In addition, Isocrates emphasizes the similarity, if not identity, between the traditional *mousikē* and his instruction to preserve the aesthetic dimension of traditional performative education and to bolster the active role of learning. Traditional *mousikē,* by virtue of its association with epic poetry, had suffered an attack from Plato, who denied it any reflective potential. Plato talks of both epic reciters and their hearers as if they are bamboozled, swept off their feet. Students who read aloud and memorized Homer and Hesiod were, in his view, no better off intellectually than the crowd spellbound by a rhapsodic singing. By contrast, Isocrates believes that the habituation afforded by the study of diverse poetic texts and discourses composed in their image only expands artistic and social sensitivity. Identification sparked by an artistically compelling performance does not block one from reflecting on the conditions that shape praiseworthy action or its consequences. Quite the opposite: by identifying with what fictional and historical characters say and do, a student grasps the repertoire of social roles and the range of situations more fully than does a person who receives lessons in moral philosophy without living its principles.

On the other hand, Isocrates' use of term *philosophia* to describe the training of the soul does not imply that he merely copies the instruction in *mousikē*. In fact, Isocrates mentions *mousikē* proper as a primer for the kind of training he offers in his school in the same passage in which he calls eristic training "a preparation for philosophy." The latter, he admits, is a "more mature subject than what children learn in schools but for the most part similar. When children have worked hard at grammar, music, and the rest of the education, they have not yet made progress in speaking better or in deliberating on public affairs, although they have become better prepared to learn the greater and more serious subjects" (*Antidosis* 266–67).

Isocrates explicitly affirms that *philosophia* is a "continuing" education, aimed at training students for a political life. Nonetheless, *mousikē*, with its combined appeal of verse and melody, serves as a crucial first step toward a study that involves reflection and application of accumulated linguistic and cultural experience. A desire to imitate the praiseworthy conduct, then, must be sparked at this stage, for Isocrates insists that a student should possess the triple ambition to speak well, to persuade, and to seize the advantage before embarking on a study of *philosophia*. As the following section will show in more detail, Isocrates shares with Aristotle a presumption that *mousikē* combines sensual pleasure and didactic content. The critical difference between the two authors lies in the trajectory beyond *mousikē*. For Isocrates, the dynamic of praise and blame that shapes a person's aspirations in younger years continues on a level of political practice in the adulthood. That is why, I think, we cannot discriminate between internal and external ends of Isocrates' discursive education. The mimetic circle of speech-thought-action remains unbroken. Not so with Aristotle, who separates and disciplines *mousikē,* poetry, and rhetoric in order to make them amenable to the ends of a life of virtue and contemplative leisure.

Mimēsis *in Aristotle*

Like Plato, Aristotle ponders possible benefits and dangers of traditional Greek instruction in *mousikē* and the role of poetic *mimēsis* in contemplative life. He also seeks to discredit what I take to be the Isocratean understanding of political *mimēsis*. For Isocrates, mimetic identification productive of desire for a good reputation is continuously renewed, as a person living the political life demonstrates his commitment to the polis over and over again. A citizen's identity is not shaped once and for all but is reaffirmed throughout one's life by the polity. Aristotle would find such life, dependent as it is on contingencies of audiences and situations, burdensome and even vulgar. His approach is to limit the role of performative *mimēsis* to early stages of education in *mousikē* in the *Politics*, and to style (*lexis*) in the *Poetics* and the *Rhetoric*. By contrast, *mimēsis* as representation is elevated in the *Poetics* to the status of philosophical learning and inference. The distinction between internal and external ends allows Aristotle to construct a hierarchy of *mimēsis* and, along with it, a hierarchy of legitimate disciplines in which the *Poetics* and *Rhetoric* occupy separate and unequal positions.

In the *Politics*, guided by considerations of utility versus leisure in the choice of proper training for the young, Aristotle selects *mousikē* as the most compatible with noble leisure. Aristotle consults the tradition regarding the advantages of *mousikē* not granted to other types of traditional instruction:

> That is in fact why those of former times gave a place to *mousikē* in education —not because it was something necessary (for there is nothing of that sort in it); nor because it was useful, in the way letters are, for business and household management and learning and a host of other political activities . . . ; nor again because it was useful, like *gumnastikē*, for health and military prowess (for neither of these do we see resulting from *mousikē*). What is left, then, is that *mousikē* is for cultured pursuits of leisure. (*Politics* 1338a13–21)

This position is prima facie evidence of Aristotle's disagreement with Plato's aesthetic austerity and distrust of poetic influence on the young and old alike. Yet Aristotle does not endorse instruction in poetry and music across the board. The case of *mousikē*, he admits, is ambiguous: "It is not easy to determine what is its power or for what purpose one should participate in it" (*Politics* 1339a15). Therefore, Aristotle canvasses various types of *mousikē* in order to separate the more noble and liberal of its functions from more base ones. He finds three possible applications of *mousikē*: for play, for education of character, and for cultured pursuits. For Aristotle, play (*paidia*) is a state of rest from toil, accompanied by pleasure. The effect of music is akin to sensual delights of other recreational pursuits; these, Aristotle writes, are "not included among things serious, though they are pleasant and, as Euripides says, 'put a stop to care.' That is in fact why people give a like place to, and make a like use of, all of these things: sleep, drinking, and music (and dancing too is added to them)" (*Politics* 1339a16–21). In this passage, we again hear a familiar analogy between rhythmic speech and pleasurable intoxication, employed, however differently, by Gorgias and Plato.

The sensual pleasure, sought because of its "restful" nature, is the least salutary for the young citizens. "Educating the young should not be for the sake of play," Aristotle demands, "for, since learning is painful, they are not playing when they learn" (*Politics* 1339a26). If they listen to performances and enjoy them as a sweet respite from schooling, the young aristocrats risk turning into effeminate barbarians, like the kings of the Medes and the Persians (*Politics* 1339a34–36). On the other hand, there is another concern that has to do with the social stratification between the "free and educated" and the "vulgar mechanics": Aristotle does not wish the young belonging to the free class to become vulgar by cultivating technical performance skills (a similar disdain, one should note, runs through Aristotle's account of rhetorical performance and excesses of poetic style in the *Rhetoric*).

He finally settles on a compromise that combines the exertion of performance and singing with more noble goals of character training and the formation of correct aesthetic judgment. The young will benefit from performance as long as they do not continue performing beyond a certain age, do not acquire "vulgar" professional skills for competition and crowd pleasing, and do not play certain musical instruments such as pipes (*Politics* 1341a17–1341b20). To use an imperfect modern analogy, children should pursue violin or cello so they can appreciate classical music and fine leisure when they grow up but should not be allowed to play drums or bass guitar in a garage band or attend heavy metal concerts, let alone become rock-and-roll musicians themselves.

Aristotle's treatment of character training through music is remarkable for its portrayal of mimetic identification as both a psychological and a social phenomenon. However, it is uncertain whether such identification is due to the recognition of "likenesses" or because the hearer is put in a certain emotional state. Thus Aristotle speaks of the verisimilitude between representations of "decent characters and noble deeds" and "real natures," as if "getting used to taking pleasure in likenesses is close to being in the same state with respect to reality" (*Politics* 1340a14–27). On the other hand, the effect of pleasure or pain is induced by tune and rhythm, with different tunes affecting the emotions in a distinct way, the Lydian mode putting the listener in a condition of "grief and apprehension," the Phrygian making one enthused, the Dorian delivering the audience into a "middling and settled condition" (*Politics* 1340a38–1340b9). Our distinction between major and minor—the latter more melancholic and the former more uplifting—provides but a pale analogy with the musical variety that apparently survived well into the fourth century.

Still, the three modes above do not exhaust the emotional diversity and social coloring of music. According to Aristotle, there are also "base" modes, corresponding to base characters of the unleisured class, which consists of "vulgar mechanics, laborers, and the like": "Just as their souls are twisted from the natural condition, so there exist modes that are deviant and tunes that are strained and highly colored, and what gives pleasure to each is what is akin to his nature. Hence, those who perform in contests and in front of such spectators should be conceded the right to use some such type of music" (*Politics* 1342a20–26). Aristotle's views on the value of *mousikē* at this point parallel those of Plato's *Republic,* in which the "variety" of poetic style correlates with the mottled and shifty character of a democratic audience. Unlike Plato, however, Aristotle approaches *mousikē* not because he must face it as a dangerous cultural force to be suppressed, but as an institution that is intrinsically valuable in the ideal state. David J. Depew (1991) insists that Aristotle is actually more idealistic than Plato when it comes to the vision of the perfect state. While such a state in Plato is predicated on a "belief that the highest function of political life is the repression of desire" (378), in Aristotle contemplative life is conjoined with political activity, conceived as the rotational self-rule of aristocrats whose desires have been conditioned toward intrinsically good things.

Aristotle's discussion of *mousikē* also can be read as an attack on Isocrates' conception of *paideia* as a lifelong pursuit of an honorable reputation through civic performance. Aristotle conceives of *paideia* as the moral inculcation of the young, beyond which lies a life of active learning (*mathēsis*), which should not be confused with mere habituation. At first sight this might seem like a perfectly Isocratean point. But for Isocrates, as I have argued, honorable reputation is both the means and the end of a political life. It is in this sense that a citizen is required to perform, in word and in deed, to the satisfaction of a political community. To Aristotle, being in a position of constantly proving one's political worth and leaving one's reputation at the mercy of an audience resembles more a life of professional entertainer rather than philosopher. Aristotle's demand that the young cease performing after they reached a certain age, lest they become "vulgar mechanics," displays exactly this attitude: "For the spectator, being crude, is wont to introduce changes in the music, and the result is that he imposes a certain character . . . on the artists themselves as they perform in front of him" (*Politics* 1341b15–17).

To avoid such devolution, Aristotle conceives of paideia telescopically: the character forming function of *mousikē* provides habituation (*ethismos*) out of which a life of contemplation spent in active pursuit of cultured leisure can emerge. Children, Aristotle notes, are not "complete" and hence cannot fully partake in contemplative activity (*Politics* 1339a30). The habituation induced by the performance of proper tunes and verses is a stage that is not entirely cognitive. It is nonetheless integral to moral and intellectual conditioning, because "education is to be in habits before it is in reason" (*Politics* 1338b4). Therefore, "taking pleasure aright," which consists in the repeated recognition of the right sorts of tunes and of "decent characters and noble deeds" (1340a13–18), is a cultivation of desire rather than its suppression. By this logic, "cultured pursuits" of free adults is an activity that is fully contemplative and is enjoyed for its own sake not because the intellect has successfully suppressed passions but because properly cultivated passions freely grant the rule to the life of the mind. Aristotle's political agent in the ideal city is thus "ordered" the same way as the polis itself: both the agent and the polis share a hierarchy in which contemplative leisure rules by consent of the properly cultivated passions (politics).

If we take Aristotle's view of *mousikē* as the cultivation of desire in youth oriented toward contemplative leisure in adulthood, we are in a good position to appreciate Aristotle's difference from both Plato and Isocrates with respect to the role of poetry in the polis. The departure from the Platonic view does not lie in Aristotle's acceptance of cathartic release of emotions in response to poetic performance, as was commonly thought.[13] There is no place for Bacchic ecstasy in the ideal state or, for that matter, in the *Poetics*. Aristotle thinks of such stimulation as base and belonging to the banausic laborers. No, a properly conditioned human agent approaches poetry and drama not to satisfy a desire for vicarious experience but to learn. Learning (*mathēsis*) here does not mean learning by imitating the characters, gathering information or acquiring skills; it is an intrinsically good contemplative activity characteristic of a mature philosophical life. In this way, Aristotle departs from the Isocratean *philosophia*, which upholds a life of continuous mimetic reinforcement between the political agent and the polis. By contrast, Aristotle's agent, as long as the conditions of proper habituation have been met, should not need it. While Isocrates thinks of poetry and political artistry in terms of their aesthetic and didactic power, the pleasures of tragic learning for Aristotle are quite different.

In the light of this analysis, one can expect that Aristotle's *Poetics* follows the orientation toward the contemplative life outlined in the *Politics* and therefore cannot be considered only as a manual for composition and criticism of poetry written by a philosophical theatergoer. Though *Poetics*, like *Rhetoric*, belongs to the category of productive arts, Aristotle's discussion of the role of *mimēsis* in learning and of the function of tragic drama seems to be shaped by his commitment to a philosophical ideal of contemplation. Moreover, the gradation of *mimēsis* in tragedy explains why rhetoric, severed from *Poetics*, ends up on the bottom of the hierarchy of legitimate disciplines.[14]

Aristotle's argument about the role of *mimēsis* in learning is set forth in *Poetics* 4, after the chapters that establish classification of poetry according to the means, objects, and manner of *mimēsis*. "Imitation and the joy derived from it are natural to human beings since childhood," he begins, "and human beings differ from other animals in that they are the most imitative (*mimētikōtaton*) and learn their first lessons by imitation (*dia mimēseos*)" (*Poetics* 1448b5–8).

Here, learning appears as a natural, instinctive process that is more akin to a child's spontaneous response to delightful tunes and rhythms rather than a mature contemplative activity. Next, we see *mimēsis* described in terms of representation: "For we enjoy looking at accurate likenesses (*tas eikonas*) of things which are themselves painful to see, obscene beasts, for instance, and corpses" (*Poetics* 1448b9–11). The two passages are nonetheless consistent if we regard them as a compressed account of how human beings are habituated to become like philosophers in their capacity not only to imitate but also to judge representations rendered by others. Aristotle himself confirms this interpretation:

> Understanding gives great pleasure not only to philosophers but likewise to others too, though the latter have a smaller share in it. This is why people enjoy looking at images, because through contemplating them it comes about that they understand and infer (*manthanein kai sullogizesthai*) what each element means, for instance, that "this person is so-and-so." For, if one happens not to have seen the subject before, the image will not give pleasure *qua* mimesis but because of its execution of color, or for some other such reason. (*Poetics* 1448b13–20)

The pairing of the terms "to learn" (*manthanein*) and "to infer" (*sullogizesthai*) leaves little doubt that Aristotle has in mind a fully cognitive process. Furthermore, the discriminating rationality is removed from the object of observation by virtue of the separation of the copy from the original.[15] Is this objective state a pinnacle in human cognitive development, as the progression from instinctive *mimēsis* to rendering correct judgment about representations implies?

This genealogical explanation is plausible, especially if we take the following story of poetry's natural development as analogous to the development of a youth into a reflective judge of likenesses:

> We have, then, a natural instinct for imitation (*mimeisthai*) and for tune and rhythm . . . , and starting with these instincts men very gradually developed them until they produced poetry out of their improvisations. Poetry then split into two kinds according to the poet's nature. For the more serious poets represented fine doings and the doings of fine men, while those of inferior nature represented the actions of inferior men, at first writing satire just as the others wrote hymns and eulogies. (*Poetics* 1448b20–28)

The first stage of imitation is similar to a play in which judgment is not present yet. As poetry evolves, it becomes more discriminating about the objects and manner of imitation. The cause or beginning (*archē*) of poetry, then, is our spontaneous identification with and mimicry of sights and sounds, but its ultimate end (*telos*), like the end of musical *paideia,* is learning and inferential thinking.

For Aristotle, the more developed the poetic form, the truer it is to the object of representation. The story of the "growth" of tragic drama is a good example. With its origin in "improvisation," tragedy "gradually evolved as each of its elements that came to light was added, and, having gone through many changes, tragedy stopped when it had found its own natural form" (*Poetics* 1449a14–15). "Nature herself," says Aristotle, discovered the iambic as "the proper metre" (*Poetics* 1449a24–25). The iambic is the most proper (*oikeion*) because it is the most conversational of all meters: it imitates ordinary dialogue. The adjective *oikeion* in Aristotle's vocabulary also means "literal"; it stresses verisimilitude of the verbal medium. By contrast, tetrameter, the iambic's predecessor, was more suitable for dancing (1449a22–23). Aristotle thus charts a course of tragic *mimēsis* from a spectacular performance style to the one that is most representational.

If the story of poetry's evolution echoes Aristotle's views regarding aesthetic and moral habituation in the direction of contemplative life, the definition of tragedy and the relative value of its component parts in the *Poetics* reflects the process by which a mature agent (as distinct from an average Athenian spectator) partakes in tragic learning. The argument can be summarized as follows: Aristotle splits tragic drama into constituent parts in order to identify its essence as one part, the plot (*muthos*). As an arrangement of events depicting a piece of action, plot works to produce in a viewer (or reader) the effect of catharsis, or clarification. Tragic learning, as a cathartic recognition of cause and effect of action mimetically reproduced by the plot, can take place in the absence of such "external" performative elements as diction, singing, and spectacle. In other words, a person who is cultivated in the way envisioned by Aristotle can get the tragic effect by reading a script. Therefore, while ostensibly reporting his observations of the structure and effects of contemporary Greek tragedy, Aristotle adapts his account to the ends of philosophical learning, which is more syllogistic than empathetic.

We can now flesh out these claims, starting with the definition of tragedy: "Tragedy is a mimesis of an action that is elevated, complete and of magnitude; in language embellished by distinct forms in its sections, employing the mode of enactment, not narrative, and through pity and fear accomplishing a catharsis of such emotions" (*Poetics* 1449b24–28). Aristotle immediately qualifies this definition to point out which elements constitute the means of representation and which pertain to the action represented. Referring to the performance of tragedy on stage, he lists three external elements: the spectacular effect (*opsis*), song making (*melopoiia*), and diction (*lexis*). The other three elements—thought (*dianoia*), character (*ēthos*), and plot (*muthos*)—form the substantive core of tragic drama. Of the last three, thought and character are "natural causes" of the action depicted, whereas plot is a representation (*mimēsis*) of action (*Poetics* 1450a8–12). The way Aristotle divides tragedy into external and internal parts is already a sign of a chasm between the performative apparatus and the object of representation. But the division does not stop there. Announcing at the beginning that the most important of all these is the arrangement of the incidents, that is, the plot, Aristotle aims at discounting those elements that exceed the confines of a perfect sequencing of cause and effect.

If "the incidents and the plot are the end at which tragedy aims" (1450a21–22), however, what is the principle that prioritizes the remaining parts? Why does Aristotle insist that "character study" is less important for the tragic effect than the plot, which he honors as "the first principle" and the soul (*psuchē*) of tragedy (1450a38)? The privileging of the plot over character rests on several grounds. Character makes people what they are, whereas their actions make them happy or unhappy. Plot represents a piece of action, hence the depiction of character is ancillary to the development of the plot (*Poetics* 1450a19). The next argument modifies the preceding one by shifting the emphasis from representation (*mimēsis*) to function (*ergon*). If a poet "writes a series of speeches full of character and excellent in point of diction and thought," claims Aristotle, "he will not achieve the proper function (*ergon*) of tragedy nearly so well as a tragedy which, while inferior in these qualities, has a plot or arrangement of incidents" (*Poetics* 1450a28–32). Aristotle resorts to an analogy with painting to magnify the contrast between the character and the plot: "If someone lavishly applied the most beautiful colors (*pharmakois*), it would not give as much delight as representations in black and white" (*Poetics* 1450b1–2).

This analogy is suggestive, because it explains metaphorically why Aristotle stacks up the elements of tragedy the way he does. He describes painting with colors as rubbing or anointing a body with potions—an image that suggests soothing the body through the application of medicinal substances.[16] This implied effect of colorful painting stands in opposition to the proper function of perception, which, according to the analogy, is a more cognitive pleasure of seeing the outlines of a representation. It follows, then, that "speeches full of character and excellent in point of diction and thought" are like potions in that they work on the somatic level, while the arrangement of incidents in the plot clarifies why a person of certain character suffers or perishes. It is for this reason, I believe, that Aristotle pays such great attention to the arrangement of incidents, noting the necessity to establish a tight progression of cause and effect.[17] The term *catharsis* thus can be translated only by a word indicating intellectual illumination rather than a release or purging of bottled up emotions. Yet even among commentators who agree about "clarification" there has been a disagreement as to how emotional this clarification really is.[18] In both *Politics* and *Poetics* Aristotle envisions the education of emotions in a manner that does not set desire in conflict with the highest mental capacities of contemplative learning and inference. If we take seriously his stress on learning and inference brought about by mimetic representations, the proper function of tragic plot does not reside in the stirring of emotions. Rather than making us sob in pity or tremble with fear, tragedy is supposed to clarify why we should feel these emotions. The effect of tragic illumination, argues Stephen Halliwell, "requires the preexisting intelligibility of action and life in the world: mimetic art may extend and reshape understanding, but it starts from and depends upon already given possibilities and forms of meaning in our perceptions of the human world" (1990, 507).

The statements Aristotle repeatedly makes about the relative insignificance of live performance of tragedy support this conclusion even further. "Indeed the power (*dunamis*) of tragedy does not depend on its performance by actors," he declares (1450b17–19). Arguing toward the end of the *Poetics* that the tragic *mimēsis* is better than its epic counterpart, Aristotle insists that "tragedy can fulfill its function even without acting . . . , and its quality can be gauged by reading" (*Poetics* 1462a11–13). The pleasures of tragic learning have therefore little to do with a complicated and multifarious machinery of dramatic performance.

By now, it should be clear why, for instance, such elements as spectacle and song making do not register on a scale of proper tragic effects. Though singing is the most important of the "seasonings" (*hedusmata*) and spectacle is the most alluring (*psuchagogikon*), they are merely parasitic upon the substance of tragedy. Referring again to a live performance, Aristotle comments that "fear and pity sometimes result from the spectacle and are sometimes a result of the arrangement of the events, which is preferable and a mark of a better poet" (*Poetics* 1453b1–3). We observe Aristotle in the act of separating the genuine tragic effects from those that exceed the proper *ergon*. To this end, he claims that spectacle is inartistic, that is, falls outside the art of poetry: "Spectacle, while highly effective is the least artistic (*atechnotaton*) and has the least to do with poetry" (*Poetics* 1450b16–17). Furthermore, one should not seek all kinds of pleasure offered by a tragic performance, but only the proper pleasure (*Poetics* 1453b10–11).

The principle of proper tragic pleasure orders the remaining hierarchy of character (*ēthos*), thought (*dianoiia*), and diction (*lexis*). When measured against the "soul" of tragedy, their function is superstructural. "Character" is important insofar as it gives impetus to action, which is the requisite object of dramatic depiction. "Thought" dresses up action by displaying the character's ability to say what is possible and appropriate. "Diction," in turn, embellishes thought. Such an arrangement is all the more interesting because thought, character, and diction constitute a shared ground between poetics and rhetoric.

It is ironic that the rhetorical elements of tragedy are conceived of as more performative and "atechnical" than the genuinely poetic craft of the arrangement of incidents.

Aristotle observes that "thought," as a vehicle for disclosing the choice made by characters, is to be found in "speeches which argue that something is or is not or in general give an opinion" (*Poetics* 1450b10–12). But as a function of the statesman's or the rhetorician's art, thought falls outside of tragic *mimēsis*. Aristotle refers the reader to the treatise on rhetoric, since "the subject is more congenial to that inquiry" (*Poetics* 1456a35). But whereas Aristotle could discount spectacle as *atechnotaton,* there is an obvious problem of peeling *dianoia* off the core of tragic representation without affecting this very core. Thus Aristotle cannot help accepting that the effects produced by the language are essentially equal to the ones generated by incidents: "In the case of the incidents, too, one should work on the same principles, when effects of pity and terror and probability have to be produced" (*Poetics* 1456b2–4). What he does not acknowledge, however, is that his concession puts in jeopardy the hierarchy in which plot is at once the "soul" and a sketch augmented by speeches, singing, stage movement, and scene design.

The principle underlying the stripping of tragedy down to its core is at work in the *Rhetoric* as well. As I argued in chapter 1, Aristotle's *Rhetoric,* thanks to the insulation of the forms of proof (*pisteis*) from style (*lexis*), displays a similar hierarchy. However, if in the *Poetics* the knowledge or ignorance in the matters of style or diction "brings upon the poet no censure worth serious consideration" (1456b10–12), in the *Rhetoric* style commands the philosopher's attention because of irreducibly diverse and irredeemably popular character of the audience. When Aristotle says that style is of great importance due to the corruption of the hearer (*Rhetoric* 1404a9), he is not discussing rhetoric as a philosophical method or a form of discourse suitable for contemplative life.

It is possible now to grasp with more precision why Aristotle is able to proclaim poetry as more philosophical than other forms of cultural discourse. I have proposed that he can accomplish that because he can analytically detach poetic *mimēsis* as representation from the performative *mimēsis* of style and the identificatory *mimēsis* of the audience. Aristotle saves poetry from Plato's assault in the *Republic* in at least two ways: he establishes poetic art as a legitimate object of philosophical inquiry and grants emotions cognitive value. But in the process Aristotle transforms tragic drama from a powerful public performance into a linear story whose most profound effects should ideally follow from the structure of events and can in principle be achieved by reading. Paradoxically, the rhetorical elements of tragedy—thought, character, and diction—emerge as more performative than poetry. This performativity, in turn, makes rhetoric less congenial to theoretical contemplation and ethical deliberation.

Mimēsis *and Performance*

Isocrates preserves the performative and politically constitutive thrust of the traditional poetic *paideia* by incorporating it into his educational program under the name *philosophia*. Moreover, he appears to do so in direct opposition to Plato's agenda of curtailing psychological and political influence of poetic performance. By making character and political identity contingent upon recurrent performance addressed to the polis, Isocrates may be said to have successfully synthesized the traditional poetic *paideia* with the political emphasis of his public performance.

Given the Isocratean synthesis of poetry and *philosophia,* one can speculate about Aristotle's motives for placing poetry above the performative *mimēsis* that had vexed Plato and attracted Isocrates. Aristotle conceives of poetry in terms of representation rather than performance or audience identification because he seeks to insulate a properly conditioned, ethical human agent from the contingencies and excesses of performance. The focus on representation permits him to sort the befuddling variety of cultural discourses according to their subject matter rather than their social function or historical significance.

However, Athenian public oratory still presents a problem for a system of knowledge conceived of and prioritized in terms of abstract topics. In the case of rhetoric, performance and audience involvement do not lend themselves as easily to the same procedure as universalizable actions represented by tragic *muthos*. Aristotle aspires to overcome this obstacle in his formulation of a theory of rhetorical genres whereby he is able to limit the scope of public performance to three arenas and genre-specific functions. As distinct from this segmentation of public address into reified genera and species, Isocrates' education in all culturally relevant forms of speech prepares his students for opportunities to intervene in public life.

Three

BETWEEN *KAIROS* AND GENRE

Aristotle's separation of poetics and rhetoric can be read as an implicit response to the Isocratean defense of the politically constitutive character of poetry and oratory. If Isocrates regards self-reflexive imitation and performance of culturally prominent forms of speech as integral to one's ethical habituation and civic identity, Aristotle, like Plato, rejects an identity bound to performance. In setting up rhetoric as a *technē* distinct from the poetic craft, Aristotle disengages the instrumental function of public speech from a nobler and more philosophical tragic *mimēsis*.

Aristotle's taxonomy of public discourse in the *Rhetoric* suppresses its role as an artificer of culture and politics and redescribes the goals of rhetorical performance in terms of a priori determined ends. In so doing, Aristotle abstracts rhetoric from the sociolinguistic mechanism of cultural memory and political ideology. His formulation of the three genres of rhetoric transcends the culture of *kairos*, in which social actors achieve recognition and negotiate the ends of political decision making through speech. In support of this claim, the first section of this chapter examines how Aristotle sorts public address into deliberative, forensic, and epideictic genres. As we trace the classificatory procedure in the *Rhetoric*, it will become apparent that the basis for classification is informed not so much by Aristotle's observation of contemporary Athenian oratory as by a desire to neutralize oratory's ideologically constitutive power. Similar to the *Poetics*, in which the genre of tragic drama is defined so as to make tragedy serve moral philosophy, the three rhetorical genres are given their respective ends by political theory. This theoretical, deductive approach to public discourse limits its legitimate scope as a domain of social knowledge and therefore implicitly disavows the politically constitutive power of language.

In opposition to Aristotle's reified genres, some contemporary scholars have sought to theorize the ancient Greek notion of *kairos* as a concept that captures the radical fluidity of the "right moment" and grants speech the power to define both the rhetorical occasion and the proper response to it. Because of its resistance to literary and social formalization, *kairos* seems the opposite of genre. However, one should be cautious about championing *kairos* as genre's antipode. For while it insists on the revolutionary novelty of discourse, *kairos* cannot be realized, or even be conceived of, without relative social permanence of discursive elements. This relative stability, found not in some abstraction but in historical conditions of communication, is best reflected in the notion of speech genres. Developed by Russian literary critic Mikhail Bakhtin, the concept of speech genre permits us to account for social and cultural recalcitrance while paying attention to unique, situational features of poetry and prose. Spanning the spectrum from the quotidian to the literary, speech genres act as reservoirs of social knowledge, rather than as abstract *topoi*.[1] As such, speech genre seems a fitting "third term" mediating the dialectic between *kairos* and genre. The remaining two sections of my argument, then, explore a conception of "speech genres" as a mediating link between the fluidity of the opportune moment and the abstractness of a theoretically reified occasion.

Isocrates' pedagogical advice on how to co-opt heterogeneous speech genres to craft a *kairos*-appropriate logos not only defies Aristotle's generic taxonomy but also illuminates the connection between public performance, cultural memory, and political invention. Instead of molding his compositions in accordance with thematic and stylistic dictates of a particular species of oratory, Isocrates proceeds by creatively reenacting already uttered and memorable discourses. Whereas Aristotle limits invention to supplying discursive means to extrarhetorical political ends, Isocrates indicates that social invention is the ultimate goal of persuasive discourse. Unfortunately, just as Isocrates' *logos politikos* was discounted by Aristotle as epideictic display, Isocrates' idea of discursive knowledge became fragmented and marginalized in Aristotle's *Rhetoric*.

Aristotle's Generic Taxonomy and Extrarhetorical Knowledge

The enduring appeal of Aristotle's formulation of the three genres resides in its pragmatic orientation: each genre plays a distinct function within a polis. In a key passage of book 1, one finds a designation of species of rhetoric on the basis of what appears to be the historical division of roles assumed by audiences in Athenian public sphere:

> The species [*eidē*] of rhetoric are three in number; for such is the number [of classes] to which the hearers of speeches belong. A speech [situation] consists of three things: a speaker and a subject on which he speaks and someone addressed, and the objective [*telos*] of the speech relates to the last (I mean the hearer). Now it is necessary for the hearer to be either a spectator [*theōros*] or a judge [*kritēs*], and [in the latter case] a judge of either past or future happenings. A member of a democratic assembly is an example of one judging about future happenings, a juryman an example of one judging the past. A spectator is concerned with the ability [of the speaker]. Thus, there would necessarily be three genera of rhetorics; *symbouletikon* ["deliberative"], *dikanikon* ["judicial"], *epideiktikon* ["demonstrative"]. (1358a35–1358b7)

The use of expressions "necessarily" and "by necessity" indicates the statement's theoretical strength. Here, Aristotle undoubtedly emphasizes rhetoric as addressed to particular types of audiences. This strong link between the speech's end (*telos*) and the hearer (*akroatēs*) reassures us that when we classify a rhetorical "artifact" as this or that genre we still retain the sense of the influence the text or speech in question has on the audience. Even as we analytically dissect a speech, we assume that words do things to live people: they exhort or dissuade, accuse or defend, praise or blame (*Rhetoric* 1358b7–12). Aristotle thus seems to authorize the perception of the rhetorical discourse as a domain of social action.[2]

This impression, however, loses its certainty as Aristotle goes on to elaborate on the elements appropriate to the three rhetorical genres. Although the division of rhetorical speeches is marked as a distinction between the functions of hearing in certain performative situations (i.e., assembly, courts, and festivals), these occasions and audience expectations in each seem taken for granted. Indeed, the very concept of occasion is absent from the generic matrix of speaker-subject-hearer. A telltale sign of this reification of situational concerns is Aristotle's attempt to rearticulate the *telos* of each genre not in terms of the hearer but in terms of the utterance's content. Striving for precision in the definition of each species of rhetoric, Aristotle has to explain the overlap between speech-acts that jeopardizes the tripartite categorization. He therefore shifts the emphasis from the act to the *telos*:

> The "end" of each of these is different, and there are three ends for three [species]: for the deliberative speaker [the end] is the advantageous [*sumpheron*] and the harmful (for someone urging something advises it as the better course and one dissuading dissuades on the ground that it is worse), and he includes other factors as incidental: whether it is just or unjust, or honorable or disgraceful; for those speaking in the law courts [the end] is the just [*dikaion*] and the unjust, and they make other considerations incidental to these; for those praising and blaming [the end] is the honorable [*kalon*] and the shameful, and these speakers bring up other considerations in reference to these qualities. (*Rhetoric* 1358b21–28)

Significantly, the stress is now not on a verb designating action (*sumbouleuei*) but on a neuter noun designating substance (*to sumpheron*). Aristotle justifies this theoretical move by adducing examples showing that "sometimes the speakers will not dispute about the other points": a person on trial will never admit to having acted unjustly; the deliberative orator will omit considerations of justice if the course of action is expedient; the epideictic speaker will bracket the expediency of a hero's action to praise it as a deed of honor (*Rhetoric* 1358b30–1359a2).

Despite the ostensible grounding in practice, however, the conceptual vocabulary employed by Aristotle points away from the speech-act and its circumstances toward its propositional, topical content. As a result of this classificatory maneuver, genres are conceptualized as entities possessing either essential or accidental characteristics. Thus, for example, deliberative oratory is *defined* by its focus on the expedient and the harmful; if a particular instance of the genre introduces concerns about justice or honor, these interventions would be accidental, that is, theoretically unnecessary to produce conviction regarding expedience or harm of a proposed future action.

The change of focus from the occasional to the thematic has led commentators such as Friedrich Solmsen (1941) to conclude that in his division of rhetoric into *tria genera causarum,* Aristotle is guided "by a deductive reasoning which is Platonic in form and method" (42). Whether or not one accepts Solmsen's conclusions about the *Rhetoric*'s grounding in Platonism, it is evident from the text that Aristotle invokes particular examples of oratory to illustrate general logical divisions rather than forms his generalizations inductively from actual examples of oratory. Moreover, Aristotle fails "to quote from or allude to the text of a single deliberative or forensic speech" (Trevett 1996, 371) or to illustrate the blame aspect of the epideictic genre (Roundtree 2001).[3] These omissions point to the reification of rhetorical occasions, audience roles, and speeches' form and substance.

The case in point is Aristotle's explanation of the deliberative orator's preference for expediency (*to sumpheron*) over questions of justice (*to dikaion*). Deliberative orators, says Aristotle, "often grant other factors, but they would never admit that they are advising things that are not advantageous [to the audience] or that they are dissuading [the audience] from what is beneficial, and often they do not insist that it is not unjust to enslave neighbors or those who have done no wrong" (*Rhetoric* 1358b34–38). Though the example does not mention a specific historical exigence, the Loeb edition's editor insists that the reference is to "the cruel treatment by Athens of the inhabitants of the island of Melos (416 B.C.) for its loyalty to the Spartans during the Peloponnesian war" (Aristotle 1991, 36 n).

It is not at all clear that Aristotle has the Melos episode in mind. But if he does, the choice of the Melian "debate" as a representative case of deliberative oratory is surprising at best. For in this exchange, at least in the version of it given by Thucydides, Athenians are not deliberating among themselves about the expediency of enslaving other *poleis*. With their fleet and the army encamped in Melos and ready to ravage the land, Athenian representatives give the Council of the Melians reasons for surrendering without a fight: "You, by giving in, would save yourselves from disaster; we, by not destroying you, would be able to profit from you" (Thucydides 1968, 5.7). The question of justice is laid aside because, as Thucydides makes the Athenians say, "the standard of justice depends on the equality of power to compel and that in fact the strong do what they have the power to do and the weak accept what they have to accept" (5.7). In this situation, Athenian speakers are not addressing a deliberating body of the demos, they are dictating their conditions to the leaders of a polis threatened with annihilation and slavery. The advice is in fact an ultimatum, and this scenario is hardly an ideal case study for deliberative oratory.[4] In Aristotle, however, the *kairos* has lost its historical and political specificity. What remains is a set of prescriptive commonplaces from which a deliberative orator may launch a discourse of admonition.

Even more reductive than the description of deliberative genre is Aristotle's treatment of epideictic.[5] Starting with the hearer, who functions both as a spectator (*theōros*) and as a judge (*kritēs*) of the speaker's ability, Aristotle assigns epideictic a very narrow and inconsequential role. Compared with the institutionally constrained yet still action-oriented contexts of court and assembly, the discourse of praise and blame does not lend itself to a classification according to an easily recognized pragmatic exigence. In book 3 of the *Rhetoric,* Aristotle even remarks that "the epideictic style (*epideiktikē lexis*) is most like writing (*graphikotatē*); for its objective (*ergon*) is to be read" (1414a15).

By the same token, the limiting of the end of epideictic to display highlights the rigidity in the classification of deliberative and forensic situations. In a forensic setting, the hearer is a judge of the past; in a deliberative, of the future; in an epideictic, of the present (insofar as the display of the speaker's ability is productive of nonreferential amplification). As we shall see shortly, Aristotle's discussion of the resources of epideictic oratory further exposes the theoretical artifice of the shift from action-based to content-based classification of rhetorical speeches. This shift, implicit in the nominalization of the *telos* of each genre, becomes explicit at 1359a7, when Aristotle concludes: "It is evident from what has been said that it is first of all necessary [for a speaker] to have propositions [*protaseis*] on these matters" (1359a7). Accordingly, the next several chapters of book 1 deal with the propositions appropriate to each genre. Again, the terms associated with the construction of propositions—"necessary signs" (*ta tekmēria*), "probabilities" (*ta eikota*), and "signs" (*ta sēmeia*) (1359a7–8) —belong to the conceptual lexicon of Aristotle's logical treatises.[6] Such exposition accords with the opening announcement that rhetoric is a counterpart of dialectic, since both are concerned with proving opposites and constructing arguments on any subject matter.

The logical division of the rhetorical species and their corresponding ends is not the sole objective of Aristotle, however. The point of generic classification is not simply to shoehorn previously existing speech practices into well-demarcated types for the sake of theoretical orderliness. Rather, the objective is to limit as much as possible the claim of public speech to political knowledge all the while preserving its claim to power.

Having isolated rhetorical genres, Aristotle must provide the *topoi* peculiar to each of them; however, according to his own criteria, in granting rhetoric specific *topoi,* he risks promoting *technē rhētorikē* to a higher position in the hierarchy of knowledge. Before he begins to enumerate the subjects of deliberative oratory and the resources for construction of propositions about the expedient and the good, Aristotle qualifies his procedure:

> It is not necessary at the present moment to enumerate these subjects accurately, particular by particular, and to divide them into species on the basis of what is customary in deliberation or to say what would be a true definition of them, since that is not a matter for the rhetorical art but for a more profound and true [discipline]—and much more than its proper area of consideration has currently been assigned to rhetoric; for what we said earlier is true, that rhetoric is a combination of analytical knowledge and knowledge of characters and that on the one hand it is like dialectic, on the other like sophistical discourses. In so far as someone tries to make dialectic or rhetoric not just mental faculties but sciences, he unwittingly obscures their nature by the change, reconstructing them as forms of knowledge of certain underlying facts, rather than only of speech. (*Rhetoric* 1359b3–16)

Aristotle thus reveals that the knowledge upon which a deliberating or any other orator draws lies outside the domain of rhetoric. In contrast with Isocrates, whose *logos politikos* welds together political speech-acts and political deliberation, Aristotle separates the domain of "mere words" from the sciences of "things" such as politics and ethics. Arguing against some recent interpretations of Aristotle's rhetoric as constitutive of politics, Arthur Walzer (2000) explains Aristotle's delineation of genre-appropriate subject matter as an example of attenuation of rhetoric by politics. Walzer points out that for Aristotle it is a constitution, "itself the product of philosophical discussion under the auspices of dialectic," that sets the parameters of a rhetorical transaction, including the appropriate subject matter (51).[7]

Having nominalized and circumscribed the subjects of the deliberative, epideictic and dicanic oratory, Aristotle creates an impression that the materials of persuasion he is serving up are not tainted by the influence of discourses that produce and preserve them. In spite of the various proverbs, poetic citations, literary references, and historical anecdotes contained under the rubrics of the three genres, Aristotle has little to say about their discursivity, as if their stylistic and compositional traits have no effect whatsoever on the way they may influence the audience's perception of the subject matter. On the contrary, in some cases he even consigns explicitly poetic and literary resources of proof to an "atechnical" category. For instance, quotes from Sophocles' *Antigone* and examples from Homer and Herodotus are listed as illustrations of "inartificial" (*atechnoi*) proofs proper to forensic oratory (1375b27–1376a4).

Whereas deliberative and forensic genres, in the way Aristotle conceives them, allow for the dimming of the power of linguistic form in the interest of propositional content, epideictic rhetoric is more difficult to dismember in this fashion. The brevity of treatment of epideictic discourse signals that Aristotle does not have much to offer with respect to extrarhetorical knowledge.[8] Because its *telos* is confined to praise and blame, epideictic for Aristotle constitutes a catch-all category for speeches that do not seem to do much outside what they say.[9]

However, this very feature compels Aristotle to acknowledge, in addition to praiseworthy virtues and blameworthy vices, the language of praise (*logos epainos*) and its performative circumstances. The language of praise is based on the assumption that "qualities that are close to actual ones are much the same as regards both praise and blame" (1367a32–34). Aristotle offers the following justification for suspending the referentiality of language: "Since praise is based on actions and to act in accordance with deliberate purpose is characteristic of a worthy person, one should try to show him acting in accordance with deliberate purpose. It is useful for him to seem to have so acted often. Thus, one should take coincidences and chance happenings as due to deliberate purpose; for if many similar examples are cited, they will seem to be a sign of virtue and purpose" (1367b21–28). It follows that such a discourse is a work of artistic interpretation, and its success depends not on the actions themselves but on the manner in which they are made manifest. Indeed, Aristotle uses this very term—*emphanizon,* "setting forth"—to characterize *logos epainos*. The setting forth of an action happens by way of amplification (*auxēsis*), whereby a deed is depicted in the most attractive fashion (1368a26).

Aristotle does not pursue the subject of the nonreferential potential of language beyond the ability of speakers to display their stylistic repertoire, nor does he dwell on extended examples of it. He brackets amplification by saying that "among the classes of things common to all speeches, amplification is most at home in those that are epideictic; for these take up actions that are agreed upon, so that what remains is to clothe the actions with greatness and beauty" (1368a26–29). The discourse of praise, in this account, is an ornament added to an already existing (and presumably extrarhetorical) social agreement between the rhetor and the audience rather than as a full-bodied argument.

Yet this discounting of epideictic is troublesome, since Aristotle also mentions, albeit in passing, the difference among the way audiences are disposed toward a certain manner of praise or blame. As a proof of this, Aristotle appeals to Socrates' remark in the *Menexenus:* "For if it were a question of eulogizing

Athenians before an audience of Peloponnesians, or Peloponnesians before Athenians, there would indeed be need of a good orator to win credence and credit" (235D). As usual, the author of the *Rhetoric* neither cites verbatim nor takes into account the situational overtones inherent in the reference but simply states "As Socrates used to say" (1367b8). He therefore recommends: "One should speak of whatever is honored among each people as actually existing [in the subject praised], for example, among the Scythians, or Laconians or philosophers" (1367b8–10). If, however, barbarians expect an entirely different social custom for the performance of praise, if oligarchic Lacedaemonians are unreceptive to an Athenian *logos epainos,* and if philosophers require a separate type of praise from the hoi polloi, there must be something more serious about the business of setting forth of a virtue than mere rhetorical showmanship. Aristotle simply does not entertain a possibility that discourse may play a key role in setting up the very cultural and institutional contexts of which he wants his audience to be aware.

Aristotle does admit, also in passing, that praise may have practical application: "Praise and deliberations are part of a common species [*eidos*] in that what one might propose in deliberation becomes encomia when the form of expression is changed" (1367b37–1368a1). Usually this passage is taken as a token of Aristotle's approval of mixing generic elements. However, it may also be regarded as a moment when Aristotle's scheme of generic classification becomes stifling. Epideictic forces Aristotle back to the consideration of the performative dimension, when a deliberative situation is called forth by the turning (*strephein*) of linguistic form of an utterance: "When, therefore, we know what should be done and what sort of person someone should be, [to use this in deliberative oratory] we should change the form of expression and convert these points into propositions: for example, that one ought not to think highly of things gained by chance but of things gained through one's efforts. When so spoken, it becomes a proposition; but as praise [of someone] it takes the following form: 'He did not think highly of what came by chance but of what he gained by his own efforts'" (1368a4–7).

The "turn" is confined to a change of syntax, but by suggesting the potential of epideictic praise to morph into a discourse of admonition, this tangential remark threatens Aristotle's orientation toward the extrarhetorical grounding of rhetorical ends. Epideictic, relegated in the *Rhetoric* to a catch-all status for "display," calls into question the categorization of deliberative and forensic genres as speeches concerned with things and deeds outside rhetorical performance.[10]

If in book 1 epideictic is granted the status of a separate genre, in book 3 display elements, qua stylistic embellishments, are dispersed among the three genres. The *Rhetoric* disengages the performative elements of rhetoric from historical situations in which they functioned as summons and exhortations, thereby reducing them to style and formal arrangement. The addition of style, however, does more than simply increase or diminish the listener's attention to the subject matter. In spite of its theoretical subordination to demonstration (*apodeixis*), the "amplification" (*auxēsis*) seems to permeate and transform the subject matter itself by transforming the audience's perception of the situation at hand.

For example, one of the functions of *prooemia* is "to attack or absolve and to amplify or minimize" (*Rhetoric* 1415b). Aristotle qualifies this advice by pointing out the hearer's poor judgment and willingness to give ear "to what is extrinsic to the subject" (1415b4–6). At the same time, he includes, as a method of removing suspicion, an appeal to the listener's dislike of false accusations: "Another is to use [the nature of] slander as a basis of attack, considering what a bad thing it is, and this because it alters legal judgments and does not rely on the fact" (1416a34–36). The arousal of the audience's indignation at the magnitude of this evil, however, remains a stylistic function. While Aristotle keeps separating the propositional core of a rhetorical speech from the nonreferential language, the function of representation from emotional identification, the artificial divider keeps collapsing under the weight of rhetorical practice.

Similarly, epideictic amplification (*auxēsis*) keeps finding its way into other genres, compromising the stability of the tripartite classification. Commenting upon the potential use of narrative (*diēgēsis*) in deliberative oratory, Aristotle advises: "If there is narrative, it is of events in the past, in order that by being reminded of those things the audience will take better counsel about what is to come (either criticizing or praising). But then the speaker does not perform the function of an adviser" (*Rhetoric* 1417b12–16).

The orator who switches to the amplification mode of praise or blame while giving advice about the future thereby exceeds the function of a deliberative speaker because praise and counsels in Aristotle's generic matrix are tied to atemporal notions of the noble (*to kalon*) and the expedient (*to sumpheron*), rather than to a historical *kairos*.

In the light of the marginalization of epideictic, the piecemeal treatment of Isocrates' discourses in book 3 of the *Rhetoric* reveals an inherent tension between the generic division according to fixed subject matter and reified political function on the one hand and the stylistic apparatus of a particular rhetorical performance on the other. Isocrates is called upon to exemplify the rousing of emotions after the manner of "impassioned" orators (1408b15–16); the correct use of periodic style (1409b34–1410a20) and antithesis (1410b30); the appeal of vivid language (1411a30); the function of proomion in epideictic speeches (1414b27); the resort to accusations against adversaries when at a loss for topics (1418a30); the introduction of laudatory episodes into epideictic speech for the sake of variety (1418a32); and the insertion of friendly testimony of others when defending one's ethos (1418b28).

This anatomical exposition accords with Aristotle's principle that the propositional core of a speech constitutes a magnet around which stylistic elements should coalesce.[11] His inclusion of stylistic matters (along with the discussion of traditional parts of speech) is called for by his conviction that ordinary hearers should be made tractable through appropriate sensory stimulation:

> Emotion is expressed if the style, in the case of insolence, is that of an angry man; in the case of impious and shameful things, if it is that of one who is indignant and reluctant even to say the words; in the case of admirable things, [if they are spoken] respectfully; but if [the things] are pitiable, [if they are spoken] in a submissive manner; and similarly in other cases. The proper *lexis* also makes the matter credible: the mind [of the listener] draws a false inference of the truth of what a speaker says because they [in the audience] feel the same about such things, so they think the facts to be so, even if they are not as the speaker represents them; and the hearer suffers along with the pathetic speaker, even if what he says amounts to nothing. As a result, many overwhelm their hearers by making noise. (*Rhetoric* 1408a16–26)

Here, as in the *Poetics,* the performative dimension (*lexis*) receives short shrift in comparison with the propositional core. Yet whereas tragic drama possesses an internal end as a species of poetry, the respective ends of the three rhetorical genres are provided externally. The function of each genre is to shape a discourse in accordance with an abstract principle—expedience, justice, or honor—that an orator must grasp in advance through habituation and study of Aristotle's dialectic and political theory. Rhetoric's job is to furnish the means to these ends, not to constitute them.[12]

Still, the theory of three genres, as it is developed in the *Rhetoric,* manifests the uncertainties of classification that arise from the clash between philosophical categories and the practice of oratory. As Jacques Brunschwig (1996) remarked, "Rhetoric is a plant growing in the open air of the city and the public spaces. This is why it smashes abstract schemas into fragments; it offhandedly makes fun of the most respectable theoretical distinctions" (51). In spite of the reification of the contexts and ends of oratory evident in Aristotle's procedure, one cannot help noticing the difficulty that accompanies his efforts to divorce the materials of persuasion from their ideological and cultural freight.

Kairos *and Speech Genres in Ancient Greek Culture*

Besides the reification of *kairos* in *tria genera causarum,* the applicability of Aristotle's generic taxonomy is complicated by a remarkable fluidity in the typology of discourse in ancient Greek culture. Recall, for example, Gorgias's claim that poetry is speech with meter and his parodic play with the elements of encomiastic and court speeches in the *Helen*. Isocrates too has long befuddled commentators who sought to fit his compositions into Aristotle's tripartite scheme (e.g., Dionysius 1974; Photius 1960; Wolf 1570; Munscher 1916; Kroll 1940; Rademacher 1951; Kennedy 1963). Indeed, fifth- and early-fourth-century B.C.E. rhetorical culture seemed to value novelty and variety in speechmaking as a sign of cleverness and political acumen. The notion of *kairos,* the right moment, stood for spontaneity and inventiveness in confronting social situations. Because *kairos* appears as an antipode of genre, some scholars have chosen it as an alternative to the traditional Aristotelian matrix. While *kairos* offers an avenue for theorizing the radical contingency of quotidian, literary, and theoretical discourses, alone it does not explain how such "performances" are enabled socially and linguistically.

The word *kairos* in ancient Greek appears in a variety of contexts and means "the right moment" or "the opportune." The etymology of these meanings, according to Eric White (1987), is twofold:

> In archery, [*kairos*] refers to an opening or "opportunity" or, more precisely, a long tunnel-like aperture through which the archer's arrow has to pass. Successful passage of a *kairos* requires, therefore, that the archer's arrow be fired not only accurately but also with enough power for it to penetrate. The second meaning of *kairos* traces to the art of weaving. There it is the "critical time" when the weaver must draw the yarn through a gap that momentarily opens in the warp of the cloth being woven. Putting the two meanings together, one might understand *kairos* to refer to a passing instant when an opening appears which must be driven through with a force if success is to be achieved. (13)

As a self-conscious rhetorical term, *kairos* finds its articulation in the late fifth to early fourth century B.C.E. in sophistical practice (Poulakos 1995; Cahn 1989; Kinneavy 1985). *Kairos* seems inseparable from the sophistic notion of truths in opposition, *dissoi logoi* (see Robinson 1979, 65–68). Because the truth is multifaceted, the speaker temporarily resolves the tension between the many possible answers by thrusting forth the one most suitable for the moment. The radical unfinalizability of any persuasive statement is thus a condition for a continuous renewal, not a mere repetition, of rhetorical answers to situations (Heidlebaugh 2002). By the same token, a rhetorical *technē* cannot supply a definitive repertoire of *kairoi*. As White proposes, "since *kairos* stands for precisely the irrational novelty of the moment that escapes formalization, any science of 'kaironomy' would find itself incoherently promising foreknowledge of chance. To put it another way, no treatise on the occasional nature of utterance could be itself exempt from occasionality, or the inevitability of its own supersession" (20).

How, then, may one capture the elusive *kairos*? What, if anything, lies in between the intuitive grasp of the right thing to say at the right time and the three generic molds we have inherited through the Western rhetorical tradition since Aristotle? A potentially fruitful "third way," I think, is offered by an orientation that examines "Homer" as well as the host of other ancient discourses not as artifacts containing germs of later classifications, but as socially situated performances. In Richard Bauman's (1986) definition, now widely adopted by classicists, performance is "a mode of communication, . . . the essence of which resides in the assumption of responsibility to an audience for a display of communicative skill, highlighting the way in which communication is carried out, above and beyond its referential content" (3).

The performative orientation urges us to recontextualize poetic and rhetorical traditions on their own terms rather than to seek their identity within a predetermined generic taxonomy. Richard Martin's (1989) study of words for speech in the *Iliad* offers an illuminating example of how native discourse "typologies" operate in a performance culture. Martin notes that "the ethnographer of speaking who attempts to reconstruct Greek talk about words . . . will not be surprised to find a folk taxonomy of speech that is askew from the standpoint of our own notions" (12). Indeed, the terms for speech in Homer, *muthos* and *epos,* describe performative situations rather than thematically established categories: "Muthos is, in Homer, a speech-act indicating authority, performed at length, usually in public, with a focus on full attention to every detail. I redefine epos, on the other hand, as an utterance, ideally short, accompanying a physical act, and focusing on message, as perceived by the addressee, rather than on performance as enacted by the speaker" (Martin 1989, 12).

Accordingly, the term *muthos* designates "a range of speech genres": "political talk, angry speech, and affectionate recollection" (Martin 1989, 12). *Epos,* on the other hand, consistently appears when someone is said to hear and acknowledge others' words. As Martin puts it, "Epos refers to the transmission of the message, the end-product of speech process" (16). *Epea* also tend to be small and fragmented: they "travel about here and there in a wide field" and "can be batted to and fro, part of a general system of exchange" (18). What distinguishes *muthos* from *epos,* then, is not its stylistic peculiarity and propositional content but the performative modality of discourse.[13] The words that constitute *muthos,* if they reach someone either immediately or through a third party, may become commands or proposals—they assume the status of the *epea.* That is why Martin questions the ostensible synonymity of the two terms, because "when we do pay attention to context, synonymity recedes" (14).

The difference between *muthos* and *epos* is also socially significant. *Muthoi* of Homeric epics are often boastful tirades of powerful men who challenge the authority of their peers or defy words of command uttered by gods. Martin catalogues heroic *muthoi* into types according to situations: "prayer, lament, supplication, commanding, insulting, and narrating from memory" (1989, 44). He draws attention to their apparent conventionality not because he wishes to formalize them but because of their intimate connection to what Victor Turner calls "social dramas" of the archaic Greek society (ibid., 43). To be the speaker of *muthoi*, "authoritative speech-acts," is part of "the heroic imperative" (ibid., 26). By contrast, *epea* are not tied to the heroic ideal of enacting of words and deeds: "*Epos* refers to the secondary transmission of an original command by someone else" (ibid., 25–26). The former term thus comprises speeches of those in power or those endowed with a special status, while the latter indicates reciprocal social relations and the persistence of a speech beyond the occasion of its utterance. The enduring quality of speech is captured by the Homeric term *epea pteroenta*, "winged words." However, the lasting nature of such utterances does not turn them into what we may call an "artifact," an object whose density allows for its typification outside the performative situation. According to Martin, the "intensity of speaker's purpose imparts to the otherwise ordinary epea a tautness, power, and movement that makes them whir and beat, like the motion of a wing. The powerful language thus produced makes its impression because it continuously reaches the hearer's consciousness, like a wave of sound" (ibid., 37).

The dialectic of *muthos* and *epos* outlined by Martin is useful for appreciating the craft of discourse and its social function in archaic and classical periods, for *muthos* and *epos* mark the opposite points of a shifting continuum between speech as action and speech as product.[14] This dialectic explains how effective, socially powerful performances leave their mark on cultural memory. As such, it challenges the transcendental formality of traditional generic distinctions. Instead of talking about a repertoire of stylistic and thematic elements that congeal into a predictable generic pattern regardless of a historical occasion, we may talk of *muthos* as an act of enunciation and *epos* as a residue of this act. The performance of an authoritative speech-act in Homer is measured not by how well it fits the formula for a certain type of address but how powerfully this action reverberates in the hearers, both those attending recitations of Homeric poetry and those within the epic itself.[15] The "product" of performance is not a textual artifact; it is *epos*—the word designating the perceived effect of speech as well as its discursive fabric.

There is, of course, a world of difference between the notion of "speech genres" employed by Martin in his description of heroic *muthoi* and *epea* and a more traditional understanding of genre. As a term coined by Mikhail

Bakhtin, "speech genre" challenges the dichotomy of literary and ordinary language that had been postulated by the Russian formalists.[16] Opposing the idea that literary discourse operates on a plane very different from ordinary talk and hence demands to be studied apart from its sociohistorical milieu, Bakhtin turned precisely to diverse registers of "ordinary" language to interpret the novelistic prose of Rabelais, Dickens and Dostoyevsky. He offers an explanation of speech genres:

> Language is realized in the form of individual concrete utterances (oral and written) by participants in various areas of human activity. These utterances reflect the specific conditions and goals of each such area not only through their content (thematic) and linguistic style, that is, the selection of the lexical, phraseological, and grammatical resources of the language, but above all through their compositional structure. All three of these aspects—thematic content, style, and compositional structure—are inseparably linked to the *whole* of utterance and are equally determined by the specific nature of the particular sphere of communication. Each separate utterance is individual, of course, but each sphere in which language is used develops its own relatively stable types of these utterances. These we may call *speech genres*. (60)

In Bakhtin's account, speech genres are neither timeless nor general but socially concrete and heterogeneous. Rather than models of imitation, they constitute the condition of possibility for entering meaningful and socially effective communicative exchange, be it a simple, everyday interaction or a complex written composition addressed to spatially or temporally remote audiences.

Speech genres possess a certain degree of permanence that allows speakers to seize an opportune moment to intervene with their rejoinders in response to previously uttered words. No speaker, as Bakhtin puts it, can be "the one who disturbs the eternal silence of the universe" (1986, 69). Although in Isocrates there is no terminological equivalent of speech genres, he nevertheless promotes the idea of discursive knowledge (summarized by the term *philēkoia,* "love of listening") as a precondition for discerning the right moment to speak. It is this knowledge that Aristotle dismisses in the *Rhetoric* as a discourse that "slips under the appearance of politics." For Isocrates, however, it is an equivalent of political wisdom and a goal of *paideia*. The following section shows that Isocrates relies on an array of popular oral and written utterances—speech genres that range from religious to secular, from hymn to historical account—to shape a timely logos. In crafting his discourses to suit the occasion (*kairos*), Isocrates self-consciously reaccentuates what in Homeric discourse is called *epea,* the words that live beyond the moment of their utterance and keep reverberating in generations of listeners and readers.

Kairos *and Discursive Knowledge in Isocrates' Prose Performance*

In many of his extant writings, Isocrates asserts the novelty and uniqueness of his own compositional task compared with the goals of contemporary speech teachers. The early pamphlet *Against the Sophists,* which is generally regarded as an advertisement for Isocrates' recently opened school, is unequivocal in its opposition to cookie-cutter methods of "an ordered art":

> I am amazed when I see these men claiming students for themselves; they fail to notice that they are using an ordered art (*tetagmenē technē*) as a model for a creative activity (*poiētikon pragma*). Who—besides them—has not seen that while the function of letters is unchanging and remains the same, so that we always keep using the same letters for the same sounds, the function of words (*logoi*) is entirely opposite. What is said by one person is not useful in a similar way for the next speaker, but that man seems most artful (*technikōtatos*) who both speaks worthily of the subject matter and can discover things to say that are entirely different from what others have said. The greatest indication of the difference is that speeches cannot be good unless they reflect the circumstances (*kairoi*), propriety (*to prepon*), and originality, but none of these requirements extends to letters. (12–13)

That fitness for the occasion takes priority in the list of virtues of a speech teacher is doubly remarkable. First, Isocrates is setting up a contrast between "technical" speech instruction of the kind purveyed by the Sophists and a more comprehensive system of education that requires "much study" and "a brave and imaginative soul" (*Against the Sophists* 17). In this manner, Isocrates signals that his *logōn paideia* is not reducible to imitation of model speeches but can stand as a sophisticated enterprise, in fact, a *philosophia*. Second, he posits an intriguing and rich tension between speaking worthy of the subject and creating an unprecedented persuasive appeal.

This tension between the rhetor's knowledge and its opportune application is integral to Isocrates' conception of discourse, especially if one compares it with Aristotle's concern with finding existing means of persuasion for any subject (*Rhetoric* 1355b2). Both are interested in the quality of "fitness for the occasion." They differ vastly from one another in understanding the sources of invention and the nature of occasion itself. Isocrates achieves a balance between the situational demands of *pragmata* and stylistic shape of his compositions by treating his linguistic resources as already infused with social meaning rather than as "letters of the alphabet" or as abstract models of eloquence.

The kind of knowledge Isocrates advocates is not disinterested or mechanical. As Takis Poulakos (1997) remarks, "When [in *Against the Sophists*] Isocrates puts forth his own method of instruction, he turns the distinction between learning based on knowledge and learning based on the use and application of knowledge into a sequence, a progression from a lower to a higher level of study" (97). Isocrates cojoins knowledge with *kairos* rather than treating it as an autonomous repository of learning. Advising his pupil Demonicus, he presses, "Apply your life's leisure time to a fondness for listening (*philēkoian*) to discussion, for in this way you will easily learn what is discovered by others only with difficulty" (*To Demonicus* 18). The noun *philēkoia,* "fondness for listening," describes the best way to develop into someone who can speak both from accumulated wisdom and in response to circumstances. As distinct from Aristotle's treatment of the resources appropriate to the three genres, discursive knowledge in Isocrates is not amenable to formalization according to fixed occasions. Each new situation is likely to give a new configuration to the linguistic repertoire that the speaker had assimilated in the process of study and practice.

To grasp how *philēkoia* relates to Isocrates' conception of knowledge and its practical application, it is useful to compare the different valuations given to the term by Isocrates and Plato. Plato employs a related term *philēkoos,* "lover of listening," in two opposite senses. In the *Republic,* for instance, those who are *philēkooi* are deemed unworthy of the title "philosopher": "The lovers of sounds and sights (*philēkooi kai philotheamones*) delight in beautiful tones and colors and shapes and all which craftsmen have made from such; but their mind is incapable of seeing and delighting in the beautiful itself" (476b). Plato also uses the word *philēkoos* in a positive sense, but then it refers to someone who is fond of listening to a particular type of speaker—namely, Socrates himself. For example, in *Lysis,* Ctesippus is described as someone who is "singularly fond of listening" (206c). Whereas Plato hears in the sounds of poetic and rhetorical speeches a distracting cacophony, Isocrates finds a generative polyphony.

Isocrates' ideal speaker seeks out the most historically and culturally memorable types of speech even as he promotes his compositions as both unique and timely.[17] He does not invent new discourses but orchestrates the already heard and repeated utterances. Yet he must summon and deploy these utterances at the moment that would be recognized by his audience as *kairos*. In Isocrates, *kairos* exceeds the spatio-temporal limits defined by the law courts, the Assembly, and the festival, the three explicit institutions of rhetorical practice in the Athenian democracy. Even though the manuscript tradition and modern philological scholarship have compartmentalized his writings into "judicial," "political," and "epideictic," Isocrates himself is reluctant to do so.[18] Instead, he insists on the "timeliness" of his literary compositions. What kinds of occasions, then, does Isocrates identify? In his advice to Demonicus, Isocrates states that there are "but two occasions for speech—when the subject is one you thoroughly know and when it is one on which it is necessary to speak" (*To Demonicus* 41). The impulse to speak is therefore both external and internal. It is external insofar one perceives in a situation the compelling force of necessity (*ananke*); it is internal insofar one has a grasp of discourses that are fit to address the situation in question.

An example of how Isocrates establishes the necessary moment to speak and brings to his "oration" the resources of various speech genres can be seen in one of his most stylistically mixed discourses, *Panegyricus*. Its author asserts the presence of both motives for speaking mentioned in *To Demonicus:* historical urgency and the rhetor's knowledge of the subject. Published around 380 B.C.E., it is at once the most politically poignant and thematically traditional of Isocrates' pamphlets. The composition is driven by a bitter strife among Greek city-states and the rhetorician's desire to display his knowledge and experience. What is remarkable about this combination of opportunities is their ostensible supercession by a third, more ritualized occasion implied by the title *Panegyricus,* a speech composed for a public festival. A critic following the generic reading protocol would immediately point out that Isocrates fits his address into a mold of an epideictic oration of the type common at pan-Hellenic gatherings. This would not be a complete error: Isocrates explicitly identifies his discourse as a *panegurikos,* draws attention to the display of his verbal ability (*epideixis*), and relies on traditional mythological and epic themes (*ta archaia*). But to view this pamphlet only as an artful account of mythical and historical events in praise of Athens, and in so doing stress common traits of the "oration" and other ceremonial speeches, would be to miss the irony of the historical moment of its composition and the image repair Isocrates performs to reassert the Athenian claim to leadership (*hēgemonia*) among the Greeks.

Lest his readers miss the duplicity of the occasion, Isocrates invites them to see it as a clash between the enduring theme of Athenian greatness and the sorry state of Athens and other Greek *poleis* in the wake of the peace of Antalkidas.[19] Before giving his counsels "on the war against the barbarians and on concord among ourselves," Isocrates directs the attention to the opportunity opened by others' inadequate treatment of the topic and the urgency of the present condition:

> I am, in truth, not unaware that many of those who have claimed to be sophists have rushed upon this theme, but I hope to rise so far superior to them that it will seem as if no word had ever been spoken by my rivals upon this subject. . . . In the next place, the moment (*hoi kairoi*) for action has not yet gone by, and so made it now futile to bring up this question; for then, and only then, should we cease to speak, when the conditions have come to an end

and there is no longer any need to deliberate about them. . . . But so long as conditions go on as before, and what has been said about them is inadequate, is it not our duty to scan and study this question, the right decision of which will deliver us from our mutual warfare, our present confusion, and our greatest ills? (*Panegyricus* 3–6)

In arguing for a pan-Hellenic alliance under the leadership of Athens, the rhetor must negotiate a difficult path between the lore of the Athenian ancestral claims to *hēgemonia* and the divisive memory of the Peloponnesian War. Therefore, Isocrates cannot merely imitate the *topoi* of Athenian speeches in praise of the city. He needs to refashion them and other serviceable linguistic resources into a pan-Hellenic logos. Nor is it enough to appeal to the audience's practical interest by rehearsing "the misfortunes which have come upon us from our mutual warfare and the advantages which will result from a campaign against the barbarian" (15). In his own description, Isocrates is aiming at an oratory that "deals with the greatest affairs and, while best displaying the ability of those who speak, brings most profit to those who hear" (4–5). This enterprise requires an ability to reinterpret a web of oral and written discourses that have not yet lost their vibrance for contemporary audiences: "Since oratory is of such a nature that it is possible to discourse on the same subject matter in many different ways—to represent the great as lowly or invest the little with grandeur, to recount the things of old in a new manner or set forth events of recent date in an old fashion—it follows that one must try to speak better than they. For the deeds of the past are, indeed, an inheritance common to us all; but the ability to make proper use of them at the appropriate time (*en kairō*), to conceive the right sentiments about them in each instance, and to set them forth in finished phrase, is the peculiar gift of the wise" (*Panegyricus* 8–9).

Because Isocrates is not presenting his discourse orally but disseminating it among a reading audience, the promise to outdo the other rhetors appears as more than just "a conventionilized statement of the power of oratory," as Norlin puts it in the Loeb edition (1:124f). The fact that Isocrates advertises his prowess in such a manner deserves attention—a literary rhetorician frames his narrative by reiterating an oral sophistic speech genre. As it turns out, he does so in order to subvert the performative and compositional conventions of ceremonial addresses:

> I shall proceed with my theme, after first vaunting a little further my own powers. For I observe that the other orators in their introductions seek to conciliate their hearers and make excuses for the speeches which they are about to deliver, sometimes alleging that their preparation has been on the spur of the moment, sometimes urging that it is difficult to find words to match the greatness of their theme. But as for myself, if I do not speak in a manner worthy

of my subject and of my reputation and of the time which I have spent—not merely the hours which have been devoted to my speech but also all the years which I have lived—I bid you show me no indulgence but hold me up to ridicule and scorn. (*Panegyricus* 13–14)

This "boast" exposes the excessive artificiality of a typical introduction to a ceremonial speech. At the same time, it draws the reader's attention to the author's persona precisely by contrasting the formulaic expression of humility with an attitude of responsibility toward the subject and the occasion.

Isocrates' distinct balancing of stylistic resources and *kairos* may be appreciated by comparing Panegyricus with another contemporary text that purported to praise Athens: Plato's mocking imitation of the Athenian funeral oration (*epitaphios logos*) in the *Menexenus*. Though composed after 387 B.C.E. (it too mentions the Peace of Antalkidas), the dialogue is set in the Periclean era, around the time of the first year of the Peloponnesian War. In the exchange preceding the parody of *epitaphios logos,* Plato's Socrates assures his young follower Menexenus that there is nothing special about praising Athens and its slain defenders. In fact, he, Socrates, easily memorized the oration that Pericles' consort Aspasia had composed on the occasion of a public funeral (235e). Socratic parodic "performance" goes on purposefully to mix a collection of historical and mythical commonplaces with an unflattering account of the deeds of the Athenian *demos*. Epideictic oratory, in this view, is little else than the aping of well-worn formulas of praise. The orators, Socrates tells Menexenus, can impart importance to the deeds of the least worthy "with their ascribing to each one both what he has and what he has not, and the variety and splendour of their diction" (234c4–5). According to Socrates, the effect of this embellishment is overpowering: "And this majestic feeling remains with me for over three days: so persistently does the speech and voice of the orator ring in my ears that it is scarcely on the fourth of fifth day that I recover myself and remember that I really am here on earth, whereas till then I almost imagined myself to be living in the Islands of the Blessed" (235b–c). By objectifying the funeral oration, Plato's Socrates in effect turns it into a mere stylistic shell without substance. It becomes a bitter satire, a statement of despair about the lost opportunity for renewed political agency.

As distinct from many dialogues in which the language of poetry and sophistry is objectified through personae other than Socrates, Plato's attack on democracy takes the shape of Socratic imitation of its most sublime institution. Plato's dramatized mockery of the discourse of funeral oration translates into a dismissal of demotic rhetoric.[20] Plato's cold irony thinly disguises his hatred for the demos: "In truth, Menexenus, to fall in battle seems to be a splendid thing in many ways. For a man obtains a splendid and magnificent funeral even though at his death he be but a poor man; and though he but a worthless fellow, he wins praise, and that by the mouth of accomplished men who do not praise at random, but in speeches prepared long beforehand" (234c).

Isocrates demonstrates the cultural validity of speech genres of Athenian democracy that in Plato's version had long ossified into institutional commonplaces. In the *Panegyricus,* Isocrates accents his timely intervention into foreign policy and uses linguistic variety as an inventional strategy. In Isocrates' reconstruction of the Athenian claim to hegemony, the author's portrayal of the present urgency is refracted through a tightly woven sequence of speech genres pertaining to the history and political mythology of Athens.

In contrast with Plato's harsh judgment of democratic imitation as a numbing repetition, Isocrates' pamphlet presents a different kind of *mimēsis*—not a satirical re-presentation but a creative reenactment. Isocrates introduces speech genres of the Greek culture as words that have been repeated many times and hence do not properly belong to the speaker alone, a condition that makes them the property of the entire Hellas. When speaking of the good deeds of Athens toward other Greek states, says Isocrates, one must choose "not those which because of their slight importance have escaped attention and been passed over in silence, but those which because of their great importance have been and still are on the lips and in the memory of all men everywhere" (*Panegyricus* 27). Isocrates uses framing devices like the one above to demarcate the living speech genres he weaves into his argument even as he seeks, in an admittedly self-aggrandizing fashion, to create a unique and timely discourse.

It is partly because of this dialogical relationship between the author's persona and his linguistic resources that Isocrates often asks his potentially skeptical readers not to dismiss archaic tales. Isocrates grants that the most ancient of these accounts, such as the story of goddess Demeter's gifts to the city, may be questioned because of its archaic status (*Panegyricus* 30). However, the cultural value of this myth, evidenced by its transmission via the *Homeric Hymn to Demeter* and associated mystic rites that evidently carried on into the fourth century B.C.E., is more germane than the veracity of the account (30–31). The authorial presence links such "archaisms" to the *kairos* at hand and thereby contests their merely "ritualistic" quality so insidiously pointed out by Plato's Socrates in the *Menexenus*. While explicitly marking the divine benevolence toward Athens as a story transmitted through sacred rituals and poetic speech,[21] Isocrates infuses the narrative of the city's noble origin and the gifts it shared with the rest of the Hellenes with a contemporary meaning. "And is it not more fitting to exercise faith (*pisteuein*) about the things of which the oracle of Apollo speaks definitively," he asks, "and on which many of the Greeks agree, and when the words spoken long ago accord with the deeds of today, and the present events tally with the statements of the old?" (31). The form of a rhetorical question thrusts the archaic discourse into the present day as if the concord it asserts were a fait accompli. Isocrates manifests his sense of *kairos* by reaccentuating the old speech genre describing the city's beginning (*archē*) to effect a change in the present political circumstances.[22] Where Plato would expose the discourse of praise as grossly fictitious when compared with the shameful situation of the King's Peace,[23] Isocrates seizes upon winged words of popular mythology to realign past, present, and future.

Indeed, throughout the rest of the pamphlet, as the narrative progresses from the quasi-historical events to the account of not-so-distant Persian Wars, Isocrates strives to transcend the current feud between Athens and Sparta and to heal the sore remembrance of the Peloponnesian War. He does so without ignoring the feud itself or shunning the controversial theme of comparison between imperial policies of Athens and Sparta (120–28). Before appealing to the common cause of the two *poleis,* however, Isocrates qualifies the harshness of his polemic against Sparta:

> For it is not with the intention of stigmatizing the city of the Lacedaemonians in the eyes of others that I have spoken as I have about them, but that I may induce the Lacedaemonians themselves, so far as it lies in the power of words to do so, to make an end of such a policy. It is not, however, possible to turn men from their errors, or to inspire in them the desire for a different course of action without first roundly condemning their present conduct; and a distinction must be made between accusation, when one denounces with intent to injure and admonition, when one uses like words with intent to benefit. (129–30)

This passage shows the author walking a rhetorical tightrope, balancing between the anti-Lacedaemonian sentiment current in the speeches of contemporary Athenian orators and the detached (and, in some cases, pro-Spartan tenor) in the writings of democracy's elite critics.[24]

To bridge the chasm between the demos and the elites, between the Athenians and Lacedaemonians, Isocrates appeals to the Greeks' common cultural enmity toward the barbarians, which for generations has been stirred by the collective experience of *hearing* ancestral *epea:*

> So ingrained in our nature is our hostility to them that even in the matter of our stories we linger most fondly over those which tell of the Trojan and the Persian wars, because through them we learn of our enemies' misfortunes.... Moreover, I think that even the poetry of Homer has won a greater renown because he has nobly glorified the men who fought against the barbarians, and that on this account our ancestors determined to give his art a place of honour in our musical contests and in the education of our youth, in order that we,

hearing his verses over and over again (*akouontes tōn epōn*), may learn by heart the enmity which stands from of old between us and them, and that we, admiring the valour of those who were in the war against Troy, may conceive a passion for like deeds. (*Panegyricus* 158–59)

Homeric epos is a powerful institution precisely because of its iterability, its capacity to send ripples through the fabric of other discourses. Isocrates wants the reader to see *his* text as such a fabric, woven as it is from a variety (*poikilia*) of *epea*. Its force, though tied to the historical *kairos,* overflows the boundaries of the immediate occasion. Because Isocrates includes an excerpt from *Panegyricus* as a "witness" in his quasi-forensic speech *Antidosis,* it is likely that he wishes to present this and other discourses from different periods of his career as the *logoi* that have survived, like the epos of Homer, through many a transmission.

Isocrates' *logōn paideia,* both in principle and in practice, is opposed to a crude typification of rhetoric for the purpose of imitation. Upholding *kairos* as a chief criterion of politically effective discourse, Isocrates offers a nuanced understanding of discourse types. I have argued that in Isocrates there is no compartmentalization of rhetoric according to ritualized or theoretically circumscribed occasions. He often crosses the generic lines between the so-called epideictic, deliberative and dicanic oratory. But this does not mean that there is a lack of differentiation with respect to his linguistic resources; rather, Isocrates distinguishes among discourses on the basis of their social significance. Those speech genres (*epea*) that have had most enduring impact on the linguistic community are, in his hierarchy, the most serviceable and most worthy of imitation. Imitation, however, is not a mere repetition but a timely reaccentuation of already uttered speech.

Unfortunately for Isocrates, his opposition to an a priori teleology of speechmaking was later interpreted as a sign of theoretical weakness. In Aristotle's view, Isocrates is a valuable resource only because of his command of the epideictic style that promotes the audience's identification with the subject. While he singles out Isocrates as one of the eminent "Athenian rhetors" (*Rhetoric* 1418a30) and cites his works fifty-nine times (Bonitz 1955, 347), Aristotle also minimizes the political importance and timeliness of Isocrates' writings by tearing them into stylistically interesting but ultimately decontextualized fragments. Apparently, this practice did not escape Isocrates' notice. In his last extant pamphlet, *Panathenaicus,* he protests against those who gather in the Lyceum (*en to Lukeio*) to abuse his discourses, "reading them in the worst possible manner side by side with their own, dividing them at the wrong places, mutilating them, and in every way spoiling their effect" (17–18).

The arrangement of examples from Isocrates in the *Rhetoric* presents Isocrates as a "parts of speech" teacher, that is, someone interested in formal strategies of display over and against substantive considerations of argumentative demonstration (*apodeixis*). This portrait of Isocrates was subsequently perpetuated by testimonia and read back into Isocrates as evidence of his *technē*. Solmsen, for example, holds that the Isocratean school exemplified "the traditional method of organizing the rhetorical material under the heading of the *partes orationis* (*moria logou*)," a tradition whose lack of "a clear conception of the essential functions of a speech" Aristotle deplored (37). More recently, however, some have attempted to reconstruct Isocrates' treatment of parts of speech as a theory of rhetorical invention. Robert Gaines (1990), drawing upon Hellenistic sources, especially Dionysius, presents Isocrates' putative emphasis on the parts of the speech as a valid rhetorical theory. According to Gaines, Isocrates showed an implicit understanding of rhetorical intellection (*noesis*), according to which the speaker matches the objectives of the speech with functions of proem, narration, proof, and epilogue (167–68). Although Gaines's reconstruction welds together invention and arrangement, the two "doctrines" separated "under the authority of Aristotle," it also promulgates Aristotle's own portrayal of Isocrates as a formalist. But Isocrates explicitly distinguishes his teaching from both *tetagmenē technē,* with its implication of precise arrangement of discursive elements, and abstract intellection. Instead, he advocates training in all socially relevant types of speech in order to prepare his students to meet the demands of the opportune moment. A political actor, for Isocrates, is someone who recognizes that entering a *kairos* requires an understanding of the cumulative, agonistic, and provisional character of the sources of eloquence.

Four

BETWEEN IDENTIFICATION AND PERSUASION

In interpreting Isocratean and Aristotelian conceptions of discourse as distinct versions of rhetoric, constitutive and instrumental, so far the argument has engaged three different, yet overlapping frames. First, the rhetorical claims of Isocrates and Aristotle were examined vis-à-vis the cultural context in which writing was introduced into a culture previously dominated by orality. The constitutive thrust of Isocratean writing can be seen in the way the author coopts the oral resources of the mythopoetic tradition to construct an identity of citizen-rhetor through his textual performance. Aristotle, by contrast, neutralizes the oral performative dimensions of discursive practice by stressing the propositional content of his linguistic resources.

The two conceptions of discourse were then contrasted by exploring the ends and modes of civic education in Plato, Isocrates, and Aristotle. As distinct from traditional interpretations of Aristotle's alleged reversal of the Platonic indictment of poetry, Aristotle emerges as an opponent of the *Isocratean* performative conception of education. Isocratean education (*paideia*) conceives of the process of discursive imitation and performance as a never-ending and fully externalized development of a political agent. One's political reputation, on this view, is both an object of imitation and an effect of performance. Aristotle, on the contrary, separates the ethical conditioning of a youth from a mature person's contemplation of artistic representations. By pushing the performative components of tragic drama to the periphery of the poetic art, Aristotle is able to claim poetry as a more philosophical discourse than history and rhetoric. In this reshuffling of the elements of poetic performance, irreducibly rhetorical aspects—especially style—are at once exiled from and subordinated to a syllogistic structure of the plot. Consequently, the arts of poetry and rhetoric are separated not only because of different subject matter, but also because of rhetoric's tendency to expose the speaker to the corrupting (from a philosophical standpoint) influence of popular audiences.

This "vulgar" performativity is partially contained in Aristotle's *Rhetoric* by way of generic segmentation of rhetorical practice. Thus Aristotle both acknowledges the public nature of rhetorical performance and disciplines it by assigning ends and topics appropriate to each genre. In Isocrates' pedagogical and political writings, which defy Aristotle's generic classification, we find a far more expansive view of rhetoric: rather than conforming to the ends and propositions appropriate to the three rhetorical forums, an Isocratean speaker draws upon the diverse repertoire of "speech genres" of the Athenian public culture in order to respond to historically unique occasions. The "discursive knowledge" employed by the speaker in determining and confronting situations does not exist prior to and above the practice of rhetoric—it is the intelligence that derives from one's continuing and avid interaction with one's political culture.

Whereas the preceding chapters compare Isocrates and Aristotle with respect to their cultural resources, the role of discourse in the formation of political agency, and the constitution of rhetorical situations, this chapter turns to the issue of the rhetorical audience. Because persuasive discourse presupposes a transaction, the character of this transaction will be determined to a large extent by the audience's anticipated and actual response. While axiomatic, this presumption plays out differently in the two authors. Isocrates articulates the collective identity of his audience in a fashion that bridges the gap between the aristocratic and democratic ethos as well as the split between Athenian and pan-Hellenic self-understanding. As such, the Isocratean invocation of audiences stands in opposition to Aristotle's fixed conception of audience, on the one hand, and to his idea of a transcendental *philia* of like-minded philosophers on the other. The hearers' proper role in the *Rhetoric* amounts to a very limited participation in the construction of proofs, because their identification with the role is fixed by the procedural matrix of the rhetorical occasion. There is no acquiring of a new sense of collective identity, because the identity of the hearer as a judge (*kritēs*) remains unchanged. This limited role of the rhetorical audience goes hand in hand with Aristotle's view, expressed in the *Politics,* that democracy is a deviant regime in need of correction. Once clarified, the politically instrumental view of audiences in the *Rhetoric* will be contrasted with the recent scholarship's conflation of the functionally bracketed relationship between the rhetor and the audience in the *Rhetoric* and the unconditional friendship (*philia*) in Aristotle's ethical treatises.

Two master terms allow me to capture the distinction between the Isocratean and Aristotelian approaches to audience: "identification" and "persuasion." The contrast between these terms is relatively new, first appearing in the work of Kenneth Burke and later elaborated by rhetorical scholars and social theorists. While the term "identification" became crucial for rhetorical theory only in the twentieth century, "persuasion" has a convoluted classical pedigree. Before delving into the problem of the audience in Isocrates and Aristotle, then, it is helpful to inspect the historical and theoretical background of these key terms.

From Peithō to Persuasion to Identification

In Greece of the archaic period, the goddess Peithō was worshiped as one of the Muses. Prior to the "technologizing" of rhetorical practice in the fifth and fourth centuries B.C.E., Peithō personified the power of speech, its seductive effect on the listeners, and the skill necessary to achieve persuasion. Classical Greek poetry and drama preserve this image of Peithō, sometimes giving it an explicitly erotic aura. For example, in *Lysistrata* (203–4), Aristophanes shows how the women bent on stopping the war plead with a goddess of persuasion to help them to seduce their men in order to change their minds (see Buxton 1982).

In a world in which concepts do not possess an existence apart from their material instantiations, persuasion's socially beneficent and harmful sides are represented by the external characteristics of immortal agents. Peithō is an ambivalent deity, as her various guises attest: "wearing the mask of Thelxinoe, she is one of the Muses; when disguised as Thelxiepeia, she is one of the Sirens" (Detienne 1996, 77). The idea of persuasion in archaic Greece therefore comprises a broad range of linguistic powers without dividing them sharply into those that seduce and those that achieve consent by appealing to reason.

Judging by his appeal to the Athenians' respect for Peithō in the *Antidosis*, this polymorphous understanding is still alive in Isocrates. Defending his occupation and his pupils' desire to pursue eloquence, Isocrates points out that the traditional worshipful attitude toward Peithō is at odds with public suspicion directed toward practitioners of rhetoric: "They regard Persuasion (*Peithō*) as a god, and they see Athens sacrificing to her every year, but they claim that those who wish to share in the power that the goddess has are being corrupted by desire for something evil" (*Antidosis* 249). While gesturing toward an archaic religious ritual, Isocrates places the power of logos within a distinctly anthropocentric frame. At length, I will explore how Isocrates' "Hymn to Logos," which follows the invocation of Peithō in the *Antidosis,* underscores speech as an architect of the entire culture. Logos in Isocrates works as both a would-be creator of a culture that allows human agents to exert their influence and an act through which this influence is exercised. In other words, our speech has significant impact as long as we are constituted by and symbolically beholden to the linguistic community.

In Aristotle's hands, by contrast, *peithō* is converted into a tool of influencing opinion of a given audience. The function of rhetoric, claims Aristotle, "is not so much to persuade (*peisai*), but to observe (*idein*) in each case the existing means of persuasion (*ta huparchonta pithana*)" (*Rhetoric* 1355b10–11). The conceptual shift is drastic.[1] Persuasion has ceased to represent a cultural force, as the transmutation of a feminine subject into a neuter object (*to pithanon*) intimates. Further, as an art that allows one to survey the existing means of persuasion, it is now fragmented into a prescriptive set of devices that can be dissected and anatomized apart from the action they perform. By turning culturally acceptable ways of addressing social and political exigencies into general and specialized topics and propositions, Aristotle normalizes persuasion but at the same time limits its application to specific cultural sites and procedures. He replaces Isocrates' constitutive discourse of culture and politics with an ostensibly referential ideal of logos that reflects the "natural" purposefulness of the polis.

In the twentieth century, Kenneth Burke expanded the definition of "rhetoric" to recognize the constitutive function of language in all spheres of human activity: "For rhetoric as such is not rooted in any past condition of human society. It is rooted in an essential function of language itself, a function that is wholly realistic, and is continually born anew; the use of language as a symbolic means of inducing cooperation in beings that by nature respond to symbols" (1969, 43).

Burke's definition of the "realistic function of language" has it that human responsiveness to symbols is a basis for a capacity to become "one" with other members of a linguistic community. However, susceptibility to persuasion is not a sheer means of "inducing cooperation." Though the response to symbols comes to human beings "naturally" and thus seems to be ontologically prior to "cooperation" as a symbolically crafted unity, it is still contingent upon the continual rhetorical effort. In other words, to be persuaded, one must be ready to identify with the language of persuasion. The logic of this statement may appear circular, but it captures the paradox of "symbol-using animals": on the one hand, we acquire intelligibility thanks to an already existing function of language; on the other, the power of discourse to name and to persuade relies on our consent, which is connected with how we identify ourselves as members of a symbolic community.

The traditional Aristotelian understanding of persuasion has been tied to enthymematic reasoning. As a "relaxed" form of deductive reasoning that is distinct from strict logical demonstration (Burnyeat 1996), enthymeme not only operates in the domain of the probable but also "asks" the listeners to supply the premises omitted by the speaker (e.g., Bitzer 1959). Much has been written about enthymeme as a form of discourse whose completion and efficacy depends on the participation of a rhetorical community. Unlike neo-Aristotelians, Burke extends the notion of audience participation to theorize the constitution of audience itself. Reviewing the traditional principles of rhetoric, Burke acknowledges the listeners' cooperation. But he shows how it exceeds the parameters of an enthymeme. Pointing beyond Aristotle to Longinus's treatise on the sublime, Burke observes, "Longinus refers to that kind of elation wherein the audience feels as though it were not merely receiving, but were itself creatively participating in the poet's or speaker's assertion. Could we not say that, in such cases, the audience is exalted by the assertion because it has the feel of collaborating in the assertion?" (1969, 57–58).

Burke answers this question by examining the function of the stylistic apparatus, rather than the sheer propositional content of rhetorical utterances, in shaping the audience's response. "You persuade a man," he begins, "only insofar as you can talk his language by speech, gesture, tonality, order, image, attitude, idea, *identifying* your ways with his" (1969, 55). He illustrates aesthetic identification through the appeal of form, pointing out how traditional stylistic devices transcend differences between speaker and audience. Thus the aspect of "flattery" that typically describes extraneous stylistic embellishment in the vocabulary of Plato and Aristotle takes on a more profound character in Burke's rereading of the classical canon. "But flattery can safely serve as our paradigm," he writes, "if we systematically widen its meaning, to see behind it the conditions of identification or consubstantiality in general" (ibid.).

The emphasis on identification does not stem from Burke's appreciation of rhetoric's aesthetic dimension alone. Identification is also a socially productive function of language; it characterizes not only a spontaneous and willing participation of the listeners in the completion of a rhythmical or visual pattern but also the constitution of the audience as such. Not surprisingly, Burke finds Aristotle's (and Cicero's) view of "audiences purely as something given" severely lacking (1969, 64). Burke's own historical situation compels him to theorize the contingent character of the audience in such diverse manifestations of rhetoric as Nazi propaganda and "the systematic attempt to carve out an audience" by modern advertisement.

In order to conceptualize the audience as contingent, as hailed into existence by the act of speaking, rather than given a priori, Burke radicalizes (in the sense of looking at the root) the notion of substance: "A doctrine of *consubstantiality,* either explicit or implicit, may be necessary to any way of life. For substance, in the old philosophies, was an *act;* and a way of life is an acting-together; and in acting together, men have common sensations, concepts, images, ideas, attitudes that make them consubstantial" (1969, 21).

Identification as a theory of rhetorical "oneness" is perhaps Burke's most profound contribution to contemporary social thought. Developed against the backdrop of political upheavals and the expansion of the culture industry in the thirties and forties, Burke's notion of identification seeks to explain both progressive social movements and reactionary politics in terms of rhetorically crafted unity. "Identification is affirmed with earnestness," he notes, "precisely because there is division. Identification is compensatory to division. If men were not apart from one another, there would be no need for the rhetorician to proclaim their unity. If men were wholly and truly of one substance, absolute communication would be of man's very essence. It would not be an ideal, as it now is, partly embodied in material conditions and partly frustrated by these same conditions; rather, it would be as natural, spontaneous, and total as with those ideal prototypes of communication, the theologian's angels, or 'messengers'" (1969, 22).

Metaphorically speaking, rhetorical identification concerns itself with the state of "Babel after the fall" by forging allegiance out of the condition of disunity. Inverting the Western philosophico-religious model, according to which disunity is a mark of degeneracy, Burke defiantly asserts the provisional and unstable, as opposed to the given and immutable, character of human sociality.[2] The realm of identification, then, extends from the most "private" act of consubstantiality of a spectator participating in the unfolding of a story on a movie screen to the constitution of social order on a large scale.

Burke's work on identification anticipates the discursive turn in contemporary social theory. Burke reviews the rhetorical tradition not only to expand the application of rhetorical devices within areas typically considered to be extrarhetorical; his emphasis on identification leads us to question the very presumptions upon which we base our understanding of individuality and collectivity. Informed by a similar appreciation of the formative role of discourse in the construction of the subject and the social order, most debates in social theory continue to revolve around the issue of power. "Power" is a tantalizingly ambiguous term; it may refer to a force that oppresses from the outside, to a condition of one's emergence as a subject, or to a subject's own exercise of his or her agency. All these different senses of power are anchored in the function of language to produce, through a web of social practices, willing compliance in individuals. Consent, in turn, makes individuals into subjects in both social and discursive senses. This understanding of power as a productive rather than merely oppressive mechanism of socialization is now shared by many social theorists. But the debate about constraining and enabling aspects of power continues. As representative voices in this ongoing debate, Louis Althusser and Judith Butler are of particular interest with regard to the identity-shaping power of language.[3] Althusser's notion of interpellation posits a structure of power relations to which the subject is ineluctably subordinated. Butler's is a more performative and, as such, more rhetorically productive theory: she imagines the subject as a crucible of negotiation of power relations, not as a mere receptacle of the voice of authority. According to Althusser (1971), we are literally called into being as subjects through our recognition and acceptance of the call of a dominant ideology. Illustrated by the now (in)famous hypothetical example of a pedestrian obediently stopping in his tracks and turning around when hailed by a policeman, Althusser's notion of "interpellation" presumes a mechanism of subjection that works simultaneously from the outside and inside. Although for the purposes of demonstration his "little theoretical theater" presents the hailing and the turning in a form of a sequence, "with a before and an after," Althusser asserts that "the existence of ideology and the hailing or interpellation of individuals as subjects are one and the same thing" (174–75). An individual's willing and repeated consent to interpellations constitutes the process of reproduction of power relationships and of subjects who are at once subordinated to and given intelligible existence within these relationships. For Althusser, one cannot be "a free subject" unless one acts as a "bad subject": the one who refuses to recognize the hailing as meaningful. However, this is a tactic that leaves the bad subject disempowered precisely because one has to abandon, along with subordination, the very place from which to speak. By contrast, Judith Butler (1997) ponders the possibility of a subject who does not simply repeat the conditions of his subjection but turns power into an agency "exceeding" them. Her critique of Althusser's theory of interpellation is particularly instructive for our understanding of identification. Butler suggests that Althusser's "recourse to the example of the divine voice that names, and in naming, brings its subjects into being" equates the origin of power to "the divine performative" (110). She writes: "The inevitable structures of ideology are established textually through religious metaphor: the authority of the 'voice' of ideology, the 'voice' of interpellation, is figured as a voice almost impossible to refuse. The force of interpellation in Althusser is derived from the examples by which it is ostensibly illustrated, most notably, God's voice in the naming of Peter (and Moses) and its secularization in the postulated voice of the representative of state authority: the policeman's voice in the hailing of the wayward pedestrian with 'Hey you there!'" (110).

Butler thus points out the central drawback of Althusser's theory: its failure to conceptualize the locus of power within the subject. She goes on to argue that the repeated process of subjection is not unidirectional, as Althusser's model implies; rather, "the iterability of the subject . . . shows how agency may well consist in opposing and transforming the social terms by which it is spawned" (29). In other words, the process of identification (to use Burke's term) is constantly thwarted by a possibility of failure, of refused or subverted identification. The problem Butler locates in Althusser's illustration—the postulated existence of an already formed subject who turns willingly toward the sovereign voice of authority—should strike a familiar note for students of classical rhetoric. An earlier discussion of Plato's attack on the poetic tradition (chapter 2) and the discourse of funeral oration (chapter 3) pointed to a similar trend in Plato's treatment of poetry and rhetoric. From Plato's perspective, the voice of authority emanating from the "inspired" poet is absentmindedly performed by a rhapsode and passively yet ecstatically received by the listeners.

Plato assigns the same pathological identification to the democratic crowd that delights in the numbing repetition of praise for anonymous Athenians fallen in battle. The direct consequence of this chain of identifications is the weakening of the authenticity of self and its substitution by a fictitious identity. Plato's objection to poetry and rhetoric is that the divine inspiration that sets in motion poetic and rhetorical *mimēsis* is corrupted as it is passed down the performative chain to the audience. In Althusser's Marxist view of identification, the subjects are reproduced thanks to the *unfailing,* repetitive functioning of the mechanism of interpellation. If for Plato performance gets in the way of truth, for Althusser it is performance, in the basic sense of acting out an already scripted part, that ensures the perpetuation of power. Whereas Althusser decries the fact that the subjects who reproduce power relationships do so willingly, Aristotle sees in it the sine qua non of a well-ordered polis. The rhetorical transaction for Aristotle should, ideally, fall in the already given grid of political roles and relationships. In Isocrates, however, there is no such a priori structure; social roles of both the speaker and the audience are constituted and sustained through discourse.

Logos as Hēgemōn *and the Rhetoric of Identification*

Many of Isocrates' pamphlets are composed as if they were records of speeches he presented to live audiences. Because of this illusion, commentators of old were led to believe that Isocrates addressed his fellow Athenians directly on several occasions. But once we realize that the majority of extant texts by Isocrates were circulated among a reading public, the question inevitably arises: What audience does Isocrates have in mind? Does he address an elite crowd of readers who already share his political views or does he reach out to audiences whose affinities are unknown? Moreover, why does Isocrates "imitate" democratic rhetoric if his readership is qualitatively different from the crowds in the courts, the assembly, and the festivals? Although it may not be possible to establish the identity of his audiences with historical precision, we can ascertain Isocrates' *attitude* to the question of the audience. This attitude is evident in his explicit and implicit defense of logos as both the creator of culture and the source of individualized acts of cultural critique. Isocrates approaches his audience as a community to be called into existence rather as something purely given, because for him logos is etiologically prior to community. Human social bonds are an effect of speech rather than a consequence of a primordial need. The clearest articulation of this position is Isocrates' famous passage in the *Nicocles* dubbed "Hymn to Logos," which he proudly reiterates as one of the best arguments in defense of his profession in the *Antidosis*. The story of human progress as told by Isocrates in many aspects resembles the traditional account favored by Greek tragedy and philosophy: logos enables humans to distinguish themselves from animals and to establish a civilized order through laws and other institutions. "Since we have the ability to persuade one another and to make clear to ourselves what we want," begins Isocrates, "not only do we avoid living like animals, but we have come together, built cities, made laws, and invented arts. Speech (logos) is responsible for nearly all our inventions. It legislated in matters of justice and injustice, and beauty and baseness, and without these laws, we could not live with one another" (*Nicocles* 6–7). The trajectory of the progress from animal nature to human culture generally resembles that of Protagoras's "Great Speech" in Plato's *Protagoras* and Aristotle's account of the rise of a community (*koinonia*) in the *Politics*. Yet Isocrates' version extends the tradition by virtue of its portrayal of speech as both the means of creating political community and the leader (*hēgemōn*) in all public and private deliberations. The uniqueness of Isocrates' depiction of speech has been amply pointed out by Takis Poulakos (1997) in his interpretation of the "Hymn to Logos." Poulakos suggests that Isocrates resorts to the conventional mythical line "in order to firm up the connection between logos and civilized life" precisely because this tie was becoming increasingly vulnerable. For example, in his dialogue *Protagoras,* Plato seeks to undermine the role of logos in the maintenance of social bonds by having the Sophist relate a story in which respect (*aido*) and justice (*dikē*), rather than speech, are causes of civilized life. He puts into Protagoras's mouth a narrative that ultimately serves the purpose of proving that political virtue cannot be taught by a Sophist. Poulakos contrasts the two versions of the story, by "Protagoras" and Isocrates, to demonstrate that even the difference in the word choice for "coming together" (*sunerchesthai* in Isocrates and *hathroizesthai* in Plato) in the account of the founding of cities connotes divergent attitudes toward the process of social unification. Isocrates stresses the act of coming together willingly and deliberately, but Plato's usage refers to "a type of togetherness formed and sustained solely out of the basic need to seek refuge in numbers (16). According to Poulakos, besides its connotation of "forming an integrated whole," Isocrates' phrasing also reveals another crucial nuance that is lost in the Loeb English translation: "The original, *sunelthontes poleis oikisamen kai nomous ethemetha kai technas heuromen,* favors the more causal construction, 'having come together, we founded cities, and made laws, and invented arts'" (1997, 16–17). Poulakos sees in this attribution of causality a sign of Isocrates' effort to expand the reach of logos beyond the realm of mere practical skills.

There is more to be said about Isocrates' rendition of the great myth. In addition to framing the narrative of human progress in a way suggesting the constitutive, rather than merely instrumental, role of speech, he also gives a synchronic, if you will, explanation of the power of logos:

We regard speaking well to be the clearest sign of a good mind, which it requires, and truthful, lawful, and just speech we consider the image (*eidōlon*) of a good and faithful soul. With speech we fight over contentious matters, and we investigate the unknown. We use the same arguments by which we persuade others in our own deliberations; we call those able to speak in a crowd "rhetorical" (*rhētorikous*); we regard as sound advisers those who debate with themselves most skillfully about public affairs. If one must summarize the power of discourse, we will discover that nothing done prudently occurs without speech (logos), that speech is the leader (*hēgemōn*) of all thoughts and actions, and that the most intelligent people use it most of all. (*Nicocles* 7–9)

Rather than stating that speech is simply useful and therefore occasionally productive of positive social outcomes such as a salutary piece of legislation or a wise political decision, Isocrates insists that logos leads us by influencing conduct and shaping reflection. Most important, the image of a leader (*hēgemōn*) projects the idea of a discursively crafted unity. Lest one objects that the progress toward a more civilized existence is but a series of successful but entirely serendipitous acts of persuasion, Isocrates insists that the function of logos is both external and internal; it is not confined to speechmaking in the narrow Platonic (and later, Aristotelian) sense of *rhētorikē* but involves deliberation in the broadest possible sense. Isocrates provocatively puts together the verbs *agōnizometha* (contend) and *skopoumetha* (investigate) (*Nicocles* 8) to promote the idea that both public disputes and private deliberation are grounded in the recognition of linguistic and cultural community. In the passage above, even grammatical form of verbs functions as a strategy of calling the audience into being. That Isocrates uses first person plural only underscores the shared nature of all the acts undertaken under the aegis of logos.

It is tempting to treat Isocrates' statement as a theoretical deification of the linguistic unity undergirding all intelligible and civilized acts in the polis. Thus Poulakos's interpretation, in spite of its attention to various symbolic *events* that constitute the "coming together," urges us to see collective self-understanding as "a *structure* from which a given deliberative utterance may draw its unifying potential and acquire its guiding force" (1997, 18–19, emphasis added). Pointing to a passage in which Isocrates describes the institution of laws (*Nicocles* 7), Poulakos comments: "The progress toward civilization is not so much punctuated by a series of discrete events in time as it is conveyed by means of a range of attitudes. . . . What is conveyed here is neither action nor eventfulness but rather a self-understanding, a way of conducting oneself and of relating to one another in the city" (1997, 21).

For Poulakos, the demand for a "structural" explanation stems from a necessity to explain Isocrates' defense of logos vis-à-vis Plato's critique of sophistic relativism. As Poulakos explains, "The gap separating the use of logos to make things intelligible and the conception of everything cultural as arbitrarily made was closing rapidly. Conventions and customs, but also institutions and laws, became understood as arbitrary creations, makings of an ever-pliable language and results of relative uses" (1997, 24). Approached in this light, Isocrates' locution seems to posit an existence of an overarching structure that exceeds the sum total of individual and collective acts of persuasion. By stressing the continuity and stability of this construct, Isocrates renders logos immune to charges of randomness and arbitrariness.

I disagree, however, with Poulakos's structural interpretation of "self-understanding." By favoring structure over eventfulness, Poulakos invokes the Althusserian notion of interpellation as a theoretical paradigm, to which Isocrates' "Hymn to Logos" seems to conform: "The logos he celebrates throughout his narrative is a signifier for utterances that not only successfully created exigencies around a disorderly, fragmented, and isolated existence but also successfully interpellated audiences as political agents" (1997, 21). This articulation, though it seems to balance the external and the internal function of logos—to influence actions and to shape self-understanding—nonetheless lends itself to the same critique as Althusser's theory of interpellation. The original act of coming together, in which the codes of civil coexistence are laid down, becomes the "sovereign" performative endlessly and invariably reinstated with each generation. On this reading, the collective self-understanding, once created, continues to power the acting-together of a community.

This interpretation thus favors structure over contingency. However, the emphasis on structure that gets replicated in a series of socially productive linguistic acts minimizes the provisional and performative character of political self-understanding and thereby misjudges the aim and strategy of Isocrates' interventions. In other words, it explains interpellation as a fait accompli rather than as an ongoing process. I propose, by contrast, that Isocrates' citizenly discourse, *logos politikos,* is constituted precisely by a series of pleas in which unification is urged and common identity affirmed in response to division and strife. Moreover, Isocrates' call for unity relies less on the sovereign authority of laws and political institutions than on aesthetically influential performance. While engaging the nonreferential capacity of logos to name and mold the political by delineating the just and the unjust, Isocrates shows, in the "Hymn to Logos" and in other compositions, that the activation of these abstractions as part of the audience's collective identity is the means and the end of political performance.

Isocrates' depiction of logos as *hēgemōn* reinforces an image of a unifying communal exchange. In this picture, agonistic deliberation and introspective contemplation are continuous with each other rather than segregated into discrete areas of the public and the private. The passage also implies, thanks to the use of the present indefinite tense, that acts binding a community together take place with a reassuring regularity. I take it that Poulakos's reading of the "Hymn to Logos" in terms of a common structure relies on this expression of habitual practices that ensure social stability. Yet if Isocrates were content with the ritualistic affirmation of unity, he would not emphasize the leading role of logos in motivating the audience to rethink its collective self-understanding.[4] On the contrary, his *mimēsis* of democratic discourses points out that identity-shaping performance is anything but mere repetition. *Areopagiticus,* in which Isocrates extols wise governance under representative democracy, is a good example of a discourse that adopts identification as both its goal and its manner of appeal to the audience. If approached as a testament to Isocrates' political conservatism, *Areopagiticus* may give an impression that the rhetorician considers the Athenian self-understanding of the "good old days" preceding the direct democracy of his times as an ideal to which Athens must return. However, Isocrates not so much urges the restoration of the status quo ante as he beseeches his compatriots to reflect on their self-perception as a community among other Greek cities. By invoking the past, he impresses upon his readers an appreciation of the frailty of any community that acts impulsively and without examination of its internal motives.

Isocrates begins by speaking of a city as if it were a human being: "I see cities that think their circumstances are best making the worst decisions, and those which are particularly confident soon finding themselves in the greatest dangers. The reason for this is that no good or evil comes to mankind of its own accord; wealth and power produce and are accompanied by senselessness (*anoia*) and lack of restraint (*akolasia*), while poverty and humble circumstances bring moderation and restraint" (*Areopagiticus* 3–4). The Athenians, similarly, went through a period of sobriety and caution "after Athens had been overtaken by the barbarians" and consequently became "leaders of Greece" (6). Yet as a result of the Peloponnesian War, which broke out primarily because of Athens' imperialistic policy toward other Greek *poleis,* "we were nearly enslaved" (7). A brief look at the peripeties in the life of cities like Athens and Sparta should make anyone circumspect, but as Isocrates points out, his fellow citizens are living in a state of insensitivity (*anaisthesia*) (9).

The thrust of Isocrates' objection is that the Athenians are carrying on without pausing to reflect on the mistakes of the past and engage in rituals that affirm their power without realizing its fragility. The general state of confusion manifests itself in lavish public decorum that is not balanced, in Isocrates mind, by enough introspection: "In such conditions, we have twice made sacrifices celebrating the arrival of good news, but when we discuss these matters in the Assembly, we are less serious than men who have achieved all they want" (*Areopagiticus* 10). Using, as in the *Nicocles,* first person plural to underscore the sense of acting together, Isocrates does not distance himself as an elite rhetor from his audience but creates an exigency out of the state of collective amnesia. The remedy, given such a diagnosis, can only come from an improvement in the polity at large, rather than from scattered policies or actions of virtuous leaders: "Nothing can turn out well for those who do not plan well about all aspects of government, but if they have success in some actions, whether through good fortune or through some man's virtue, they soon slip up a little and again find themselves in the same uncertainty (*aporiai*). Anyone can learn this from our own experience" (*Areopagiticus* 11).

Isocrates' discursive construction of the polity (*politeia*) as the city's soul (*psuchē*) both builds on the tradition of Athenian democratic rhetoric and extends its scope in order to create identification among nondemocratic and non-Athenian audiences. Consistent with the claim about the leading role of logos in *Nicocles,* the rhetoric of *Areopagiticus* promotes social concord as an effect of a communal self-understanding shaped through discourse.

To amplify the difference between a good polity and material conditions or legal statutes, Isocrates employs a key *topos* in the Athenian discourse of identification: an idea of the city that exceeds the physical boundaries of its location. This *topos* dates back to Aeschylus's *Persae*, in which the Athenians are described by the "barbarian" characters as the people whose polis lives on despite the devastation of the actual city by the army of King Xerxes. Athens is a polis that not only survived through the bravery of its defenders but also saved the rest of Greece. In *Areopagiticus,* Isocrates activates this memory in order to contrast contemporary self-understanding with Athens' powerful reputation after the Persian Wars: "We neither have nor do we really seek a government that correctly deals with public affairs. And yet, we all know that prosperity visits and remains not with those who have cast the finest and largest walls around themselves, nor with those who have gathered together with the largest number of people in the same place, but with those who manage their city in the best and most moderate manner" (*Areopagiticus* 13–14). The phrase "we all know" goads the reader to partake in the cultural memory and subtly deflects the popular audience's attention from the author's elite background. According to Josiah Ober's analysis of elite Athenian rhetors' use of history and mythology, this strategy softened the "potentially elitist thrust" implicit in such references (1989, 180–81).[5] Thematically, Isocrates is also treading over well-plowed ground. As Ober observes, "One particularly common *topos* of blame in political orations was the contrast between the Athenians of the present day and their illustrious ancestors" (1989, 319). Thus, Isocrates asserts his commitment to democracy and appeals to the audience's political memory when he says, "I have discussed a government that is not hidden but open to all, which you all know was our fatherland and was responsible for the greatest goods for Athens and for the rest of Greece" (*Areopagiticus* 59).

The distinction of Isocratean address from speeches of other rhetors is that he elects to examine the state of *politeia* not for the sake of any immediate action but in order to further the collective reflection. This apparent incongruity between the discursive form of the composition and its function is noteworthy. Despite the decorum appropriate for an oral address in the Assembly, and the elaborate defense of his anti-oligarchic stance, Isocrates is not recommending a specific policy but summons a particular vision of polity.

The anthropomorphic image of the state aids in conjuring up the ideal of control and balance:[6] "The soul (*psuchē*) of the city is nothing other than its constitution (*politeia*), since it has as much power as the intellect does in the body. For it is this that deliberates in all matters, preserves what is good, and avoids misfortune. Laws, public speakers, and private citizens all necessarily resemble it, and the fortunes of each citizen are determined by the form of constitution they possess" (*Areopagiticus* 14). This passage furthers the argument that a good polity does not equal physical or material power, which is foreshadowed by the earlier allusion to "citizens are the polis" topos of drama, historiography, and oratory. Isocrates now states, however, that *politeia* overflows the parameters of written laws as well. This, I believe, is the sum of his plea in the *Areopagiticus:* rather than resurrecting the legal codes of the restricted democracy, Isocrates urges his readers to attend to broader cultural practices conducive to citizenly identification.

In arguing for a discursive understanding of the conditions productive of social harmony, Isocrates rejects the notion that legislative art can ensure order. "A large number of specific laws is a sign that a city is badly governed," he insists, "for in erecting these obstacles to crime, people are forced to make many laws" (*Areopagiticus* 40). Instead, it is the everyday practices and customs that create a political community: "Those who are properly governed (*politeuomenous*) do not need to fill the stoas with written laws but to have justice in their souls. Cities are well governed (*oikeisthai*) not by legislation but by customs, and those who have been badly brought up will venture to transgress even meticulously written laws, whereas those who have been well educated will be willing to obey even simple laws" (*Areopagiticus* 41).

Of special significance here is the idea of continuity between private and public, manifested by the placement of terms *oikeisthai* and *politeuosthai,* the former related to the word "household" (*oikos*) and the latter to the word "state" (polis). Isocrates is driving home the point that virtue, both private and public, is advanced by habits of everyday life (40). Because for Isocrates virtuous political life is not codifiable, there is no such thing as the ideal constitution. If it were possible to draft one, he points out, "nothing would prevent all the Greeks from being alike, since written laws are easily borrowed from each other" (39). It is therefore doubtful that Isocrates either wishes to import monarchy or to restore the restricted democracy of Solon based on his "impersonation" of a monarch in the *Nicocles* and his praise of Areopagus in the *Areopagiticus*.

Another detail in the passage about the ideal *politeia* lends support to my claim that Isocrates aims to refashion the Athenian self-understanding in accordance with his *logōn paideia*. The notion of "the governed" (*tous politeuomenous*) is rendered through a middle voice participle, as distinct from the passive construction in the English translation. Governance, then, is literally a *self-governance*, a connotation that accords well with Isocrates' use of the term *sunerchesthai* in the *Nicocles* to indicate a deliberate act of coming together. Reflective self-governance does not come about through sheer repetition of good habits that someone else had laid down. It is a result of a deliberate and daily pursuit, as the use of the word *epitedeumata* (pursuits, practices) indicates. It is not so much the institutional mechanism of discipline and punish as the discursive mechanism of praise and blame that goads a polity toward virtuous conduct. Isocrates underscores the effect of "noble pursuits" and "labor accompanied by pleasure" in the process of "taming" the tempestuous souls of the young, for "these alone hold the attention of men who have been raised as free citizens and are accustomed to noble thoughts" (*Areopagiticus* 43). Steered toward the praiseworthy, and chided when they violated the ethical decorum, the young men "did not spend time in the gambling houses, or with flute girls" but "spent all their time in activities that were assigned to them, admiring and competing with the best in these pursuits" (*Areopagiticus* 48).

In a composition that ostensibly addresses all of the Athenians, to single out the type of enculturation usually linked to a privileged social status may seem strange. But Isocrates does not mean to confine the conditions of good citizenship and virtue to a particular economic class or social group, in contrast with Aristotle's understanding of good citizenship as distinct from goodness in the highest human sense (*Politics* 1277a5–14). Ober's analysis of the Athenian oratory of the fourth century B.C.E. suggests that *kalokagathia* (nobleness) and *eugeneia* (nobility of birth), terms previously attached to aristocracy, became part of democratic rhetorical repertoire: "The old aristocratic ideal of high birth as a possession of the privileged few has been appropriated and transformed into the inborn nobility of the citizen body as a whole" (1989, 262–63). Similarly, Isocrates posits the identity of an Athenian citizen as a political and aesthetic model to be emulated and embodied by whoever happens to heed his discourse. The model is, of course, based on the reputation of the best among the ancestors, since it is they who represent Athens to the rest of the world. To identify with them, in the *Areopagiticus,* means to disapprove of an Athens that is "filled with law-suits, accusations, taxes, poverty, or wars" and to endorse an order in which citizens live "at ease with one another and maintained peace with all others," earning "the trust of the Greeks and the fear of the barbarians" (51–52).

The self-understanding to which Isocrates seeks to inspire allegiance among his various audiences is more a rhetorical composite rather than a historically or geographically bound moral code. As such, this composite portrait assimilates both the features of an aristocratic ethos passed on from the archaic times through the performance of poetry and drama and the notion of answerability of a political agent inherent in a democratic political exchange. For Isocrates, then, power is not tied to or controlled by institutions; rather, it is a contingent effect of identification.

Logos, Role Differentiation, and the Rhetorical Audience in Aristotle

Because in the *Politics* Aristotle appears to articulate a conception of logos that, as in Isocrates' *Nicocles,* grants speech a place of honor within a city-state, we may profit from comparing their views on this subject. It will soon become apparent, however, that for Aristotle logos has a function of *representing* the natural division of social roles rather than, as in Isocrates, *goading* people toward a cultural collectivity. This insight, in turn, will illuminate Aristotle's approach to the function of audience in the *Rhetoric.*

At first glance, there is much similarity in the views Isocrates and Aristotle hold regarding the role of logos in a state. To begin with, Aristotle's account also is at variance with Plato's political vision. As Depew and Peters (2001) comment, Plato "proposed to replace the autonomous practical rationality (*praxis*) of freely associated citizens with governance by technical rationality (*technē*). In doing so, he reduced (at least in Aristotle's opinion) the status of the governed to herd animals, manipulated by a shepherd-like ruling class that knows what images to display to the untutored masses.... Thus when Aristotle says that humans are political animals, he means precisely that they are *not* herd animals (*zōa ageleia*), or even 'social animals' (*zōa koinonike*)" (3).[7] In the *Politics,* Aristotle explains that human beings are political animals because *anthropos* alone among the animals possesses logos. The description of the difference between animal sounds and human speech parallels Isocrates' "Hymn to Logos." Aristotle stresses that, whereas the voice of animals can signify (*semainein*) the sensations of pain and pleasure, "*logos* is designed to indicate (*deloun*) the advantageous and the harmful, and therefore also the right and the wrong; for it is the special property of *anthropos* in distinction from the other animals that he alone has perception of good and bad and right and wrong and the other moral qualities" (*Politics* 1253a14–17). It is the partnership (*koinonia*) in these that, for Aristotle, "makes a household (*oikos*) and a city-state (*polis*)" (*Politics* 1253a18).

Unlike Plato again, and still in agreement with Isocrates, Aristotle does not see a gulf between human perception of values and the speech by which these perceptions are communicated. For Aristotle, logos indicates or makes clear (hence, the verb *deloun*) human moral perceptions. It does not, however, possess the capacity to constitute a *politeia* as it apparently does for Isocrates. Aristotle's argument for the natural priority of the polis assigns logos to the function of representation of already differentiated social relationships, as opposed to the constitutive mechanism of identification valorized by Isocrates.

First, what does Aristotle mean by "natural priority"? He explains it by drawing an analogy between a living body and a state (as distinct from Isocratean comparison between a human being and a polis):

> Thus also the city-state (*polis*) is prior in nature to the household and to each of us individually. For the whole must necessarily be prior to the part; since when the whole body is destroyed, foot or hand will not exist except in an equivocal sense, like the sense in which one speaks of a hand sculptured in stone as a hand; because a hand in those circumstances will be a hand spoiled, and all things are defined by their function and capacity, so that when they are no longer such as to perform their function they must not be said to be the same things.... It is clear therefore that the state is also prior by nature to the individual, for if each individual when separate is not self-sufficient, he must be related to the whole state as other parts to their whole. While a man who is incapable of entering into partnership, or who is so self-sufficient that he has no need to do so, is no part of a state, so that he must be either a lower animal (*therion*) or a god (*theos*). (*Politics* 1253a19–29)

The vast interpretive controversy over this so-called organic argument is beyond the scope of this chapter. However, many scholars have regarded this passage as a metaphor that still leaves room for rational choice and constitutional art. As David Depew's analysis of the major claims and evidence in this debate suggests, this interpretation is a reaction to a worry that "if the analogy between *polis* and organism were taken seriously the *polis* would become a substance in its own right" (21). As distinct both from metaphorical readings and readings that overestimate the organic analogy, Depew claims to have reduced the said worry "by treating role-dividing politicality as an intrinsic attribute of individual human beings, and by showing how the set of relationships that constitute the *polis* unfolds through the cumulative effects of discursive communication on role division itself" (21).

Speaking of the role of logos, Depew elaborates: "The dynamic character of *logos* springs from the fact that rational animals regulate their interactions with their environments, including their social environments, by way of noetic representations of past, present, and future states of affairs, thereby rendering human ways of life (*bioi*), that is, patterns of interacting with each other and with the external world, highly diverse and adaptable" (n.d., 20). The key word here is "representation." It implies that speech facilitates the *intrinsic* "role-dividing" politicality of individual human beings. Logos thus assists in coordinating the already differentiated relationships, rather than producing differentiation and unity, as Isocrates would have it. Isocrates posits the polis as a cumulative, if provisional, effect of multiple identifications that forge unity out of division. Aristotle assigns to logos the function of mediating representations that characterize particular "natural" relationships (master-slave, husband-wife, parent-child) as essential for self-sufficient existence. Through logos, these asymmetrical ties become not only intelligible but also beneficial and just. Logos for Aristotle does not goad people into communities, it represents the codes of behavior that optimize the conditions of role differentiation.

Still, this account sheds light only on the first part of a story leading to the founding of distinct types of constitutions. The rise of the polis out of separate households for Aristotle creates the conditions of possibility of a good life (*eudaimonia*) that may be actualized once the necessities of self-sufficient existence have been fulfilled. As with the habituation of a youth trained for a life of contemplative leisure (discussed in chapter 2), the trajectory of the polis toward the good life follows a telescopic pattern. The natural polis that arises out of households with the assistance of speech is a foundation, characterized by differentiation of social roles and self-sufficiency, out of which a legislator fashions a particular polis. Depew outlines the distinction between "the natural polis" and "a polis":

> By the time the craftsman of laws comes along, . . . making pursuit of the good life the explicit aim of policy, the differentiated social structure that Aristotle calls a natural *polis* is already available as the proximate matter for the exercise of constitutional art under the guidance of practical reason. . . . The *polis* such a legislator brings into existence comes to be in accord with rational art, not nature. But he could not exercise reason to produce an individuated polis, set off from other such poleis as an instance of a constitutional kind (*eidos*), unless a naturally developed polis, which is a set of social arrangements that stand in contrast to the undeveloped household and village, were available as proximate matter for his art. (39)

The natural polis is, as it were, a necessary condition for the introduction of "good" constitutional forms such as aristocracy, monarchy, and constitutional regime (*politeia*), in which the highest form of humanly possible rationality can flourish. This, indeed, is the meaning of Aristotle's declaration that the polis comes to be for "the sake of life" but exists "for the sake of living well" (*Politics* 1252b29–30).

A similar line of reasoning unfolds when Aristotle invokes functional differentiation with respect to good citizenship as opposed to human goodness in general. Criteria of citizenly virtue (*aretē*), like judgments about role division in the natural polis, are based on an organic model: "Again, since the state consists of unlike persons—just as an animal . . . consists of soul and body, and a soul of reason and appetite, and a household of husband and wife and master and slave, in the same manner a state consists of all of these persons and also of others of different classes in addition to these,—it necessarily follows that the goodness of all the citizens is not one and the same, just as among dancers the skill of a head dancer is not the same as that of a subordinate leader. It is clear then from these considerations that the goodness of a good citizen and that of a good man are not the same in general" (*Politics* 1277a5–13).

Citizenly virtue can and sometimes does overlap with human virtue, but while the former is functionally tied to a specific constitutional form and hence is a relative quality, the latter transcends constitutional differences. So, for instance, citizens from a class of artisans and hired laborers can be said to possess virtue in so far as they function properly under a constitutional regime. By contrast, in an aristocratic state these classes are not entitled to civic virtue as "the honors are bestowed according to goodness and to merit, since a person living a life of manual toil or as a hired laborer cannot practice the pursuits in which goodness is exercised" (*Politics* 1278a19–21). Whereas in a constitutional government (*politeia*) a banausic laborer's citizenly virtue is different in kind from the human virtue of an aristocrat, in an aristocracy (the rule of the best), citizenly virtue and human virtue are most likely to merge in a mutually reinforcing union. For this reason, given a choice, Aristotle would not admit laborers and tradesmen to citizenship in his ideal state, even if the condition of role differentiation of the natural polis has been satisfied. This theoretical separation of political virtue from ethical virtue is an implicit defense of aristocracy, which becomes more pronounced as Aristotle gets closer to describing the ideal constitution. This split is crucial for our appreciation of Aristotle's distinction from Isocrates on the question of civic discourse. Although both Isocrates and Aristotle admittedly espouse elitist social values, they differ appreciably in their approach to the role of logos in the polis. Isocrates' depiction of logos as a leader transcends the boundaries between private and public, between ethics and politics, between aristocracy and democracy. Aristotle's functional treatment of logos as a medium of representation of social infrastructure aims to not only reinforce these boundaries but also establish them as a prerequisite for the actualization of virtue. Now, if logos is but a representation of how human relationships actually are and its function is to perpetuate and maximize the division of roles, what does *persuasion* have to do with it? How can one square Aristotle's treatise on the art of persuasion in a democratic regime with his account of conditions of inequality supposedly built in by nature? The difficulty is that rhetoric occupies an ambiguous territory between logos as a unique trait of human political animals in the account of the natural polis, on the one hand, and the distinctly political art of a legislator on the other. In the *Politics,* logos justifies the division of social roles, which Aristotle considers natural and essential for the rise of any fully independent polis. Logos works in tandem with daily habits of material life to prepare the platform for a higher, even more diversified community in which philosophical reflection, unburdened by mundane instrumental concerns, can be truly at home.

In the *Rhetoric,* however, Aristotle does *not* postulate the rules of communicative interaction among those who are engaged in a pursuit of virtue but specifies the verbal means of influencing opinion under corrupt constitutional conditions of a democratic regime. The next chapter will examine how the framing of rhetoric as a capacity (*dunamis*), rather than as praxis, enables Aristotle to protect practical rationality and virtue of a properly habituated agent from being corrupted by a democratic audience. The goal of the following discussion in this chapter, however, is to defend a claim that Aristotle disciplines the *audience* by assigning a prescribed range of responses to generically structured discourse. I propose that *The Art of Rhetoric* reflects the presumption of functional social differentiation—the one we see at work in the *Politics*—as the basis of public address. The division of rhetorical discourse into three genres allows Aristotle, at least in theory, to compartmentalize political speech not only thematically but functionally as well. This means that Aristotle seeks to correlate judgments about expediency, justice, and virtuous conduct with utterances confined to highly structured deliberative, forensic, and epideictic occasions. By structuring enthymemes in accordance with propositions derived from topics specific to each of these institutionally differentiated situations, the speaker is capable of steering the audience into an already determined subject position. Over and against readings of the *Rhetoric* that point to audience participation in the construction of enthymemes as a sign of a robust theory of civic discourse, I contend that Aristotle actually constructs rhetoric as a tool for rectifying the "unnatural" condition of democracy. In other words, rhetoric can be viewed as a discursive mechanism for redirecting a democratic audience toward the condition Aristotle describes as constitutional government (*politeia*) in his mature public philosophy.[8] In such a regime the many fulfill their functional role in the partnership (*koinonia*) for the good life without aspiring to rule.

That democracy is in need of rectification is abundantly evident from Aristotle's division of constitutions into correct ones (monarchy, aristocracy, and constitutional government) and their deviations (tyranny, oligarchy, and democracy). For Aristotle, citizenship can be claimed on the basis of at least one of three attributes: virtue, wealth, and free birth (*Politics* 1283a15–21). Under correct forms of government, citizens develop constitution-relative virtue by willingly submitting to rule, thereby creating optimal conditions for the leisured rationality of those who pursue virtue unconditionally. These regimes, whether or not they admit free laborers to citizenship, are correct as long as they are formed on the basis of partnership (*koinonia*) and exist for the purpose of good life. As Aristotle says, a city is "a community of free men" (*Politics* 1279a21). Those citizens who cannot fully participate in the pursuit of unconditional virtue (which, for Aristotle, comes only through a life of reflective leisure) still enjoy the advantage of the membership.

In deviant regimes, on the other hand, there is a lack of community in Aristotle's sense, since those who rule are pursuing only their own, rather than a collective, interest. In such a polis, the nobility, the rich, and the free-born poor do not negotiate the division of citizenly roles but usurp the power for the benefit of their class alone. Democracy thus is a deviant regime because of popular sovereignty, which entails the absence of differentiation between the ruler and the ruled and the corresponding lack of citizenly virtue. Democracy can be corrected if the multitude of the free do not hold offices but participate in deliberative and judicial procedures. Aristotle gave qualified approval to the political inclusion of the free poor:

> For it is not safe for them to participate in the highest offices (for injustice and folly would inevitably cause them to act unjustly in some things and to make mistakes in others), but yet not to admit them and for them not to participate is an alarming situation, for when there are a number of persons without political honours and in poverty, the city then is bound to be full of enemies. It remains therefore for them to share the deliberative and judicial functions. ... For all when assembled together have sufficient discernment, and by mingling with the better class are of benefit to the state, just as impure food mixed with what is pure makes the whole more nourishing than the small amount of pure food alone; but separately individual is immature in judgement. (*Politics* 1281b25–38)

Having established Aristotle's position on the limited political participation of the free poor, we can turn to this chapter's primary claim—that the *Rhetoric* aims at "disciplining" the democratic audience. That rhetoric is a tool for pushing democracy toward a more natural state of a constitutional regime (*politeia*) is unlikely to be openly announced as Aristotle's intention. A passage in *Rhetoric I*, in fact, appears to assert rhetoric's universal usefulness by stating that "the most important and effective of all the means of persuasion and good counsel is to know all the forms of government and to distinguish the manners and customs, institutions, and interests of each" (*Rhetoric* 1365b22–24). This advice, which is believed to be a later addition possibly contemporaneous with the writing of the *Politics* (Kennedy 1996, 419), need not, however, be read as a sign of rhetoric's applicability in all existing regimes. Rather, the existence of a variety of constitutional forms in close geographical proximity in the pre-Macedonian era presented constant challenge to domestic and foreign policy. General instability is a refrain of much Athenian rhetoric of the fourth century, and while Aristotle was not a native-born Athenian, the fortunes of the Academy, his "graduate" institution, were tied to the fate of this polis.

Athenian democracy itself, then, furnishes the context of a challenge to the Philosopher. As Kennedy insists, "There is no reasonable doubt that the *Rhetoric,* along with the *Poetics* and the *Constitution of the Athenians,* is one of his most Athenian works, primarily addressed to Athenians; for only in Athens did rhetoric fully function in the way he describes" (1996, 418). Throughout the treatise one finds scattered remarks about audiences that are preoccupied with personal interests, enjoy emotional stimulation, and prefer a good display to a demonstration of unadorned facts. Nevertheless, Aristotle sounds confident that hoi polloi can be persuaded to acknowledge the superiority of "truth" and "justice." Otherwise, he would not declare that "the true and the just are by nature stronger than their opposites" (*Rhetoric* 1355a22).

Where explicit statements are few, turning to imagery allows us to probe a text's covert strategies. An analogy with the art of medicine, given early in the treatise, is instructive. Comparing the artfulness of rhetoric to other *technai,* Aristotle uses medicine as an example of an art whose function is not "to create health but to promote this as much as possible; for it is nevertheless possible to treat well those who cannot recover health" (*Rhetoric* 1355b11–15). Similarly, I suggest, Aristotle hopes if not to restore democracy to the natural (and hence, healthy) condition of a *politeia,* then at least to construct a set of discursive relationships mimicking the differentiation of roles he regards essential for a good regime in his *Politics.*

From a standpoint of *technē,* making the audience fulfill its function is a matter of minimizing inartistic distractions impeding the listeners' judgment. In a passage criticizing current judicial procedures, Aristotle says:

> Those who have composed *Arts of Speech* have worked on a small part of the subject; . . . these writers say nothing about enthymemes, which is the "body"

of persuasion, while they give most of their attention to matters external to the subject; for verbal attack and pity and anger and such emotions of the soul do not relate to fact but are appeals to the juryman. As a result, if all trials were conducted as they are in some present-day states and especially in those well governed, [the handbook writers] would have nothing to say; for everyone thinks the laws ought to require this, and some even adopt the practice and forbid speaking outside the subject, . . . for it is wrong to warp the jury by leading them into anger or envy or pity: that is the same *as if someone made a straightedge rule crooked before using it.* (*Rhetoric* 1354a12–25, emphasis added)

It is noteworthy that Aristotle singles out the judicial context to attack contemporary writers of rhetorical *technai* and to assert the centrality of enthymeme as "the body of proof," since later he rates judicial genre second to the nobler deliberative discourse. The reasons for this spotlight on judicial oratory are multiple and likely to be shared by most elite critics of democracy. Aristotle indeed expresses a sentiment that mirrors that of Isocrates, whose dislike for the meddlesomeness (*polypragmasynē*) of litigious sycophants is well known. More remarkable, however, is Aristotle's promotion of enthymeme in connection with a metaphor of the audience as a measuring instrument (*kanon*). This link, I suggest, points to a previously unnoticed but important sign of Aristotle's motive of disciplining democracy by disciplining rhetoric.

First, however, we need to examine what may be called "expansive" interpretations of enthymeme. Aristotle introduces enthymeme in order to assist the ordinary juror in learning something new in a quick fashion, as the court is no place for elaborate instruction. Modern theorists of rhetoric have focused on the notion of enthymeme as a classical precursor of informal logic and argumentation. On this view, when presented with an enthymeme, the audience fills in the missing premise and thus takes on an ostensibly active role in decision making. A turn toward audience was a major shift in argumentation studies after the publication of Stephen Toulmin's *Uses of Argument* (1958) and the English translation of Chaim Perelman and L. Olbrechts-Tyteca's *New Rhetoric* (1969). Anticipating this shift, Lloyd Bitzer's 1959 essay on Aristotle's enthymeme in the *Quarterly Journal of Speech* proposed that "the audience itself helps construct the proofs by which it is persuaded" (408).

In Aristotelian studies, the centrality of enthymeme was particularly emphasized by William Grimaldi's (1980, 1988) commentary on the *Rhetoric*. As distinct from the earlier commentary by Edward Cope (1970), Grimaldi argued that in spite of Aristotle's repudiation of emotional excitation as external to *pisteis,* the description of enthymeme does not narrow down rational persuasion to logos alone. "If anything," he wrote, "*soma* means: the structure, the frame, which incorporates *pistis,* the 'corpus probationum'; and if *pistis* is ethical, and emotional, as well as logical, then the enthymeme is the structure which embodies them" (1980, 9). While an audience-centered understanding of enthymeme in terms of "the manner of construction" is plausible, expansive interpretations like the one offered by Grimaldi are flawed on two grounds. First, the text of the *Rhetoric* directly advises not to mix enthymematic arguments with either emotional appeals, "for it [*enthymeme*] will either drive out emotion or it will be useless," or with ethical proofs, "for demonstration involves neither moral character nor moral purpose" (1418a12–17).

Second, Grimaldi overlooks that other rhetorical forms—examples, narratives, and maxims—allow for the deployment of ethos and pathos. The logocentric character of enthymeme does not eliminate the demand for ethical and emotional appeals; it simply stamps the core of what Aristotle considers persuasion.[9] The fact that Aristotle sounds particularly proud of this innovation provides further justification for the centrality of enthymematic reasoning in his rhetorical project.[10]

To return to the image of audience as a measuring stick, what can be made of the link between enthymeme and the need to protect the dicast from being corrupted? Aristotle is not talking about the dicast's individual identity or soul but about a specific role within a rhetorical exchange. The choice of the court as a paradigm for the "medicinal" intervention of the rhetorical art springs from the assumption that the dicast's disposition should not be marked by a special interest in the matter at hand. The jury member passes judgment on others' affairs in accordance with written and unwritten laws of the land. Whether the trial is about murder or property, about a private crime or an offense against the state, the juror's proper role is to judge only whether the litigants have demonstrated the fact of the crime and its character. Elaborating on the appropriateness of enthymemes to forensic oratory, Aristotle remarks that speeches in this genre "are concerned with what are or are not the facts, which are more open to demonstration and a logically necessary conclusion, for the past has a necessity about it" (*Rhetoric* 1418a3–5). That the metaphor of "the measuring stick" describes the audience as an instrument is implied by Aristotle's discussion of style appropriate to forensic oratory: "Speaking in the law courts requires more exactness of detail, and that before a single judge even more, for it is least of all a matter of rhetorical techniques; for what pertains to the subject and what is irrelevant is more easily observed [by a single judge], and controversy is gone, so the judgment is clear" (*Rhetoric* 1414a10–13). The normative thrust of this passage is echoed in Aristotle's distinction between ordinary Athenian hearers and the *function* of hearer. The audiences, he points out, "are attentive to great things, things that concern themselves, marvels, and pleasures. As a result, one should imply that the speech is concerned with such things" (*Rhetoric* 1415b1). The audience's fickle disposition therefore needs homeopathic application of devices of which Aristotle generally disapproves and that he condones only as "remedies" (*iatreumata*) (*Rhetoric* 1415b9). Engaging the hearer's attention, then, is a steering function that falls outside the proper rhetorical transaction between the speaker and the audience. Commenting upon examples of attention getting devices, Aristotle remarks, "But it is clear that this is not addressed to the hearer in his proper capacity as hearer" (*Rhetoric* 1415b16). It follows, then, that the process by which the hearers identify with the subject differs substantially from their function as judges (*kriteis*).

The audience's creative co-construction of rhetorical proofs, then, is not so creative after all. Providing that the speaker properly constructs an enthymeme, the audience will contribute the missing premise almost automatically. To be sure, the function of "filling in" relies on the shared stock of written and unwritten cultural norms. But the audience's role is not to question the norms themselves, only their correct combination in the deployment of a syllogistic form. When judging a particular case, the audience affirms, regardless of the verdict, the justice of conventions that authorize the legal procedure. Even as the audience participates in the completion of the utterance, it acts as an agency of justice rather than as an agent. This is a truly brilliant invention on Aristotle's part: the jurors are interpellated as rational subjects whose agency lies entirely outside their individuality. The subject's rationality, however, is thoroughly tied to the procedure in which it is enacted as part of a speech plan of the litigant.

This reconstruction of "rational interpellation," of course, is purely theoretical, because Aristotle does not deny the importance of emotion and character even in a judicial context. However, the audience's function delineated by the syllogistic form works as a paradigm for all other acts of judgment. The dicast's characteristic as a rational measuring device is functionally superior to his ability to feel and to judge the speaker's character. The basis of all critical acts possible within the three arenas of rhetoric is the capacity to judge *representations* of the expedient, the just, and the noble. Yet the capacity to *recognize* these representations, as my earlier discussion suggests, does not render Aristotle's audience equal to the speaker already possessed of *phronēsis*. Recall the distinction between citizenly virtue and human virtue in the *Politics*. If my hypothesis that the *Rhetoric* facilitates the distribution of social roles proper to a constitutional regime is sound, the audience will have virtue in a relative sense, which is to say that it still would be inferior to citizens of the leisured classes who can cultivate virtue above and beyond politically necessary interactions.

One may object that the consent given by the audience to the propositions peculiar to the three genres does not exhaust the range of possible responses. After all, the catalog of popular morality in the second book of the *Rhetoric* speaks to the relevance of ethos and pathos as integral parts of persuasion. Yet the manner in which various emotions are analyzed leaves little doubt that emotions, too, are rational. For instance, to rouse the audience to anger, "it might be needful to put [the audience] in a state of mind of those who are inclined to anger and to show one's opponents as responsible for those things that are the causes of anger" (*Rhetoric* 1380a1). Similarly, to produce a representation of ethos, the orator must study propositions regarding virtues, "for a person would present himself as being of a certain sort from the same sources that he would use to present another person" (*Rhetoric* 1378a16). Aristotle introduces ethical and pathetic proofs in order to complement, rather than displace, the logocentrism of the enthymeme.

To believe, as some scholars do, that Aristotle ascribes to the audience the sort of practical rationality he wants his speaker to possess is therefore to conflate the functionality of a rhetorical transaction with the relationship of like-minded, virtuous equals. It must be acknowledged, however, that the concept of such discursive parity, like the political ideal of equality it seems to bolster, is inspiring. Many rhetorical theorists and critics have enthusiastically embraced the idea of the audience's participation in building arguments as a new paradigm for rhetoric. In the sixties and seventies, a shift of scholarly attention toward the audience was a welcome challenge to a theory of argumentation previously mired in formal logic.

Among rhetoricians, Thomas B. Farrell has been the most influential advocate of the Aristotelian paradigm for the invigoration of public discourse. Following Bitzer, Farrell (1976) developed in his earlier scholarship the notion of "social knowledge" in an effort to question technocratic obsession with empirically derived information and to revitalize public dialogue. Farrell defined social knowledge as a complex of "conceptions of symbolic relationships among problems, persons, interests, and actions, which imply (when accepted) certain notions of preferable public behavior." In so doing, he explicitly reacted against the "knowledge of observation," a technocratic ideology that assures us of the knower's objective stance (4–5). Advocating the twofold nature of social knowledge as "an object to be known and as constituted by a unique kind of relationship to knowers," he proposed that such consensus-based knowledge can "transform society into a community" (11).

For Farrell, a community is a "conscious and civilized audience" whose "collective nerve endings are alive to the interests of others within a society" (1976, 8–12). This ideal, espoused by the best of American progressives, including Dewey and Mead, posits a relationship in which the human community is an extension of self and self is a reflection of the other. Farrell, too, sees his concept of social knowledge as "merely the surface tracing of a deeper identity, between the self and its conscious extension—the human community"

(13). This is a powerful and ameliorative vision. However, if it is indeed indebted to Aristotle, as Farrell claims, this ideal has little to do with the type of discourse Aristotle calls rhetoric.

In Aristotle's corpus, we do find a description of the community of enlightened others, but this community and the one which provides the conditions for an individuated polis are distinct in Aristotle's view. Whereas the former is a "consubstantiality" to which Aristotle grants the status of true friendship (*philia*), the latter is an articulated organism with different parts working in agreement among themselves. In the *Eudemian Ethics,* Aristotle praises the advantages of a friendship built upon mutual admiration and respect. Contrasting instrumental *philia* with a more reciprocal relationship between persons of virtue, he concludes that "a friend is not for the sake of utility or benefit but that one loved on account of goodness is the only real friend. For when we are not in need of something, then we all seek people to share our enjoyments, and beneficiaries rather than benefactors; and we can judge them better when we are self-sufficient than when we are in need, and we most need friends who are worthy of our society" (1244b15–20). Aristotle goes against the Platonic ideal of rational self-sufficiency and proposes instead a relational vision of good life. He prefers "the life of perception and knowledge in common" (1244b25–26) because he sees in it a condition for reflexive attainment of *eudaimonia.*

In this respect, Farrell and the philosophical tradition he relies on are on target: Aristotle states that "to perceive and to know a friend . . . is necessarily in a manner to perceive and in a manner to know oneself" (1245a35–36). It is also clear, however, that Aristotle does not extend this *philia* to "the human community" at large. Besides the definition of true friendship above, consider the following gradation of shared pleasures: "Consequently to share even vulgar pleasures and ordinary life with a friend is naturally pleasant (for it always involves our simultaneously perceiving the friend), but more so to share the more divine pleasures; the reason of which is that it is always more pleasurable to behold oneself enjoying the superior good" (*Eudemian Ethics* 1244a36–1244b1).

The moral amelioration via shared *theoria* is not, at least for Aristotle, the goal of a rhetorical art, even if this art furnishes propositions regarding virtues. Nor is rhetoric designed, because of its place within Aristotle's hierarchy of disciplines, to foster the self-reflexivity peculiar to *philia*. Farrell nonetheless sees the *Rhetoric* as a necessary complement to Aristotle's ethical treatises insofar as rhetoric seems to promote judgment characteristic of practical rationality.

In this spirit, Farrell (1993) argues that in reaching out to a particular audience, the rhetor in fact tries to think and feel like the audience—an exercise that engenders the rhetor's self-reflection. Indeed, Farrell paints a portrait of an Aristotelian speaker who approaches the audience as if it were an extension of self: "To really think *as an audience* cannot be a morally neutral activity. Aesthetically speaking, it may be to see people in assembly as better than they are, thereby allowing us to address them in such a way that they and we may become better than we were" (71). This is a fascinating insight into the intersubjective dimension of *philia,* but I doubt it can be extended to Aristotle's rigid repertoire of audience's roles in the *Rhetoric.* Interestingly enough, the speaker's *mimēsis* of the audience Farrell so deftly describes is the very point that Isocrates, not Aristotle, repeatedly makes in his defense of aesthetic *paideia* and performative politics.

Farrell's noble intention—to find a theory of discourse that "allows us to envision the audience as something more distinctive than the popular contemporary models of 'target,' 'market,' 'mass,' or 'voyeur'"—projects onto the *Rhetoric* some of the constructs that Aristotle reserves for ethics. Because Aristotle calls the hearers of public speeches *kriteis,* "judges," Farrell reads it as a sign of conceptualizing the audience as "an agency capable of deliberative insight" (1993, 80). It is true that the role of rhetorical audiences is to render *krisis,* but their judgment is already circumscribed by the occasion and discursive procedure. Moreover, while he demands that the speaker possess *phronēsis,* Aristotle does not grant the audience practical wisdom.[11] At best, the hearers can put aside their personal interests and contribute to deliberation by "filling in" the formula-like utterances of the speakers.

Farrell is not alone in wanting to elevate rhetoric's status among other works by Aristotle as well as among contemporary philosophers and political scientists. In recent years, scholars from a variety of disciplines have turned to Aristotle in the hope of finding a model of practical rationality that can also accommodate the discourse of democracy. Unfortunately, Aristotle's discussions of virtue and practical wisdom are not easily reconcilable with his discussion of rhetoric as a technical capacity (*dunamis*). His vision of discursive power, while it tames the violence and arbitrariness of logos described by the likes of Gorgias, nevertheless resists bringing together virtue and democracy.

Five

BETWEEN SOCIAL PERMANENCE AND SOCIAL CHANGE

In a book written during the Great Depression, Kenneth Burke observed how every new generation reinterprets already existing vocabularies in order to generate "the device of living and thinking by which the faulty emphases of their day may be rectified" (1984, 182). "The desire to recharacterize events," he writes, "requires a new reading of the signs—and though men have ever 'looked backwards,' the backward-looking of the 'prophets' is coupled with a new principle of interpretation, a new perspective or point of view, whereby the picture of 'things as they *really* are' is reorganized" (180).

Burke's point is germane for interpreters of rhetorical history, because their labor of reading and articulating the relevance of historical documents is informed by contemporary disciplinary and political concerns. When we approach classical discourses, their contemporary appropriations form both a background and an interpretive challenge. On the other hand, as Terry Eagleton (1983) once asserted in his advice to literary critics, rhetoric sees "speaking and writing not merely as textual objects, to be aesthetically contemplated and endlessly deconstructed, but as forms of *activity* inseparable from the wider social relations between writers and readers, orators and audiences, and as largely unintelligible outside the social purposes and conditions in which they were embedded" (206). In the case of classical rhetorics, the chasm between original historical contexts of ancient texts and their contemporary usage seems so great that some scholars have opted to distinguish between "historical reconstruction" and "contemporary appropriation," the former designating philological fidelity to extant textual evidence and avoidance of anachronism, the latter referring to rendering of ancient theories through some sort of contemporary theoretical lens.[1] To be sure, importation of classical models cannot be a simple matter of matching an ancient author's "theory" to our current scholarly and political agendas in the same way two transparent sheets of celluloid are superimposed upon each other. At the same time, if we self-consciously cultivate an "ironic" stance toward our scholarly vocabularies, objects of study and goals of interpretation, we do not have to sacrifice historical rigor for contemporary relevance and vice versa. An "ironist," as Richard Rorty (1989) puts it, is "the sort of person who faces up to the contingency of his or her own beliefs and desires—someone sufficiently historicist and nominalist to have abandoned the idea that those central beliefs and desires refer back to something beyond the reach of time and chance" (xv). From this perspective, then, it is important to examine both the cultural conditions of emergence of a particular ancient theory and the context of our own theoretical and political biases.²

The aligning of *logos* and power in the title of the book is no doubt motivated by a *contemporary* concern with theorizing the political through a discursive lens. Given the continuing importance of the classical tradition in the legitimation of power relations in the West, however, this perspective also demands that we focus on heretofore downplayed aspects of the "canon." Indeed, refracted in the ancients' vocabulary one finds a remarkable, if fragmentary, strand: from Gorgias to Isocrates to Aristotle there is a consistent association between the words for discourse and the words for power. Gorgias refers to logos as *dunastēs* (ruler) and as *bia* (violent force); Isocrates names logos *hēgemōn* (leader); and Aristotle designates rhetoric as *dunamis* (power or capacity). By stressing the pivotal role of these terms, I do not wish merely to engage in an etymological exercise. Abiding by an "ironic" perspective, I want instead to inquire into the implications of these acts of naming for both ancient and contemporary rhetorical practices. Accordingly, while attending to the contextual grounding of the terms for rhetoric in Gorgias, Aristotle, and Isocrates, I will also consider how they have been appropriated by contemporary scholarship. In comparison with Gorgias and Aristotle, the Isocratean paradigm arguably offers us a notion of discursive power that at once challenges the received contemporary assumptions about political rhetoric and provides a valuable alternative to the classical visions of logos as irresistible force on the one hand, and a pliable instrument of a fully ethical agent on the other.

Logos as Bia *and the Question of Agency*

As far as we know, Gorgias did not leave behind authoritative written versions of his speeches. But his fragmentary record has been compensated by his enduring fame in the Hellenic world. An itinerant yet highly influential teacher, Gorgias has become virtually synonymous with the sophistical movement and the fifth-century wave of democratization in several city-states.³ Responding to the crisis of aristocratic political power, Sophists like Protagoras and Gorgias seem to have enabled an unprecedented radical pluralism of the Athenian democracy. Small wonder that in the last thirty years, the years following the 1960s, Gorgias and the sophistical movement he represents have become attractive to many American intellectuals, whose own political sensibilities had been shaped by the decade of the civil rights movement, women's liberation and student protests against U.S. military policy in Vietnam. Animated by a desire to update the classical liberal education, an impressive group of scholars has attempted to reread the Sophists in order to find a more pluralistic conception of discourse and power than the one yielded by traditional histories of rhetoric.[4] The Sophists now appear as nomadic or cosmopolitan intellectuals, eternally playful and irreverent toward any social order. The so-called Sophists seem to personify social change as a radical process.

Such a sketch is not unfaithful to what Gorgias reportedly said about the power of speech in his *Encomium of Helen*. He treats the power of the mythopoetic logos with ambivalence: on the one hand, speech is likened to violence (*bia*); on the other, the speaker treats his own composition as a plaything (*paignion*).[5] Gorgias exposes logos in its untamed arbitrariness, which is akin to a tyrant's lack of accountability and direction in dealing out favors and punishments (*Helen* 8). Yet this arbitrariness now characterizes not the rule of kings but speechmaking in a democratic polis. Calling logos *bia* and *dunastēs*, Gorgias employs the imagery of the archaic past, but his description of verbal artists of various types points toward the wrangle of the Athenian democracy of the late fifth century.

Although Gorgias's motives for composing *Helen* cannot be known with certainty, the extant text's many levels of meaning allow for a symptomatic reading. Like Thucydides in his *Histories* and Aristophanes in his comedies, Gorgias gives us a stylized glimpse of attitudes toward public speech among the Athenians of the second part of the fifth century. *Helen* portrays a culture of agonistic display of linguistic prowess in which discourses topple one another and the authority of a persuasive speech is higher than any divine or human law.[6] Gorgias's "rationalistic" treatment of a traditional mythopoetic topos reveals that even such stable cultural truths as the myth of Helen's abduction by Paris can be shown to rest on a series of deceptive acts of persuasion.

The decentering thrust of the *Helen*, therefore, relies not only on its subversive attitude toward the mythopoetic tradition, but on the criticism of doxastic cultural practices made possible by the powers of speech. Gorgias shows truth (*alētheia*) to be a product of opinion (*doxa*). Yet his most remarkable move is to show how *doxa* can masquerade as *alētheia*. The myth of Helen is *defamiliarized* in order to display new *possibilities* of the logos. The dynastic power of the latter nonetheless contains a reactionary potential that can transform a discourse from a state of doxa to a state of *doxa* qua *alētheia*. As distinct from other fifth-century critics of the excesses of democracy such as Thucydides and Aristophanes,[7] Gorgias does not advocate linguistic temperance. Asserting the all-encompassing power of logos, Gorgias leaves open the possibilities of its application.

In this context, we cannot discount the "mythologization" that took place alongside the new "rationalism" of the fifth century with which the Sophists are associated. One cannot presume, in other words, that the rationalizing tendency did away with the ongoing political influence of mythopoesis. In the wake of the Persian Wars, Athenian democracy produced its own myths, such as the myth of Athens as the savior of Hellas that emerges in Aeschylus's *Persae* (472 B.C.E.) and is echoed throughout classical Athenian funeral orations as well as in the so-called rational historiography of Herodotus and Thucydides. In her work on the Athenian funeral oration, Nicole Loraux (1986) has even referred to the transcendence of Athens as "the spell of an ideality" (263). These discourses were public performances that furthered cultural reproduction just as much as Homeric epic recitations. The new political mythology did not, in fact, displace the old world of epic but wove it into the existing cultural texture. For instance, Herodotus intermingles historical and mythical details in the narrative about the origin of the feud between the Greeks and the barbarians. In a similar fashion, American democracy created its own civil religion without displacing traditional religious practices (Bellah 1967). One only needs to recall Frank Capra's famous World War II "documentary" series *Why We Fight* in which the ideal of Liberty and of the United States as the land of Liberty crystallize as a divinely sanctioned social order and a bastion against the dark forces of fascism around the globe. In classical Greek usage, *eleutheria* (freedom) also became one of the terms that not only distinguished a particular political constitution but also characterized public and private conduct.[8] It is precisely this ideological spell, with its assertion of Athens' cultural uniqueness, that Aristotle attempted to transcend in his naturalistic view of politics and with which Isocrates had to grapple in order to orient the Athenian audience toward a more pan-Hellenic ideal.

To be sure, the Sophists self-consciously functioned within the ambiguous domain of opinion (*doxa*), in a way that was ruled by the "principle of contradiction" (Detienne 1996, 117). Yet the educational and political practice founded on such ambiguity admits of both social permanence and social change. Thus Takis Poulakos (1994) sees *Helen* as a text symptomatic of the crisis of aristocratic power and suggests that Gorgias introduces a socially decentering possibility of "opposition to aristocracy" (75). At the same time, the rule of logos, which supplanted the rule of aristocratic blood, made it possible for elites to get their way by "voicing" the culturally embedded attitudes of the demos. According to Josiah Ober's (1989) description of the relationship between elite rhetors and their democratic audiences, "Athenian politicians were well aware of the climate of public opinion in which they operated, and no public speaker could afford to contradict central principles of the Athenian belief structure very often" (315). Though Gorgias's phrase "substituting opinion for opinion" (*Helen* 13) suggests that *doxa* were easy to uproot, "the Athenian belief structure," a continually reinforced ideology of the Athenian imperial democracy, constituted a conservative cultural force that a rhetorician could exploit but not easily challenge.

Playfully unveiling the illusory tactics of poets, philosophers, and rhetoricians, Gorgias's *Helen* performs the very rhetorical and political ambiguity that is the object of the discourse. His ambivalence, communicated by the word *paignion* (*Helen* 21), promises a possibility of a self-reflective agent who is neither fully autonomous from nor entirely vulnerable to the influence of persuasion. Yet this ambivalence also precludes a definitive answer about the political trajectory of his performance. However fascinating the self-reflexive potential of his verbal artistry, Gorgias brackets the question of the social function of discourse, leaving us in awe of the magical powers of logos.[9]

Dunamis *and Instrumentality of Rhetoric*

Aristotle's rhetorical project aims to disambiguate the magic of logos and to systematize the existing means of persuasion. It remains to be seen, however, what social ends are being served by the enabling power of rhetoric. The *Rhetoric* has puzzled modern critics as an intriguing mix of Aristotle's own philosophical principles and a catalogue of indiscriminately assembled bits and pieces of popular Greek wisdom.[10] It is possible that Aristotle, faced with something as arbitrary and unsystematic as the speech practices of a democracy, loosened his theoretical standards to accommodate the heterogeneous norms of the culture. I do not, however, share this view. I have argued that in spite of its seemingly empirical character as a compendium of accepted public expression, Aristotle's *technē rhētorikē* actually atomizes and reassembles these fragments of culture so as to make them amenable to his intellectual and political agenda. The *Rhetoric* appears as a kind of compromise between the philosopher's commitment to a particular vision of good life in the polis and historically concrete and heterogeneous norms of a democratic culture. But with a trade-off such as this, one cannot help asking what is being compromised and why. The *Rhetoric,* as the following argument regarding Aristotle's designation of rhetoric as *dunamis* will show, severely limits the role of discourse in the formation of a political subject, furnishes the existing means of persuasion, linked to the traditional forums, to an already properly habituated moral agent, and thereby marks other discourses of culture as extrarhetorical.

The word *dunamis* is one of the most commonly used terms in Aristotle. Not surprisingly, the various contexts in which it appears render it polysemous. For instance, *The Constitution of the Athenians,* which purports to be an account of the rise of democracy in Athens, employs *dunamis* at least in three senses, all of them taken from the vernacular: as a political influence of a certain class, as a legislative act, and as state power linked to the growth of the navy (12.1, 22.2–3, 27.1).[11] In Aristotle's theoretical inquiries, however, *dunamis* is a very specific and univocal concept: it designates "potentiality" with respect to nonhuman objects and animals and "ability" with respect to humans. The distinction between ability and activity, potentiality and actuality (*energeia*) is crucial in Aristotle's entire philosophical apparatus. Mere ability does not necessarily lead to activity. It is this sense of "ability" as opposed to "activity" (*energeia*) that Aristotle attaches to the notion of rhetoric as an art: "Let rhetoric be [defined as] an ability (*dunamis*), in each [particular] case, to see the available means of persuasion. This is the function of no other art, for each of the others is instructive and persuasive about its own subject" (*Rhetoric* 1355b26–30). Yet the ability in question does not result in the kind of logos Gorgias so vividly describes in the *Helen*. With Aristotle, we are far removed from the notion of discourse as violence and from an understanding of speaker as a seducer. Discursive power has been transformed into a technical ability that may or may not be actualized. Indeed, the ability Aristotle promises through his art may never result in an act of public persuasion at all. In *Nicomachean Ethics,* Aristotle states emphatically that "an art never produces an activity, but the capacity for an activity" (1153a25).

Why does Aristotle take care to define his subject in such a tentative way? What assumptions about political agency are riding on the term *dunamis*? Eugene Garver's *Aristotle's Rhetoric: An Art of Character* (1994) attempts to recover rhetoric as a civic art by overcoming the limitations presented by the name *dunamis*. As a classical philosopher, Garver fully appreciates the theoretical gap between art and practice, between ability and activity implied by Aristotle's use of terms *dunamis* and *technē*. He knows, accordingly, that the treatise is not meant as a new and improved training manual for budding orators. What, then, is its application? Garver's answer is instructive with respect to our claim about the formation of political subjects: "Through the *Rhetoric,* the politician can intelligently rule on the place of rhetoric in the polis. Such an inquiry tells citizens and lawmakers what they need to know about the art for a variety of political purposes, from legislation about rules of evidence to questions about education and discursive proficiency. It will be useful for politicians to know about the relations of one art to another, so that they can know which problems are unique to rhetoric and which are shared by other arts. They might value the products of some art without wanting to be practitioners or experts themselves, in which case a professional art at most, not a civic one, will be possible" (1994, 19). Garver suggests that the *Rhetoric* enables a legislator to understand how rhetoric works in the polis without imposing the necessity to employ it, since the act of persuasion—or, rather, its external end—

is not as noble as a detached (internal) understanding of how persuasion works. Garver refers to Plato's *Protagoras* to distinguish between the lowly, professional practice of rhetoric and a more cerebral appreciation of the art: "Hippocrates at the beginning of the *Protagoras* is a paradigm. He is troubled by Socrates' suggestion that learning from a sophist will make him into one too, and Socrates lets him off the hook by distinguishing learning *epi technei,* in order to become professional like his teacher, and studying *epi paideiai,* which is suitable for free and wealthy young men (312b). If something is a civic art, then it will be valued for more than its results" (1994, 19).

Garver's overall claim is that rhetoric is a civic art that is valued and valuable for its own sake whether or not its practice produces conviction in the audience. Aristotle's views of rhetoric, on Garver's reading, lift it up from the status of "mere rhetoric" (to which Plato had reduced it) to a civic *technē* that can, if practiced well, play a crucial part in the formation of character. However, according to Garver's first passage quoted above, the legislator or the statesman already occupies a position of power, presumably thanks to his excellence in deliberating about things political. Therefore, the understanding of the workings of rhetoric in various civic arenas fortifies his already sufficient aptitude to cope with contingent particulars. This interpretation is not at odds with Aristotle's description of practical rationality (*phronēsis*) as a nonscientific grasp of the right thing to do in circumstances that escape lawlike generalizations (*Nicomachean Ethics* 1140a32). Persons like Pericles are called *phronimoi,* says Aristotle, "because they are able to observe what things are good for themselves and for humankind" (1140b7–10). However, Garver hopes to see the *Rhetoric* as an art that not only serves but somehow substantively enriches *phronēsis.* The overriding achievement of the *Rhetoric,* he claims, "is to align art, argument, and *ethos* so that we primarily make discourse ethical by making argument artful" (184). It is on this basis that Garver distinguishes between "cleverness" of the sophistic "professional" art and *phronēsis* of Aristotle's "civic" art (184–85). Although Garver's attempt to give *phronēsis* a rhetorical grounding is worthwhile, I believe he is looking for a model of discursively constituted character in the wrong place. It is Isocrates' *logōn paideia* that conjoins *phronein* and *legein,* prudent deliberation and eloquence, in the act of rhetorical performance. Aristotle, on the contrary, takes care to position practical wisdom (*phronēsis*) precisely below scientific knowledge (*epistēmē*) and above art (*technē*) (*Nicomachean Ethics* 1140b1–5).

Aristotle's motives for framing rhetoric as an art productive of a capacity (*dunamis*) can best be grasped in the light of his explicit desire to limit inevitable contingencies of political life and to have most practical public decisions follow from established laws. Rhetoric comes into play when the situation exceeds the parameters circumscribed by law. In a passage from the opening chapter of the *Rhetoric,* Aristotle lays out the political raison d'être of his inquiry:

> It is highly appropriate for well-enacted laws to define everything as exactly as possible and for as little as possible to be left to the judges: first because it is easier to find one or a few than [to find] many who are prudent and capable of framing laws and judging; second, legislation results from consideration over much time, while judgments are made at the moment [of a trial or debate], so it is difficult for the judges to determine justice and benefits fairly; but most important of all, because the judgment of a lawmaker is not about a particular case but about what lies in the future and in general, while the assemblyman and the juryman are actually judging present and specific cases. For them, friendliness and hostility and individual self-interest are often involved, with the result that they are no longer able to see the truth adequately. (1354a32–1354b12)

Aristotle draws a sharp distinction between those who establish laws and the multitude who vote in a democracy on everyday matters in the courts and the assembly. Of particular interest is the contrast between the legislator's sovereign subjectivity, untroubled by petty desires, and the deficient state of mind of the regular judge. Especially telling is the fact that Aristotle assumes these conditions as a natural point of departure rather than as consequences of rhetorical practice. The legislators' deliberative rationality and reasoned judgment with respect to the law *are prior to* their involvement in the mundane business, just as the regular member of the assembly and the dicast *are already* in a state of confusion before they cast their vote for a particular decision.

To be sure, Aristotle faults other *technologoi,* the writers of rhetorical handbooks, for emphasizing "how to put the judge into a certain frame of mind" over the facts of the case (*Rhetoric* 1354b20). But his sentiment that they are pandering to an already corrupted set of hearers is transparent. Appeals to emotion fan the flames of the audience's innate excitability. Other statements in the *Rhetoric* affirm the presumption of an a priori deficiency of the hearers who form the deliberating body in a democracy. Aristotle ascribes the popular appeal of "political contests" to the "corruptness of governments" (1403b34–35) and laments the necessity of employing style (*lexis*) due to "the corruption of the audience" (1404a9).[12] The condition of "corruptness" (*mochthēria*) characterizes not only subjects in a democracy but also the form of government itself, which entails that the legislator is no longer a sovereign subject but a product of a particular constitution. However, for Aristotle the discourse of constitution and the art of rhetoric must remain separate. That is why he not only insists on the boundaries between rhetoric and ethics and between rhetoric and politics (*Rhetoric* 1356a) but also subordinates rhetoric to politics as the most controlling science in the sphere of praxis (*Nicomachean Ethics* 1094a27–28). Unlike Plato and Isocrates, Aristotle does not want to leave the formation of political identity and social organization to a particular form of discourse. This may appear inconsistent with my earlier argument that Aristotle disciplines democracy by disciplining rhetoric. However, it is not the political identity Aristotle is trying to influence but the differentiation of citizen roles. In other words, he does not seek to reinforce the audience's self-understanding as a democratic polity but to compartmentalize it according to specific goals of a discrete occasion.

For Aristotle, social roles in the polis are (or at least, should be) natural, with the leisured classes having the most potential for developing the practical wisdom (*phronēsis*) required for prudent government and deliberation even when the many are legitimate members of the body politic. His discussion in the *Politics* of the difference between the ideal constitution and other forms of government, especially democracy, is instructive in this regard. Rather than following Plato's lead in throwing out poetic *paideia*, whose aesthetic influence corrupts the polity's character, Aristotle sets up discrete conditions of citizenship and corresponding functions of political subjects for various types of constitutions. In order to have self-sufficiency (*autarkeia*), each polis must have classes corresponding to the six necessary functions: production of food supply, handicrafts, armed forces, monetary supply, the service of religion, and, "most importantly, a provision for deciding questions of interests and of rights between the citizens" (*Politics* 1328b6–14). In the ideal state, which is the most conducive to a life of happiness in accordance with true virtue (*aretē*), the citizens must necessarily own property, "for the artisan class has no share in the state, nor has any other class that is not 'an artificer of virtue'" (*Politics* 1329a19–20). The free multitude does not partake in the ideal state, since it is most likely to be fixated on the pursuit of what Aristotle terms *bios apolaustikos*, "life of enjoyment," as opposed to the two nobler types of living, *bios politikos* and *bios theōrētikos*, "political life" and "life of contemplation" (*Nicomachean Ethics* 1095b15–31). Not that for Aristotle wealth automatically guarantees that the rich will develop moral and intellectual virtues. *Nicomachean Ethics* stresses that the life of enjoyment has been glorified only because "many persons of high position share the feelings of Sardanapallus," a mythical Assyrian king personifying greedy pursuit of bodily pleasures (1095b21). Similarly, in the *Politics* Aristotle distinguishes between oligarchy and aristocracy on the basis of virtue: the former is ruled by those who are merely wealthy, the latter by those who by birth and demonstrated excellence have proved themselves worthy of ruling and being ruled in turn (see Ober 1991). Nonetheless, Aristotle's use of Plato's phrase "the artificer of virtue" (*Republic* 500d) signals his conviction that a "mechanic and mercantile life" is "inimical to virtue" and that "leisure is needed both for the development of virtue and for active participation in politics" (*Politics* 1328b38–1229a2). In a democracy, on the contrary, a free but largely indigent male population prevails over the propertied class because of sheer numbers. *Dēmokratia,* in this Aristotelian sense, means the political domination based on "equality according to number, not worth" (*Politics* 1317b1–3). This form of governance, in which no one (save slaves, women, metics, and barbarians) is barred from performing a miscellany of functions, from tilling the land to bearing arms to voting and legislating, clearly threatens the conditions of individuation and forms of collectivity that Aristotle considers normal, that is, differentiated according to ability and virtue. Following Plato's sarcastic description of the democratic man in the *Republic* (559d–562a), Aristotle comments with alarm on a twist in the popular application of the term freedom (*eleutheria*). As a proclaimed principle of the democratic form of constitution, *eleutheria* has come to mean "to live as one likes, for they say that this is the function of liberty inasmuch as to live not as one likes is the life of a slave" (*Politics* 1317b11–13). From there, Aristotle points out, "has come a claim not to be governed, preferably by anybody, or failing that, to govern and be governed in turns" (*Politics* 1317b13–16). What Aristotle describes here is the dominant motif of democratic ideology at the time when Athens was commanding naval superiority, a theme that goes back to Thucydides' unflattering portrayal of the conflicting desires of the deliberating *demos* (3.1–50) and of the violent temper of the poor who manned the ships (8.84.3).[13] Besides communicating a concern of an elite critic in the face of the volatile power of the *demos,* Aristotle's account demonstrates a certain degree of frustration with the theoretical confusion created by the democratic political self-understanding. Instead of developing skills appropriate to one's function (excelling in farming or crafts, for instance) and moral virtues to match, a democratic subject is "free" to live as he wishes. As Plato's portrayal of the democratic man in the *Republic* goes, such a person imitates whoever strikes his fancy: "And if military men excite his emulation, thither he rushes, and if moneyed men, to that he returns, and there is no order or compulsion in his existence, but he calls this life of his the life of pleasure and freedom and happiness and cleaves to it to the end" (561d). For the same reason, Aristotle is more sanguine about democracies with a large population of free farmers: "For owing to their not having much property they are busy, so that they cannot often meet in the assembly, while owing to their having the necessaries of life they pass their time attending to their farmwork and do not covet their neighbours' goods but find more pleasure in working than in taking part in politics and holding office" (*Politics* 1318b11–15). To have an identity guided by desire for a variety of roles is like having no identity at all. It is partially because of this presumed confusion, I believe, that Aristotle refuses to equate rhetorical discourse with the discourse of civic education. For in doing so, he would risk putting on the same plane "equality according to worth," which undergirds aristocratic ethos, and the democratic "equality according to number." Aristotle offers the matrix of rhetorical discourse to arm elite rhetors against the changing winds of democracy. As a *dunamis,* rhetoric can be used as a buffer between the rhetor and the *demos.* After all, in Aristotle's *Politics, dēmokratia* is a corrupt form (*parekbasis*) of constitution, distinguished by popular sovereignty, rather than by the "partnership of free men" (*Politics* 1279a 21). Aristotle uses the principle of "common interest" (*to koinon sumpheron*) to distinguish between the proper and corrupt types of government (*Politics* 1279a 28). Corrupt states aim at the goal of the ruler alone, whether an individual or a class, not at the shared goal of ruler and the ruled. By contrast, democracy's correct counterpart, *politeia,* acknowledges the demands, even rights, of wellborn prudent citizens along with the desires of the multitude. If an elite orator succeeds in securing consent of the poor masses, the pendulum of power may indeed swing toward a *politeia,* a more "natural" political regime in Aristotle's account.

In the light of his position about the democratic identity being essentially a state of confusion about one's proper role in the polis, Aristotle's articulation of rhetoric as a capacity (*dunamis*) to discern existing means of persuasion is unlikely to describe an art of virtue. If the *Rhetoric* is indeed intended for the purposes of analysis and production of persuasion in a democratic polis like Athens, it is unlikely that Aristotle would champion the discourse suitable for such a polis as the language appropriate for socializing "artificers of virtue." In *Nicomachean Ethics,* Aristotle asserts that "it is difficult to obtain a right education in virtue from youth up without being brought up under right laws" (1179b32–33). But in the absence of proper public regulation (such as that of Sparta), "it would seem to be the duty of the individual to assist his own children and friends to attain virtue. . . . But it would seem to follow from what has been said before, that he will be more likely to be successful in this if he has acquired the science of legislation" (1180a29–34). Aristotle obviously gives paternal discipline, enlightened by the true science of legislation, all of the authority in the matter of *paideia,* just as he denies it to "the sophists who profess to teach the science" (1180b34–1181a2).

Garver apparently thinks that Aristotle's *Rhetoric* can be interpreted as a civic art of character as long as one studies it, in Plato's phrase, not *epi technei* but *epi paideiai,* for the sake of education rather than professional skill. Garver thus invites us to think of rhetoric as part of *paideia,* in the general sense of "culture."[14] There are plenty of good reasons to want to integrate rhetoric as the discourse of political culture into the moral habituation of citizens. For as a discourse concerned with contingencies of political existence, rhetoric seems particularly well suited for instilling an appreciation of ambiguity of cultural norms and precariousness of any social collectivity. However, Aristotle does not endorse any such inclusive view of rhetorical *paideia* either in the *Rhetoric* or in other parts of the corpus. His exposition of moral habituation through *mousikē* in the *Politics* and of adult learning through poetic illumination in the *Poetics* presents a rather rarefied portrait of a culture. When speaking of training in poetry and instrumental music, Aristotle does not want children to be exposed to a broad variety of poetic and musical forms, only to those that can teach them to "take pleasure aright." Again, when discussing tragic drama, Aristotle insists that one should not seek from it all kinds of pleasures, but only the proper one. Most important, the structure of moral habituation of an aristocrat, as Aristotle conceives it, permits training by imitation and performance only until a certain age. After that, cultivation of performance skills is considered vulgar. We may also recall from the *Politics* that Aristotle considers performance in front of an audience a corrupting influence on one's character. For the listeners are wont to alter one's repertoire and style—and, by extension, one's very character—in the way that would be pleasing to them. In this disapproval of performance, then, Aristotle reflects a longstanding aristocratic bias against technical skills that we also find in the passage from Plato's *Protagoras,* to which Garver turns for the difference between *paideia* and *technē.*

The formulation of rhetoric as a *dunamis* rather than as a practice or activity seems to reflect this concern with upholding distinctions between "liberal" education and "illiberal" training. As a *dunamis,* Aristotle's *technē rhētorikē* concerns itself with influencing opinion (*doxa*) of the multitude in areas where law is ambiguous or silent rather than with the shaping the rhetor's or audience's identity. Even in an epideictic setting, where the opportunities of hailing into being or reinforcing a particular civic identity through the language of praise or blame are the greatest, Aristotle assigns the audience the role of a spectator judging the speaker's verbal ability (*Rhetoric* 1358b5). The narrow description of epideictic in Aristotle is, as it were, a formal nod to the performative culture's assumption about the bond between eloquent speech and praiseworthy conduct. But performance in this case is detached from the invocation or renewal of identity. As a fragment of popular morality, the speech-conduct pair is mentioned in the *Rhetoric* among other taken-for-granted "good things" (*agatha*): "Capacity to speak and to act, for they are productive of many goods" (1362b23–24). Despite its appearance on the list of *agatha,* the formula *legein kai prattein* has lost its centrality for Aristotle. His public philosophy can be described as a sustained effort to disengage conditions of moral and civic habituation from exigencies of political performance.

If rhetoric furnishes the linguistic tools, the already constituted moral agency of the speaker supplies the power that turns these inanimate tools into artful utterances produced in deliberative, judicial and epideictic contexts. Garver is correct to assert, then, that if practiced well, the art of rhetoric is an instantiation of deliberative rationality. It is in this spatially and temporally restricted and linguistically formalized way that one can be artful without being persuasive (i.e., failing to convince a particular audience in a specific situation). "The species of rhetoric . . . are essential kinds of practical activity, while the instances of rhetorical practice that fall outside these kinds . . . have no such central place in our practical life," Garver notes. "To anticipate, it is the species, not rhetoric in general or great individual acts of persuasion, that best exhibit the *forms* and function of persuasion, and hence the *ends* of rhetorical activity. Other examples of rhetoric that fall outside the three species might be needed because of the weaknesses or exigencies of audiences, but the three kinds of rhetoric are instances of practical rationality functioning well, because in the precise sense they are instances of practical rationality *functioning*" (55).

Garver's reading of rhetoric as an art of practice pushes the boundaries of Aristotle's terminology to accommodate a more rhetorically inflected theory of ethics. He shows how one can be ethical and still practice rhetoric. But he does *not* show how this practice substantively enriches the agent's practical rationality (*phronēsis*) and the character traits that undergird it. If I possess *phronēsis*, my linguistic acts, crafted in accordance with my rhetorical *dunamis*, will display my practical rationality to those who can recognize it. But the point is, I must have *phronēsis* before I engage in rhetorical activity that would instantiate my ability to grasp what is good for myself and for the polis in each particular situation.[15] To put it in terms of speech-act theory, Garver succeeds in showing how a rhetorical utterance is artful as an illocutionary speech-act regardless of its perlocutionary effects.[16] Rhetorical performance instantiates but does not exceed or transform rhetorical *dunamis*. Along with other philosophical rhetoricians, Garver is caught between his commitment to an art of civic discourse informed by ethical standards and Aristotle's refusal to allow rhetoric to be more than a productive art subordinated to politics and ethics. The following quotation from Ronald Beiner (1983), whom Garver cites at length in an endnote to *An Art of Character,* captures this concern in a particularly poignant fashion:

> As even Habermas concedes, "the difference between what we always claim for our rationality and what we are actually able to explicate as rational can in principle never be eliminated." But for the demands of situated praxis, this is simply not enough. One must act as if unreflectively, embodying a sure sense of what is good and right; one must command a kind of practical assurance that even the strictest, most rigorous set of arguments fails to supply. This is something made available only by character and habituation, never by

rational argument as such. As an Aristotelian would say, in order to live virtuously and to make the right choices, one's soul must be shaped by certain habits of virtuous conduct, in a way that renders superfluous recourse to strict arguments. Judged by these purposes, the achievements of theory always fall short. (1994, 267)

Aristotle aspires to make the public language of democracy, with its conflicting values and its tradition of display and contest, conformable to the purposes of a properly habituated moral agent. In my critique of Garver, I explained how Aristotle uses the term *dunamis* to demarcate the domain of rhetoric from the conditions of subject formation as well as to subordinate it to the power structure of the state. As a neutral capacity, Aristotle's rhetoric cannot stand on its own as a discourse of civic identity and political deliberation. To become such a discourse, it must be animated by *phronēsis,* which is autonomous from and superior to *technē*. The rhetorical agent arrives on a scene that had already been settled through extrarhetorical means and uses existing means of persuasion (arranged by Aristotle into logical, pathetic and ethical *pisteis*) to bring the unsettled matters in line with the status quo. Rhetoric as a *dunamis* is thus a politically and ethically reactive, rather than constitutive, power. Though based on publicly negotiated norms of discursive conduct, it nevertheless cannot function as a discourse of deliberation regarding the *ends* of political life.

Hegemony and the Ambivalence of Political Performance

Over and against Aristotle's brand of technical rhetoric, Isocrates implicates himself, as a citizen and an educator, in the act of negotiating the political and rhetorical legacy of the Athenian democracy. This active mode of intervention into the life of the polis posits a double problem for modern interpreters. On the one hand, his oeuvre is inseparable from the context of the rhetorician's relationship with the agonistic display culture of the Athenian democracy. The second difficulty is related to the performative character of Isocratean writings: what Isocrates says about the power of logos is not easily separable into the propositional, theoretical core and the communicative, situationally contingent elements. However, it is precisely because of the performative thrust of his compositions, that Isocrates' vision of *logos politikos* is not locked into a predetermined political path but constitutes the condition of possibility for a pluralistic rhetorical polis. On its face, such a claim may sound overly optimistic. Unlike the Older Sophists, whose oral practices are inextricably connected with democratic institutions, Isocrates is a literary rhetorician, seemingly removed from daily concerns of the assembly. He distances himself from the public places of democracy and instead creates a new, literary forum for the discussion of cultural and political issues. By construing logos as hegemonic, Isocrates responds to the strife and cultural disintegration in the wake of the Peloponnesian War and the peace treaties of the fourth century B.C.E. But with this response to political instability he seems to defy the agonistic principle that had sustained the radical Athenian democracy. His vision of logos as a civilized force, at once a principle of social unification and a mechanism through which this unification is achieved (*Antidosis* 253, *Nicocles* 5–9), seems to require the exclusion of voices that threaten unification.[17] The power of language, on this view, is no longer an untamed force amenable to heterogeneous political ends. It is instead personified by prudent political agents like Isocrates himself, as well as his students, many of whom were aristocrats and monarchs from various parts of the Greek world. An advisor and tutor to kings, Isocrates does not fare much better politically than Aristotle, a teacher of Alexander the Great.

The very aspect of Isocrates' rhetorical practice that has the most resonance for a theory of civic discourse—the constitution of the author's political identity—is also one of the key reasons Isocrates remains a controversial figure in the rhetorical tradition. While we know that the words of Gorgias and Aristotle have been reported and probably altered by others and through this dissemination have achieved immortality apart from their supposed creators, we cannot *not* hold Isocrates accountable for what he had written. Whereas Aristotle's reputation as the Philosopher has been nearly sanctified by generations of scholars, Isocrates' legacy seems much less illustrious. Therefore, before considering the viability of Isocrates' vision of logos as an alternative to Gorgias's *bia* and Aristotle's *dunamis,* one must address the arguments that see his texts as little more than a cautionary tale about the dangers of political aesthetics.[18]

Isocrates' use of mythopoetic tradition to craft his public identity and to promote cultural unification in the context of the agonistic Athenian democracy has provoked criticism from contemporary historians of rhetoric. Isocrates seems to lend himself to accusations of elitism and cultural imperialism by buying so freely into Athenian and Greek identity politics. These charges are expressed most forcefully in Victor Vitanza's *Negation, Subjectivity, and the History of Rhetoric* (1997). Vitanza (who singles out Gorgias as a premodern inspiration for a poststructuralist "Third Sophistic") argues that Isocratean *paideia* and his vision of the logos lead to the class bias of the modern European educational system and, in retrospect, justify the ideology of the Third Reich. These claims cannot be dismissed simply by calling attention to the critic's anachronistic (or "metaleptic" as he prefers to call it) "reading protocol" (1997, 140). After all, by invoking the past—archaic, classical, or medieval—we illuminate our present condition in order to better articulate terms that constitute our pedagogical and political "equipment for living" (Burke 1973, 293).

However, we need carefully to distinguish between reactionary appropriations of Isocrates' corpus and the potential of his vision of civic performance in a contemporary democracy.

The claim of "elitism" associated with Isocrates' appeal to the past is canonically expressed in M. I. Finley's 1972 lecture, later reprinted under the title "The Heritage of Isocrates" in Finley's *Use and Abuse of History* (1975). In it, the author critiques the nostalgia of modern historians for "traditional" education, of the sort often connected to institutions like Oxford and Cambridge. Finley links Isocratean literary *paideia* to the socioeconomic bias of educational institutions "designed for members of the ruling elite, a socially and culturally homogeneous group, whose common values were formed and repeatedly reinforced by their continuous association and shared experience" (208). For Finley, such *paideia,* if it serves merely as a "common code," a mark of social status, inevitably degenerates into a "cult of the past" (210). As an example of such cultlike elitism, he quotes Dean Gaisford of Christ Church, who is "supposed to have said early in the nineteenth century that a classical education 'enables us to look down with contempt on those who have not shared its advantages'" (203).

What Finley wishes to teach to modern students is "a relevant past" as opposed to a reified encyclopedia of historically remote facts (1975, 213). This criterion, however, does not render Isocrates irrelevant. Isocrates' critique of Athenian rhetorical practices and his use of the mythopoetic tradition have much to teach modern students. Ironically, the original title of Finley's lecture —"Knowledge for What?"—repeats a resoundingly Isocratean concern. Isocrates himself questioned the purpose of contemporary rhetorical education and literary exercises, faulting the former for its service to political and material self-advancement and the latter for furthering politically disinterested knowledge. Indeed, the problem with today's university training, even within the humanities, is its increasing stress on technical skills, a "general cultural drift which may reduce Anglo-American democracy to an oligarchy of expertise" (McGee 1985, 9). In the sphere of language education, the shift has been away from civic rhetoric toward the business-friendly "plain style" celebrated by Carnegie and codified by Strunk and White's *Elements of Style.* In spite of its ostensible virtues of clarity and humble simplicity, this style has naturalized some of the most pernicious constructs of the technocratic culture. As Kenneth Cmiel astutely summarizes in his *Democratic Eloquence* (1990): "The plain style also creates the illusion that language can be like glass, a medium without the infusion of a self. It pretends the facts can speak for themselves in ways that the old rhetoric never did. The very style has helped perpetuate the belief that there are technical, apolitical solutions to political problems. It is perhaps the most deceptive style of them all" (260).

The intimate connection between poetic style and political performance in Isocrates no doubt goes against the grain of the current Anglo-American linguistic norms. It is likely that the resurrection of Aristotle's *Rhetoric* as a paradigm for public discourse in the second half of the twentieth century stems from a particularly felicitous match between the great philosopher's demand for clarity and our own cultivated preference for a middling political style unmarked by class, race or gender. Isocrates' prose makes one suspicious and uneasy precisely because it violates this expectation of homogeneity. But this incongruity can also illuminate both the historical conditions of Isocrates' rhetorical practice and our understanding of contemporary democratic discourse.

In this light, Finley's remark about the "literary" emphasis, and hence, elitism, of Isocratean *paideia* is only partially justifiable. Despite their literary medium, his compositions and training were steeped in what can be called "popular culture" of the Hellenic world. Epic poetry and drama in antiquity were popular institutions. It is modern philological tradition that has severed them from their performative context, rendered their civic character into timeless expression of the Greek genius, and transformed them into a corpus of texts to be perused by the elites.[19] Isocrates' legacy did not escape this process of formalization, with the resulting attitudes of protective nostalgia on the part of the "traditionalists" and resentment toward "the dead white males" on the part of the younger generation of academics.

There is yet another, more disconcerting feature in Isocrates' record. Having adopted Finley's "elitism" claim as a point of departure, Vitanza goes on to find a more politically malevolent ramification of Isocratean pan-Hellenism: its cultural imperialism. In Vitanza's words, "It becomes a forerunner of 'manifest destiny' and the Third Reich" (1997, 140). The basis for Vitanza's causal argument is the identification of reactionary German philosophical historiography and philology with the Greco-Roman ideal. I will bracket the validity of Vitanza's "reading protocol," which, he claims, is a "language game" like any other "canonized protocol of reading" (ibid.). Nevertheless, I would like to object to the lack of differentiation between the discourses that have appropriated Isocrates to their reactionary political agenda and the ambivalent political potential of his rhetorical practice.

The association of Isocrates with proto-Nazism emerges from Vitanza's reading of Jaeger's *Paideia,* which epitomizes a rhetorical historiography predicated on "an *abstract timeless* conception of the mind as a realm of eternal truth and beauty high above the troubled destinies of any one nation" (Jaeger, quoted in Vitanza 1997, 146). Vitanza shows how Jaeger constructs two links, the "Greece-Rome-Germany continuum" and a parallel between Isocrates and himself (147). Vitanza explains the Isocrates-Jaeger construction: "The hero of *Paideia* story is not Plato, though he is commonly considered to be of a greater intellectual weight; instead, the hero is Isocrates—either the pragmatic or xenophobic political strategist—in his constant attempt to argue for Panhellenism and war against the barbarians" (ibid.).

It is easy to see how Jaeger's idealistic abstraction, or extraction of Isocrates from his historico-political context, could implicitly justify the logic of cultural chauvinism culminating with Nazi ideology, which equated culture with race. If read as programmatic philosophical or moral positions, Isocrates' references to the war of the Hellenes against the barbarians might sound unequivocally xenophobic. But so would Aeschylus, Herodotus, and Aristotle. Within the Athenian democratic imaginary of the fifth and fourth centuries B.C.E., the terms "Hellene" and "barbarian" are rhetorical place holders, ready to be filled with insignia of Greekness and its cultural (rather than ethnic or racial) opposite. The barbarian, in fact, is "invented" in order to delineate the Greek identity.[20] In Aeschylus's *Persae* (472 B.C.E.), the "barbarian" servitude to King Xerxes is depicted to highlight the freedom (*eleutheria*) of the Athenian democratic polity. Herodotus goes even further by framing the Trojan War as the conflict between the Greeks and the barbarians (3–5). In Aristotle, the opposition between the Greek and the barbarian achieves theoretical status: in the *Politics* "barbarians" are presented as "natural slaves" (1252a34).

If Isocrates resembles Jaeger, it is only because his appeal to the cultural capital of the Greeks is treated as a transcendental principle, not as a series of statements crafted in response to a concrete historical situation. As Michael McGee (1985) points out, in Isocrates the past works not as a model to be reproduced in the present, as it does in the rhetoric of Fascist nationalism. Rather, "the past is related to the present through analogy, as memory to action. The analogy does not prove—it illustrates and clarifies" (11). Distancing himself from rhetorical practices that have led to oligarchy in Athens and war among the Greek city-states, Isocrates adopts the old theme of pan-Hellenism in order to criticize the contemporary historical situation by comparing it with mythologized historical past and to remind the audience of its collective identity.[21] However, as distinct from the Homeric rhapsodes of the oral tradition, Isocrates promotes the rhetoric of political responsibility by assuming, in his writing, the identity of the "leader of words."[22]

The democratic tenor of Isocratean political aesthetics may seem suspect, for it is complicated, if not tarnished, by the nationalism of Athenian democracy and misappropriation of Isocrates' heritage by modern nationalistic historians. Yet by acknowledging both of these tendencies—one past, the other still present—we can move beyond labeling Isocrates' discourse as progressive or reactionary. Instead, we can learn from Isocrates' political performance to appreciate the subtle relationship between rhetoric and power implicit in his portrayal of logos as the force of unification. The remaining section of this argument, then, defends the contention that Isocrates offers us a conception of discourse that is more salutary for a democratic theory of civic discourse than either Gorgias's *bia* (force) or Aristotle's *dunamis* (a neutral capacity). With this goal in mind we return to Isocrates' logos as *hēgemōn*.

Isocrates offers a new version of the Greek mythopoetic narrative about the rise of civilization and social institutions. Compared with other variants of the same myth in fifth-century tragedy and even in Aristotle's *Politics,* Isocrates' account stands out due to its attention to the role of speech in the formation of institutions and the maintenance of civic ties. Coupled with the guiding role of *logos politikos* in the *Antidosis,* the "Hymn to Logos," with its assertion of the leadership of speech in private and public affairs, offers a paradigm for a constitutive understanding of rhetoric. Both of these aspects of constitutive power of discourse—to sanction the social order and to challenge it through individual rhetorical acts—marks Isocrates as a premodern prototype of a postmodern political agent. It has become commonplace to valorize linguistic self-reflexivity as a distinguishing trait of postmodern "liminal intellectuals"—artistic and academic "nomads" who constantly "transgress" various disciplinary and political boundaries. Isocrates hardly fits this portrait, partly because of his exaggerated, from a modern standpoint, commitment to the polis, partly because he was still living in a culture not yet stratified into the areas of knowledge, art, and politics. But his pedagogical and political emphasis on language as a renewable source of both community and identity resonates with the postmodern search for community in the age of lost (or renounced) foundations.

Isocrates' vision of discourse as a leader, unlike the tyrannical *bia* of Gorgias and the neutral *dunamis* of Aristotle, projects an image of an aesthetic, rather than institutional, power. From an Aristotelian perspective, Isocrates may appear callous in his disregard for the normative expectations appropriate to particular constitutional regimes. Viewed through Aristotle's eyes, Isocrates is little more than a composer of epideictic speeches designed to flatter and entertain, who vainly confuses his compositions with substantive politics. However, it is precisely the move outside the institutional constraints of the courts and the assembly that permits Isocrates to redefine *politeia* as an agency of deliberation about substantive ends, rather than as a constitutional structure that circumscribes the process of deliberation regarding the means. This point cannot be overemphasized, because Isocrates not only demonstrates the substantive character of what Aristotle loosely terms epideictic but also confronts us with an altogether different paradigm for understanding political discourse in a democracy.

Isocrates' rhetoric challenges our traditional association of politics with institutions and our equation of democracy with rational decision making by the populace. Scholars who study "public address" typically turn to genres of governance and campaign addresses to speculate why certain messages resonate with the public. Small wonder that they find Aristotle most congenial to their critical project. As Thomas B. Farrell (1993) summarizes this presumption, "If we are to keep close to the parameters—what we might call 'friendly confines'—of the Aristotelian paradigm, the relational goods of rhetorical practice should be recognizable in an institutional context. For it is there that we find the conventions and affiliative bonds that allow inferences to be constructed and enacted" (82–83). While absorbing agonistic "conventions" of democratic rhetoric, Isocrates nonetheless unhinges the discourse of "affiliation" (what may be called "identification") from its institutional, and even constitutional, frame. In many of his pamphlets he deliberately blurs the terminological lines between democracy and its ideological "others" in order to extend his addresses to multiple audiences. Through the language of praise and blame, Isocrates makes his audiences, regardless of their constitutional affiliation, consider the body politic as a volatile mixture of various forms of governance. Kathryn Morgan (2003) points out how Isocrates employs the traditional Athenian hatred toward tyranny to criticize the *demos* for endorsing tyrannical foreign policy, and addresses kings as if they were citizens. *Nicocles*, in which Isocrates impersonates a tyrant offering kingly advice to his subjects, is a case in point. Given the compositional context of this document, one may object that the "Hymn to Logos," by virtue of its utterance by a "tyrant," defends monarchy and so overturns the agonistic principle that is the sine qua non of a democratic rhetoric. This conclusion is possible only if we disregard the performative dynamics of the composition. We know that Isocrates was able to assume different identities in his pamphlets.[23] But the persona in whose language Isocrates happens to speak in a particular piece is also, if partially, his own. As distinct from epic performance and public speaking, writing allows Isocrates to be at once distinct from and identical with the "I" of the speaker. He can simultaneously inhabit the "voice" of another and retain a critical distance from it. To be sure, we should not overlook Isocrates' sympathy for monarchy, and the "tyrant" identity of the speaker may be a vehicle for attacking "the slackness and irresponsibility of contemporary democracy," as Norlin implies (*Isocrates I,* 75).

Conversely, however, *Nicocles* may be interpreted as an imposition of a democratic role upon a tyrant; for a supposedly sovereign subject is forced to *defend* his rule in an argument. In chapter 4, I suggested that Isocrates fashions the discourse of citizenship along the lines of responsibility, both collective and individual. Takis Poulakos (1997) has argued that for Isocrates "citizenship is an identity that must be reclaimed, and the problem with citizenship appears to be how to disclose that identity publicly—how a king can prove that his royal status did not violate but actually derived from his status as a citizen, or how an orator can demonstrate that his words did not originate in his interest for self-advantage but in his position as the citizen who speaks as a member of the polis" (33–34).

In contrast with Aristotle's rigid conception of citizenly virtue as a procedural function within a well-ordered state, Isocrates aestheticizes and thereby makes desirable the identity of a citizen. In so doing, he builds upon a long-standing and mutually reinforcing relationship between virtue and democratic discourse. By fusing idea of individual merit with the performative ideal of accountability to the polis, Isocrates resists the inclination of theorists such as Plato and Aristotle to disconnect the discourse of ethics from the discourse of democracy. While for Plato and Aristotle, performance, due to its low epistemological status, does not affect the ethical core of a political agent, for Isocrates identity is tied to reputation, which in turn is a contingent effect of performance. Isocrates' models of political excellence are democratic leaders of bygone generations: Solon, Cleisthenes, Themistocles, and Pericles. All of them received their reputation as doers of deeds and speakers of words, and as Ober points out, it was "democracy that provided the distinctive environment . . . in which their worthy speeches were delivered" (1998, 265). By the same token, those who do not seek the approval of the political community through their logoi, can find themselves in disrepute, like the general Timotheus, one of Isocrates' former students. We can grant, then, that for Isocrates conditions for claiming political power are not socioeconomic but discursive. To be able to claim authority, one must engage in a discourse of *therapeia,* which means to pay court to the audience. In her essay "The Tyranny of the Audience in Plato and Isocrates," Morgan is quick to point out that Isocrates refuses to characterize his advice to Nicocles as *therapeia,* but that it is what he "advises people to do with the *demos*" (forthcoming, 355). She concludes that "king-advisor relationship is marked by freedom, whereas the orator-*demos* relationship is marked by flattery (unless one interprets *therapeia* of the demos as the attempt to heal it by the excellence of Isocratean oratory)" (355–56). The binary between freedom and *therapeia* is not entirely accurate, however, since Isocrates often addresses the *demos* as a critic, not only as a servant (Clark 1996). Over the period of his long career, Isocrates sought to craft through prose an oppositional political identity that was nonetheless presented to the readership as a role vital to the welfare of the polis. Both sides of this public persona, its critical and its hegemonic aspects, are well within the range of the possible subject positions occupied by rhetoricians in democratic Athens. According to Ober, the roles of "leader, critic, opposer of people's will" were indeed salutary for the democratic balance of power: "The good orator not only praised the people, he also criticized and opposed them; orator and audience alike recognized that criticism and opposition to the will of the masses were central to the orator's political function" (1989, 323).

We may expect, then, that *Nicocles*—a piece simultaneously addressed to the king's subjects and to the Athenian audience—should exhibit *therapeia*. The arrangement of *Nicocles* is noteworthy in this regard. The praise of logos as *hēgemōn* (5–9) precedes the king's arguments for monarchy against democracy and oligarchy (14–27), which, in turn, take precedence over the tyrant's claim to ancestral right and defense of his kingly conduct (27–48). Speech is described as *hēgemōn,* and the tyrant obeys the hegemony of speech just as any democratic subject. Furthermore, the speaker's own role as a leader is far from guaranteed. It rests upon the force of the address and hence makes even the king subject to the audience's approval.[24] The verbatim citation of the praise of logos in the *Antidosis* bolsters this interpretation, because this composition is intended as the author's display of loyalty to the democratic polis and, as such, asks the audience to consider previously composed "speeches" in light of his democratic commitments.

The arbitrariness of logos, conveyed in Gorgias by the terms *dunastēs* and *bia,* is replaced in *Nicocles* with an image of a leader, *hēgemōn,* whose dynastic powers are neither sovereign nor inscrutable. Thus Isocrates poses a new vision of logos and power, in which power depends upon rhetorical performance for its legitimacy and political impact. Isocrates' own performance over time indicates that logos is productive both of dissent and unification.

The "Hymn to Logos" in the *Nicocles* combines two modes—what Kenneth Burke (1952) called "constitutive" and "admonitory" (330). It is constitutive in so far as it announces a state of being: as social actors, we are enabled by the leading role of logos to act in a civilized way toward each other. It is admonitory in that it exhorts through the repetition of first-person plural verbs signifying collective action: "we refute the bad and praise the good," "we educate the ignorant and recognize the intelligent," "we fight over contentious matters and we investigate the unknown" (*Nicocles* 7–8). In short, the passage performs the underlying message of the discourse—that logos is the basis of human consubstantiality. This parable of consubstantiality, while articulating social cohesion in terms of harmony, nonetheless leaves room for agonistic contestation. To paraphrase Burke, by putting war and peace ambiguously together, the "Hymn to Logos" furnishes a characteristic invitation to rhetoric as a constitutive discourse of culture and politics.

Six

CLASSICAL RHETORICS AND THE FUTURE OF DEMOCRATIC EDUCATION

The distinction between Isocrates and Aristotle is far more complex than a contrast between Isocrates the practitioner who composed models of oratory and Aristotle the theorist who spelled out its normative principles. Rather, I have argued that the difference between the two ancient Greek educators and their theories of discourse is best appreciated by looking at the methods and goals of their appropriation of the performance-centered culture in general and of the democratic political culture in particular. Isocrates integrates discursive training with civic education, which he regards as a lifelong pursuit not reducible to a set of procedures and commonplaces, whereas Aristotle catalogues historically and culturally specific elements of public discourse as instantiations of putatively universal principles discernable by those who already possess practical wisdom. It is, in fact, Aristotle, with his cyclical view of history and human knowledge, who bequeaths us a picture of the rhetorical art that aspires to transcend the historical specificity of received opinions (*endoxa*) out of which it arises. Instead of interpreting Isocrates' compositions through Aristotle's matrix of proofs and genres (which in traditional rhetorical studies has been read back into most pre-Aristotelian public discourses of the fifth and fourth centuries B.C.E.), I adopted a performative perspective on the two authors. Isocrates and Aristotle were cast as rivals in a debate over the character, resources, and ends of discursive education. This juxtaposition required attention to the cultural, intellectual, and political contexts in which these rival conceptions of rhetorical practice were articulated. Thus framed, Isocrates' vision of constitutive rhetoric of political identity can be understood as a reformist (although not necessarily antidemocratic) attempt to bring together democracy and virtue. By comparison, Aristotle's articulation of rhetoric as a *technē* available to a properly habituated political agent is based on a *separation* of moral education from public performance. It has been my contention that while Isocrates' educational program strives to reform Athenian democracy by the cultivation of its potential leaders, Aristotle's approach is to discipline the *demos* into substantively and procedurally restricted roles within a constitutional regime. In other words, if for Isocrates power is explicitly a product of a discursive negotiation of civic identity and authority, for Aristotle power relationships depend on nature and on the art of a legislator, not the craft of a rhetorician. To evaluate these positions historically, it is more illuminating to consider them alongside one another as strategic maneuvers in a culture war, rather than as more or less comprehensive political theories. We can no longer interpret ancient authors as autonomous voices of reason, even though some of them (like Plato and Aristotle) may have aspired to such status. Indeed, each articulation of the proper function and end of logos is inextricably tied to and productive of a particular relation of power.

Considering his overall intellectual project as a pursuit of knowledge for its own sake, Aristotle stipulated a number of political conditions necessary for a life of contemplation. In so doing, Aristotle naturalized the hierarchical divisions within a city-state and theoretically validated the aristocratic class as an artificer of virtue in the absolute sense. Offering advice on rhetorical means of persuasion in the course of his afternoon lectures at Plato's Academy, Aristotle was instructing the elites how to face the listeners who would have little regard for his explanations of their natural inferiority. In other words, rhetorical instruction was not a means of habituating wealthy Athenians and foreigners into persons of practical wisdom, but an instrument of inoculating them against the corrupting influence of democratic audiences. Although more pragmatic about the ends of learning than Aristotle, Isocrates still found much to criticize in the political culture of his native city. His pedagogical program, as Josiah Ober (1998) and Yun Lee Too (1995) point out, was an elitist correction of popular democracy in Athens; therefore, it would be misguided to propose Isocrates' version of discursive education as a replacement of Aristotle's (or, for that matter, Plato's) version in the classical rhetorical canon. Isocrates' assertion of his pedagogical and political authority as a paradigm of citizenly virtue, it seems, falls short of his own vision of a discursive *paideia* grounded in the multivoiced and fractious political culture. The politics of the Isocratean pedagogy, then, run counter to the democratic strand in his theory of *logos politikos*.

Yet it is not enough to consider what logos and power meant to elite critics of Athenian democracy. What they might mean *to us,* especially those of us who are involved in rhetorical education, is just as important. Hence my insistence on practicing an "ironic" stance, a critical dialectic that keeps one aware of the selectivity of one's intellectual lenses while attending to historical and textual data. As a historian, I have tried to avoid inconsistency and anachronism in interpreting ancient texts; as a teacher and cultural critic, I have sought to articulate a socially productive approach to rhetoric by way of rereading two different classical responses to the problem of discursive education. In this effort, I was especially motivated by a growing discomfort at the instrumentalism of contemporary higher learning and by the alarming signs of erosion of a democratic culture on which so much of formal education depends.

As communication and rhetoric professors know all too well, the instrumental character of rhetorical knowledge is built into the very structure of liberal education in the United States. Rhetoric and composition are typically "service" courses, a sort of *minimum minimorum* of linguistic expertise, added to a student's presumably robust repertoire of civic skills. "Presumably" is a key word here, for lamentably few students (usually those who attended private or wealthy, suburban public schools) are sufficiently prepared to engage in a sophisticated reflection and argument beyond the remedial level. The U.S. system of higher learning thus tacitly accepts Aristotle's premise that rhetoric is useful to someone who is already habituated in virtue and political science, thereby leaving the responsibility for discursive and civic training to others (parents, religious authorities, and various private organizations). Severed from their cultural environment, "rhetorical skills" become either a communication proficiency requirement for other professional pursuits or a focus of training in latter-day logography of public relations and advertising. The contemporary university's orientation toward vocational training in existing means of persuasion is disconcerting not only because the usefulness of rhetoric has been detached from the cultivation of individual ethics (as it was in Aristotle). It is troubling because in contemporary Western democracies this shallow version of Aristotle's *technē* has been placed atop the culture of consumption with its appeal to the individual desire and disregard for the common good. In the twenty-first century, our public culture reverberates with words and images crafted to stimulate solipsistic fantasies and urge us to purchase products and services to satisfy those desires, thereby calling upon us as consumers rather than citizens.

Today's university students grow up amid a constant hum of messages that ask them not what they can do for their country, but some variation of the McDonald's advertising jingle "You deserve a break today." Along with Disney-style "infotainment" that has permeated even the once high-minded enclave of public television programming, commercialism of mass culture constructs a narrow set of subject positions for young people to embody. Regardless of the path one takes, its goal is identified as wealth and celebrity. It is telling that today's typical role models are corporate CEOs and entertainers, not politicians or intellectuals. Even the idea of political and aesthetic dissent, once countercultural, has been thoroughly commodified in the service of consumption.[1]

Contemporary cultural *mimēsis,* like that of classical Greece, is a process by which new generations acquire intellectual skills and political identities. Unlike the Greeks, contemporary Americans are habituated by mass media into patterns of thinking and acting that often benefit not themselves or their communities, but corporate interests. The ethos such cultural reproduction fosters is that of detached cynicism and political apathy.[2] Being earnest about anything is blasé, and changing the status quo, unless it is done for profit, is likened to spitting against the wind. One of my undergraduates, writing about the prospects of an "electronic republic" in which computer technology would make direct civic participation possible, summarized her bleak vision as follows: "Electronic Republic: Buncha Lazy Bums."

Alarmed by the sorry condition of our public culture, some scholars have called upon Aristotle to revitalize the ethical grounds of civic discourse. I spent some time addressing the arguments of Eugene Garver (1994) and Thomas B. Farrell (1993), whose treatments of Aristotle's *Rhetoric* are among the most influential in recent years. Garver's position, articulated explicitly to challenge the assumption of discursive instrumentality, maintains that rhetoric, providing its internal end of artfulness is fulfilled, can stand on its own as an ethical activity. The activity Garver envisions, however, must stay within the "artful" parameters of a preestablished argumentative procedure, rather than act as a response to contingencies of audiences and situations. This teleology, however, not only excludes a host of practices from the circumscribed domain of the rhetorical but also pictures a rhetorical transaction as an exchange between a virtuous speaker and an equally virtuous and rational audience. As such, Garver's argument succeeds only in reasserting the primacy of proper ethical conditioning, autonomous as it is for Aristotle from the "corrupting" influence of performance.

Farrell's *Norms of Rhetorical Culture,* as distinct from Garver's "internal ends" thesis, attempts to integrate ethics and rhetoric from a dialogic perspective, influenced by G. H. Mead and Mikhail Bakhtin. Farrell produces a remarkably appealing and richly layered image of what a rhetorical act would be like, if conceived as both a moral and aesthetic invocation of an audience and a timely response to social exigencies. Such rhetoric would at once express and foster civic friendship (*philia*) and thus provide optimal conditions for democratic conversation. As I have pointed out, Farrell chooses to ignore that Aristotle reserves *philia* for a relationship among aristocratic equals, whose conversations do not spring from exigencies of interdependence as they do in a (corrupt) democratic regime. Aristotle repeatedly emphasizes the asymmetrical relationship between the rhetor and the audience, whereby the audience's judgment (*krisis*) is influenced by the rhetor's projection of a good character, not the other way around. Indeed, only epideictic occasions, even as refracted through Aristotle's generic lens, promote the kind of intersubjective cultural bond Farrell attributes to deliberative situations. Importantly, it is Isocrates' record, albeit in a fragmented fashion, that exemplifies achievements of epideictic discourse in Aristotle's *Rhetoric.* I have argued that Isocrates' model of rhetorical education and political performance deserves our recognition as Aristotle's historical and dialectical "other." Admittedly, this "otherness" may at first sight seem too uncongenial to a modern sensibility, for Isocrates presents himself not as a detached observer but as a partisan critic of Athenian democracy. It is precisely this particularity of his civic persona that prevents us from adopting Isocrates as a "normative voice" of the classical age. By the same token, the rootedness of this voice in the culture's aesthetic tradition, its performative contingency and answerability to the political community offer us a compelling alternative to a rhetorical education based either on atemporal models of excellence and disinterested rationality or on narrow professionalism.

How, then, can one adapt the Isocratean vision to the purposes of today's discursive education, given that the cultural and political context of this education is so different from classical Athens? To be sure, no sole teacher can undo the cumulative effects of the culture industry on our students' self-image as consumers of knowledge. However, it is possible, by relying on the Isocratean vision of logos as an artificer of culture and identity, subtly to turn students toward an appreciation of their milieu as a complex process of inculcation of personal and social values. The goal of this *paideia* is not a mere acquisition of technical proficiency in composition and public speaking or a pursuit of social privilege through the knowledge of the "tradition." Rather, it is a cultivation of our critical relationship with the symbolic worlds we inhabit. Cultural critics of various stripes urge teachers to make their students think hard, so that they liberate their minds from the oppression of common opinion. Hard thinking is typically equated with the rigors of argumentative analysis—the skills of isolating and testing claims and their support. Habituated by this exercise, pupils supposedly learn how to question their own decisions and thereby become emancipated citizens. This approach, grounded in Aristotle's premise of disinterested rationality, tends to ignore the deep impact of the cultural-historical context on students' subject positions. The teaching of categories and types of proof as resources of critical decision making often bypasses the questions of discursive agency and ideological function of discourse. More often than not, it results in the glorification of discursive omnipotence of the kind one finds among high-priced U.S. attorneys as a model of political agency.

As we know from the criticism of the eristics advanced in the *Antidosis*, Isocrates holds that learning the anatomy of argument is little more than mental gymnastics, a preparation for what he calls "philosophy." The Isocratean pedagogy requires us to go beyond the mechanics of discourse composition and analysis. While building upon the existing repertoire of analytical skills, it invites teachers and students to probe the ways in which verbal and visual symbolism shapes what we consider reasonable and desirable. After all, for Isocrates, the mastery of different forms of discourse was a basis for a self-reflexive performance of civic excellence, whose highest form was *logos politikos*.

Admittedly, this pedagogy does not easily translate into the modern context. To achieve mastery of all forms in which "logos expresses itself" (which prepared Isocrates' students for kairotic interventions into the life of the polis) seems difficult in the face of the sheer volume and diversity of discourses that clamor for our attention. Nowadays, the forms of discourse we may want our students to study and emulate as well as models of civic excellence are not easily agreed upon, for modern university curricula are torn between the demands of the preservation of (Western) intellectual tradition and the affirmation of cultural diversity.[3] The choice of texts, therefore, becomes a matter of political deliberation on the part of academic departments and individual teachers. Amid the controversy over the cultural resources of education, however, it is easy to forget that these models, whether novels of Dostoyevsky, speeches of FDR, or films of Spike Lee, are not artistic or political blueprints but portals into ethical and political dilemmas of different historical moments. They are, as Kenneth Burke would put it, "stylized answers" to questions posed by the situation in which they arose (1967, 1).[4]

Isocrates' emphasis on the constitution of values and identity by discourse suggests that we do not separate our beliefs from the stories and images that produced them. Rather, we should seek exposure to many different stories and images to test our convictions. To find this "otherness," one need not flee from contemporary cultural products to a safe haven of literary classics, however. For example, if film and comic book are the forms that students consider the most valuable, a resourceful teacher and a good media librarian should be able to summon the "texts" necessary for a rich discussion of visual iconography and narrative. Even advertising, when one views it within its historical and cultural context, can motivate critical thinking about social values. To wipe the mental slate clean by declaring mass culture, our students' default educator, hopelessly inauthentic and antidemocratic, would yield no positive result. For an ironist, Isocratean pedagogy calls for sympathy toward the common cultural denominator as a starting point of critical inquiry the goal of which is learning to question the limits of cultural knowledge. This is not to suggest that debunking dominant ideology should be the goal of such inquiry, since debunking entails a search for "true" discourse untarnished by political bias. Instead of seeking a replacement of dominant ideology (such as liberalism), discursive education should aspire to furnish a range of subject positions that would enable political intervention beyond voting in the next election, sitting on a jury, or running for office.

Political performance need not be confined to traditional forms of public address but can encompass a spectrum of symbolic responses to cultural, economic, environmental, and international issues. Thus, for example, an antiwar activist can write petitions, post photographs of public protests on the Internet, and work as a disc jockey at a college radio station. A student of film production can make a documentary about the excesses of consumption on campus. A writer for a college newspaper can interview her classmates about their spring break in order to contrast the moral satisfaction of Appalachian volunteers with the sunburn of Florida escapists. Communication and rhetoric classrooms, too, can cultivate students' political impulse by introducing role playing in various genres of public culture, from a cartoon to an advertising clip.

This list of examples is neither categorical nor exhaustive. Rather, it illustrates the interventionist possibilities of "speech genres" that are not typically considered "mainstream." These genres of mass culture, however, constitute a shared mythology and as such exercise perhaps greater influence on young people's political imagination than the speeches of President Kennedy or Martin Luther King Jr. This mythology is not, as a classical Marxist would say, a form of "false consciousness." As Frederic Jameson (1979) has argued, popular culture contains within it longings that are subversive of the status quo. A democratically oriented rhetorical education, therefore, should aim at pointing out these longings as well as actualizing them through the lexicon and iconography of the culture.

Isocrates' theory of discursive education is also a theory of political action in a democratic community. By linking private deliberation and public conduct, individual political impulse and political accountability, normative cultural ideals and social criticism, Isocrates offers a comprehensive yet flexible model of education. To be sure, my rereading of this model in the context of the postmodern consumer culture is preliminary. If political engagement with a view to social change is to remain a normative ideal of education, however, we stand to learn from Isocrates the teacher, Isocrates the "philosopher," and Isocrates the critic.

NOTES

Introduction

1. On Plato's role in delineating the nature of "rhetoric" by using the term *rhētorikē,* see Schiappa (1990a). The word "philosophy" also became attached to the brand of Platonic-Aristotelian studies, although Isocrates used it to name the goal of his discursive education. See Timmerman (1998).

2. For instance, in the introduction to *Rereading Aristotle's "Rhetoric,"* Alan Gross and Arthur Walzer propose: "Whitehead's observation that the history of philosophy is one long footnote to Plato can be for us transferred to the *Rhetoric:* All subsequent rhetorical theory is but a series of responses to issues raised by that central work" (2000, ix). The centrality of Aristotle in the historiography of rhetoric, however, has less to do with the reception and pedagogical applications of *The Art of Rhetoric* from antiquity through the present than with the disciplinary efforts of speech and composition educators (usually marginalized in the modern humanities curriculum) to associate themselves with a prestigious classical figure. See Poster (1998).

3. In asserting this discontinuity, I am opposing a view held by some historians of rhetoric that there was a monolithic Hellenic "paradigm." See, for example, Campbell (1984).

4. For a critique of the theory/practice binary, see Atwill (1993).

5. For studies that question the attribution of a handbook (*technē*) to Isocrates, see Barwick (1963), Cahn (1989), and Too (1995). On the other hand, contemporary rhetorical theorists urge us to pay attention to the dimensions of performance, agency, and power in ostensibly "neutral" theoretical discourse. See McGee (1990), McKerrow (1989), and Oravec and Salvador (1993). On the interdisciplinary application of the notion of performance, see Parker and Sedgwick (1995).

6. On Isocrates' "language game" with respect to the naming of his occupation and its goals, see Haskins (2002).

7. See Burke (1952, 1969) and Bryant (1953) for efforts to expand the domain of rhetoric. For the development of rhetorical theory in the second half of the twentieth century, see Lucaites and Condit (1999).

Chapter 1—Between Orality and Literacy

1. For "disciplinary" accounts of the emergence of rhetoric, see Cole (1991), Johnstone (1996b), and Schiappa (1991, 1999). Cole's position disregards "proto-rhetoric" (in particular, discursive practices of the fifth century B.C.E.) and presents rhetoric as a relatively static system of multiple, exchangeable means of transmitting extralinguistic content. His position presumes a literate condition of storage of linguistic devices as if

they were neutral letters of an alphabet. Johnstone modifies Cole's thesis about the classical invention of rhetoric to account for "earlier intellectual, political and cultural conditions in the absence of which [rhetoric] could not have developed" (1996a, 6). Nevertheless, he accepts Cole's premise about separability of form and content as a sine qua non of a systematic rhetorical theory: "Thus does mere expression become a message" (1996a, 6).

2. For a distinction between explicit and implicit rhetorical theories, see Schiappa (1999, 109).

3. For studies of implicit rhetorical theory, see Kirby (1992) on Hesiod; see Kennedy (1963) and Enos (1993) on the rhetorical typology of archaic discourse dating back to Homeric epics.

4. For example, William Harris (1989) investigates "restricted literacy" in classical Greece. Rosalind Thomas (1989, 1992) combines the discussion of general theories of orality and literacy with historical research. Also of interest are studies that focus on the relationship between literate practices and power in antiquity, such as Deborah Steiner (1994) and Alan K. Bowman and Greg Woolf (1994).

5. The *locus classicus* of the argument is Bruno Snell's *Discovery of the Mind* (1953).

6. Havelock and those who rely on his interpretation of oral consciousness in *Preface to Plato* (1963), assume that this state of the listeners' mind was passive and the poet could make the audience identify almost pathologically with the content of what he is saying. I would take such an assumption with a grain of salt for two reasons. First, Havelock is following Plato's rather hostile treatment of oral poetry, motivated by a desire to substitute the traditional *alētheia* with one of a transcendental philosophical sort. Second, the contrast between "the words without realization" and those that "accomplish the truth" in epic culture (Detienne 1996, 84) indicates a degree of uncertainty about the efficacy of speech in oralistic contexts.

7. Jean-Pierre Vernant (1983) observes that the "fundamental concepts upon which . . . construction of Ionian philosophy is based are (i) the separation out from a primeval unity; (ii) the constant struggle and uniting of opposites; (iii) an eternal cycle of change; and all three reveal how their cosmology was rooted in mythical thought. The philosophers did not have to invent a system to explain the world: they found one ready-made" (347).

8. Intellectuals classified under "the first Sophistic" differed in their attitudes toward the status of writing and its relationship to speech. Gorgias's ridicule of Prodicus's devotion to the written script is a stark, if anecdotal, example. See Neil O'Sullivan (1996, 121–22).

9. I do not wish to press the contrast between "philosophers" and "rhetoricians" (or "Sophists") in the fifth century B.C.E., since these categories were at the time still in flux. For an overview of the use of the term "Sophist" in the fifth century and earlier, see Schiappa (1999, 50–53). For a contrasting interpretation of the Sophists' identity, see Poulakos (1995, 11–52). In the fourth century, this distinction continues to be up for grabs, given Isocrates' insistence on calling his profession *philosophia*. On Isocrates' use of the term *philosophia,* see Schiappa (1999, 162–84) and Timmerman (1998).

10. "Reason," contends Vernant (1983), "is not to be discovered in nature, it is immanent in language. It did not originate in techniques for operating upon things. It

was developed from the organization and analysis of the various means of influencing men, of all the techniques for which language is a common instrument, namely, the arts of the lawyer, the professor, the orator, and the politician" (366). As G. E. R. Lloyd (1990) demonstrated in his studies of early Greek scientific discourse, much of what we now regard as early Greek philosophy cannot be separated from "the circumstances or contexts in which a certain rivalry between claimants to knowledge could and did develop" (15).

11. For a succinct analysis of the pamphlet's background and style, see Usher (1999, 302–3).

12. Of course, any translation would be idiomatic, but some idioms are more indicative of the translator's unconscious biases. Norlin's translation reveals modern positivistic bias, since "truth" is interpreted as a faithful statement of objective facts.

13. Although a fifth-century play, Aristophanes' *Birds* portrays a popular distrust of those who exploit writing for profit and political gain. See Slater (1996).

14. Isocrates' reliance on so-called *muthoi* in his compositions has received much attention. Calame (1999) insists that in Isocrates, "*muthos, qua* argument, fits neatly into deductive thinking articulated by *logos!*" (127). As shall become evident later, I am focusing on performative, identity-shaping aspects of Isocrates' use of *muthoi* rather than their value as building blocks of argumentation.

15. It is not necessary, of course, that writing leads to more elaborate composition that can be only appreciated through silent reading. As is well known, written discourse was performed orally well into the fourth century B.C.E., and Athenians especially "loved the convoluted stylistic devices" of orally presented compositions (Thomas 1992, 107).

16. The range of "ocular" experience need not be confined to "objective" observation, of course. Seeing can be just as seductive and overwhelming as aural persuasion. For instance, Gorgias draws a parallel between the ocular and oral illusions in the *Helen* (17–19). Plato, being far less sanguine about illusions, derides both "the lovers of sights and sounds" in the *Republic* (5:476b).

17. G. E. L. Owen (1986) was first to defend endoxology, an inquiry beginning with received opinions (*endoxa*), as Aristotle's method of investigation.

18. Martha Nussbaum builds upon and extends the argument first advanced by G. E. L. Owen. Owen defended a linguistic translation of Aristotle's *phainomena* as "ordinary beliefs" and "appearances." But he still demanded that *phainomena* be rendered as theory-neutral observations in Aristotle's physical treatises. According to Nussbaum, Owen's split attitude toward the term does the philosopher an injustice by charging him with equivocation "in just the area where Aristotle's precision and attentiveness are usually most striking" (1986, 244).

19. Nussbaum argues that "Aristotle's ethical views make him hospitable to tragedy and its style as sources of illumination," but she defends Aristotle's austere style as something that does more justice to poetic art than its subversion by Plato: "We might think of the ethical works as works of interpretation, orderings of the 'appearances' found in ordinary life and in tragic poetry. They do not replace tragedy: for only tragedy can give us illumination through and in pity and fear. But they supply an essential part of tragic learning, a part that Aristotle might fear losing were he to run together criticism and

madness, explanation and passion" (1986, 393). I find such drawing of boundaries between philosophical writing and tragic drama troublesome, since the "clarity" of Aristotle philosophical discourse may disguise, through its aura of scrupulous analysis, attitudes that are just as politically and culturally partisan as those of Plato.

20. In a recent commentary, Peter Simpson (Aristotle 1997) states: "The *Politics,* according to Aristotle himself, is not about a historical phenomenon, nor is it about a Greek phenomenon. It is about a *natural phenomenon* which, if prominent in ancient Greece, could in principle exist in any place and at any time and which, moreover, is necessary at every place and at every time if human beings are to attain happiness" (xxi, emphasis added).

21. Aristotle remarks immediately after that: "That is why Rhetoric assumes the character [*hupoduetai hupo to schema,* 'slips under the appearance'] of Politics, and those who claim to possess it, partly from ignorance, partly from boastfulness, and partly from other human weaknesses, do the same" (1356a26–30). Isocrates is the most likely object of attack here, for his *logos politikos* does not distinguish between the "higher" *pragmateia* of politics and the "lower" *technē rhētorikē.*

22. Carol Poster argues that the *Rhetoric* is "provided as a manual for the student trained in dialectic who needs, particularly for purposes of self-defense or defense of Platonic-Aristotelian philosophy, to sway the ignorant or corrupt audience or to understand the functioning of rhetoric within the badly ordered state" (1997, 244).

23. In book 3 of the *Rhetoric,* Aristotle summarizes the exposition of the sources of proof: "We have also stated the sources from which enthymemes should be derived—some of them being special, the others general commonplaces (topoi)" (1403b1).

24. See Aristotle's *On the Heavens,* 270b14–20, in which he states his belief in the cyclical nature of knowledge.

25. Aristotle's separation of rhetoric from poetics will be discussed in chapter 2. It must be pointed out, however, that other texts besides the *Rhetoric* indicate Aristotle's puzzlement over nonpropositional types of speech. In *On Interpretation,* he seems intrigued by sentences that cannot be verified as true or false: "A prayer, for instance, is a sentence but it is neither true or false. Let us set aside these other cases, since inquiry into them is more appropriate for rhetoric or poetics" (17a1–6).

Chapter 2—Between Poetics and Rhetoric

1. The traditionally held view that Aristotle saves rhetoric from Plato's indictments (see especially Farrell 1993) has been challenged by several scholars. Poulakos's work on Aristotle's reception of the Sophists (1996) highlights Aristotle's debts to Plato; Poster (1997) points out the Platonic tenor of Aristotle's *Rhetoric* on the grounds of its esoteric character and its many explicit negative remarks directed at rhetorical practice; Schiappa (1999) shows how Aristotle disciplines rhetoric by depoliticizing "epideictic" discourses. On the other hand, Nussbaum (1986) argues for Aristotle's radical departure from Plato on the issue of tragic learning.

2. For a comprehensive account of performance in archaic Greece, see Nagy (1996).

3. This view of mimesis as imitation and production of sounds and shapes, argues Elizabeth Belfiore (1984), is a thread that runs throughout the account of poetry (and

other forms of imitation) in the *Republic*. Belfiore thus proposes that what seems like a series of disconnected treatments of poetry actually amounts to a consistent theory of imitation. Richard McKeon (1936) insists that the ambiguity of the term *mimēsis* serves in Plato a profound theoretical purpose: "In its expansion and contraction, the word 'imitation' indicates the lesser term of the proportion of being to appearance: if God is, the universe is imitation; if all things are, shadows and reflections are imitations; if the products of man's handicraft are, his representations of them are imitations" (9).

4. Kevin Robb's *Literacy and Paideia in Ancient Greece* (1994) mentions forty-five fifth-century vases depicting scrolls, school scenes, and recitation of poetry as examples of an alliance between the oral *paideia* and writing.

5. Interestingly, even Aristotle in the *Poetics* touches upon the mimetic quality of Socratic dialogues (*tous Sokratikous logous*) (1447b10). For a contemporary argument that defends a mimetic view of Plato's dialogues, see Press (1995). Press concludes that the dialogues "do not give rise to conceptual knowledge, knowledge of a fact or judgment. Rather they create a kind of excitation, commitment, and captivated judgment, and the knowledge that we derive is in the 'form or style of knowing' rather than in the object or judgment known" (150).

6. That Isocrates "imitates" Plato's Socrates in the *Antidosis* is well established, judging by the Loeb edition's copious footnoting of passages that either repeat or echo Plato's *Apology*. But the motive behind Isocrates' strategy is still open to interpretation. In his reading of *Antidosis*, Josiah Ober (1998) states: "If the hierarchy of mimesis implies a subsidiary role for the imitation and the superiority of the original, then Isocrates seems to have put himself in a dubious position indeed" (261). Yet the presumption of an inferior status of a copy is Platonic, and Isocrates' "imitation" may be intended to subvert this hierarchy.

7. On whether Plato indeed sought such an art, see Roochnik (1996).

8. Viewed only against the backdrop of "Sophistic" speech instruction, Isocrates' *logon paideia* may seem as a watered down Platonism, albeit without Plato's strict epistemological criteria. Erika Rummel (1979), for instance, situates Isocrates "midway between the philosopher's arguments and the layman's objections" and states that Isocrates "was a professional teacher with philosophical aspirations, but also sharing the layman's bourgeois ethics and his taste for practicality" (25). Apart from the "taste for practicality," however, Rummel's portrait is too flat, for it ignores a sharp, irreconcilable split between the Platonic and Isocratean responses to their cultural tradition.

9. See G. J. De Vries (1953) in conjunction with R. L. Howland (1937) on the relationship between Plato's *Phaedrus* and Isocrates' *Antidosis*. It is likely, however, that Isocrates is reacting not only to the *Phaedrus* but also to a host of other dialogues directed at *logon paideia*.

10. See Merlan (1954–55) for a reading of this passage as one of the many veiled attacks by Isocrates on his Academic rivals. Schiappa (1999) calls for the reinscription of Isocrates in the philosophical canon because of the use of the term *philosophia* rather than *rhētorikē*, arguably Plato's term for what Isocrates professed in his school.

11. On the ideal of *kalokagathia*, see Marrou ([1956] 1964).

12. See especially the following sections of the *Republic*: 426a, 557c–558c, 604e–605a.

13. This nineteenth-century view of Aristotle's difference from Plato, now successfully challenged by Golden (1962, 1992), Nussbaum (1986), Depew (1991), and Halliwell (1990), among others, is summarized by W. Hamilton Fyfe in the preface to the old Loeb edition of Aristotle's *Poetics* (1982): "And in dealing with Emotion, Aristotle meets Plato's sensitive hesitation with hard common sense. Of course emotions are dangerous in the body politic. But what good is done by ignoring them or by heaping legislation on the safety-valve? We must face them as facts and use Art as their medicine. The soul, like the body, needs an occasional purge (*catharsis*)" (xvii). The most recent Loeb translation of the *Poetics* by Halliwell (1995) leaves the terms *mimēsis* and *catharsis* untranslated.

14. For an argument defending the *Rhetoric*'s influence on the structuring of the parts of tragic drama, see Kirby (1991).

15. Compare this statement with the praise of sight as the most discriminating of human senses in the *Metaphysics* 980a23–26.

16. Both Plato and Gorgias used the word *pharmakon* with reference to the effects of speech and writing. For a discussion of Gorgias's "magic" conception of discourse, see de Romilly's (1975). For a discussion of the ambivalence of *pharmakon* in Plato, see Derrida (1981).

17. The incidents that cause fear and pity must follow in a causal fashion, that is, they must appear as inevitable results of what has gone before (*Poetics* 1452a3–5). In chapter 17, Aristotle advises the poet to first outline the plot, taking special care of clarity and coherence, and only then insert the names of characters and episodes. J. M. Armstrong argues that the plot, by virtue of its abstractness, "is a kind of universal—an action-type—and can be instantiated many times both in real life and in make-believe contexts" (1998, 455).

18. See especially Golden (1962), Nussbaum (1986), and Depew (1991).

Chapter 3—Between Kairos *and Genre*

1. For an application of Bakhtin's notion of speech genres, see Berkenkotter and Huckin (1995).

2. Eugene Garver (1986), for example, compares Aristotle's *Rhetoric* to modern speech-act theory. From a perspective of rhetorical theory, Michael C. McGee also points out that "if we ignore the *product* of his attitudes, there is in Aristotle's *method* a process-conception and process model of rhetoric" (1982, 29). Similarly, Carolyn Miller demands that "a rhetorically sound definition of genre must be centered not on the substance or the form of discourse but on the action it is used to accomplish" (1984, 151).

3. See also Hunt (1962).

4. A much more felicitous example would be the debate between Cleon and Diodotus regarding the punishment of Mytilene, depicted at length by Thucydides in the opening sections of book 3. Diodotus is portrayed as a prudent orator advising the Athenian demos to revoke the previous day's decision to ravage the rebellious island. He indeed excludes considerations of justice and retribution and speaks of advantages of abstaining from harsh punishment. However, he does so in response to Cleon's self-serving invocation of retribution as the right sentiment on the part of the demos. The two speeches cannot be viewed separately, since both represent a response to a rhetorical

situation (the change of heart with respect to the previous day's decision to punish Mytilene), and each speech implies the agonistic presence of the other.

5. Despite the brevity of Aristotle's exposition of epideictic, some scholars have attempted to revive this aspect of his account of *technē* by postulating an affinity between the concept of *theoros* in the *Rhetoric* and the discussion of practical wisdom (*phronēsis*) in the *Nicomachean Ethics*. See especially Oravec (1976). Jeffrey Walker (2000) seizes upon "epideictic" as a key term in the history of rhetoric.

6. Aristotle establishes this connection clearly at 1357b24–27: "We have now explained the meaning of probable (*eikos*), sign (*semēion*), and necessary sign (*tekmērion*), and the difference between them; in the *Analytics* we have defined them more clearly and stated why some of them can be converted into logical syllogisms, while others cannot." The reference is to *Prior Analytics* 7a3–38, where Aristotle uses the same illustrations as in the *Rhetoric*.

7. In the next chapter, the issue of rhetoric's relation to politics will be integral to the explanation of Aristotle's conceptualization of the rhetorical audience.

8. By comparison, deliberative genre is discussed in chapters 4–8 and forensic genre in chapters 10–15.

9. I agree with Edward Schiappa's (1999, 185–206) argument that Aristotle "depoliticizes" several discursive practices—*enkomion, panegyrikos logos,* and *epitaphios logos*—by grouping them under the rubric of epideictic. As will become apparent, however, I interpret Aristotle's treatment of epideictic language as evidence of the conceptual separation of rhetorical discourse from the political knowledge across the three genres.

10. In his extensive treatment of "epideictic literature" before and after Aristotle, Theodore Burgess (1902) points out how writers such as Quintilian criticized the Aristotelian school for neglecting "the practical value" and political urgency of speeches classed under epideictic (95). Still, while he extends the scope of epideictic to cover substantive *topoi* (as opposed to mere display) and affirms the "occasional" character of much epideictic speechmaking in antiquity, Burgess's project remains largely classificatory.

11. "A speech," says Aristotle, "has two parts. It is necessary to state the subject, and then to prove it" (*Rhetoric* 1414a13.1).

12. See *Rhetoric* 1362a18 for the externality of the ends of deliberative oratory.

13. Martin's interpretive frame explicitly relies on speech-act theory as it was conceived by Austin (1962). *Muthos,* in this frame, can be described as an "illocutionary force" and *epos* as a "perlocutionary effect."

14. The term *muthos* in the later archaic period becomes synonymous with "tale, fiction, lie," while *epos* "becomes marginalized in Greek, to be replaced by *logos* in the sense of a 'single word'" (Martin 1989, 13). Lincoln's (1997) investigation of archaic usages of *muthos* and *logos* confirms Martin's description of *muthos* as a public authoritative speech-act. *Logos,* on the contrary, is used "to mark a speech of women, the weak, the young, and the shrewd" (352–53).

15. In viewing heroic speech-acts in terms of social performance, Martin defies the traditional (negative) portrait of an oral-formulaic student of Homer, who is obsessed with counting formulas. Gregory Nagy, another influential Homerist, has stressed that performance of epics in archaic and classical Greece should not be equated with

mere recitation of a fixed pattern: "The rhapsode cannot be viewed as merely 'reduplicating' what Homer had said" (1996, 60).

16. According to formalist literary theory, the object of literature, "life," is creatively distorted in art, and "ordinary speech" is "attenuated" in a literary discourse (Shklovsky 1965, 23). "Literariness" thus distinguishes verbal art from simple everyday speech. Bakhtin, on the contrary, insisted that "already discussed quality" (*ogovorennost*) of the world and the "already uttered quality" (*peregovorennost*) of language are part and parcel of the verbal artist's repertoire (1981, 331).

17. Isocrates' emphasis on uniqueness and novelty of written discourses has been interpreted by some as a manifestation of aesthetic formalism. For instance, noting Isocrates' aesthetic accomplishments and the "artifact" quality of his speeches, Andrew Ford (1993) concludes that Isocrates thereby cultivated an apolitical stance. Such a conclusion can only be reached if we disregard Isocrates' equally strong emphasis on *kairos* and if we limit the range of the political to speechmaking in the assembly.

18. Isocrates' compositions are notoriously difficult to classify if one follows traditional generic prescriptions. See, for instance, Poulakos's (1986) discussion of previous readings of *Helen*. On the problem of Isocratean genres, see Sullivan (2000). On the difficulty of classifying Isocrates' letters, see Sullivan (forthcoming).

19. Norlin thus describes the treaty: "The crowning shame of this condition of affairs was the so-called Peace of Antalkidas (negotiated in 387 B.C., mainly by Sparta), under the terms of which the Greeks submitted themselves formally, for the first time in history, to the overlordship of the Persian king, accepting him as the arbiter of their disputes and the guardian of the 'autonomy' of the Greek states in their relations to each other" (I. 116).

20. Therefore, the parodic thrust of Platonic imitation cannot be ignored, as some scholars do. See, for instance, Carter (1991).

21. Yun Lee Too states that Isocrates' "discourse of mimesis . . . ensures that 'archaisms' are never obsolete. It guarantees that myth in particular, as well as other forms of traditional language . . . will be perpetuated as a popular discourse of knowledge and culture" (1995, 59–60). This assessment is similar to the one advocated by de Romilly (1958).

22. See Poulakos (1988) for an understanding of epideictic as "site of a critique or transformation of the social order" (161).

23. As, in fact, Plato does in the *Menexenus* (245d–246a).

24. For instance, Thucydides' *History of the Peloponnesian War,* Plato's *Menexenus,* Xenophon's *Hellenica*.

Chapter 4—Between Identification and Persuasion

1. Michael Gagarin (2001) argues that Plato's and Aristotle's characterization of rhetoric as "the art of persuasion" and a subsequent preoccupation with "techniques of persuasion" has "distorted our understanding of sophistic contribution of what we call rhetoric."

2. In one of his most lucid critical essays, "The Rhetoric of Hitler's *Battle,*" first published before World War II, Burke admonished his compatriots against assuming

the rationality of democratic processes, which later became the leitmotif of such propaganda documentaries as Frank Capra's *Why We Fight* series. Burke wrote: "We are 'beyond' the stage where we are being saved from Nazism by our *virtues*. And fascist integration is being staved off, rather, by the *conflicts among our vices*. Our vices cannot get together in a grand united front of prejudices; and the result of this frustration, if or until they succeed in surmounting it, speaks, as the Bible might say, 'in the name of' democracy" (1973, 191).

3. This choice of authors is not random: in his *Speaking for the Polis,* Takis Poulakos relies on Althusser's conceptual apparatus (and its attendant assumptions) in interpreting Isocrates' "Hymn to Logos." Butler, in turn, offers a critique of Althusser's overly deterministic and procedural conception of interpellation.

4. To be sure, "The Hymn to Logos" is not univocal. It is part of an address written by Isocrates in a persona of Nicocles, the Cypriot monarch—a circumstance that is intriguing in the context of our argument about "sovereign performatives." I will save this interpretive problem for chapter 5, where I consider theoretical and political dilemmas that accompany the appropriation of classical theories of discourse.

5. Aristotle's *Rhetoric* points out this device in book 3 as something orators repeat ad nauseam but which nevertheless impresses the hearers (1408a7).

6. This is another metaphor exploited by orators and philosophers. Plato toys with this image as a bridge between the psychic and the political in the *Gorgias* and the *Republic*. For a comparison of the uses of the metaphor by Isocrates and Plato, see Morgan (2003).

7. For a distinction between herd animals and social animals in Aristotle, see Depew (1995).

8. Aristotle's treatise on rhetoric in all likelihood was written and revised over a long period of time, with later additions reflecting changes in his philosophical and political outlook. See Kennedy (1996).

9. For a critique of what I call "expansive" interpretations of enthymeme (i.e., accommodating *ethos, pathos,* and *logos*), see Gaines (2000, 8–10).

10. See Burnyeat (1996) for an interpretation of Aristotle's originality in the application of the commonly used term *enthumema*. See Walker (1994) on the "nontechnical" (i.e., pre-Aristotelian) uses of the term in ancient Greek sources.

11. At *Rhetoric* 1357a13, Aristotle states that "the judge is supposed to be simple person."

Chapter 5—Between Social Permanence and Social Change

1. See, for example, the exchange between Schiappa (1990b, 1990c) and Poulakos (1990) regarding the reconstruction of Sophistical rhetoric in several issues of *Philosophy and Rhetoric*.

2. For a useful discussion of this issue as it applies to classical studies, see Falkner, Felson, and Konstan (1999), and Too and Livingstone (1998).

3. On the interdependence of the Sophistic movement and democratic political change, see de Romilly (1992), Farrar (1988), Kerferd (1981), and Poulakos (1995). In his *Protagoras and Logos* (1990), however, Schiappa objects to grouping various sophists together as a theoretical or political movement.

4. See Crowley (1979), Farrar (1988), Gronbeck (1972), Jarratt (1991), J. Poulakos (1995), T. Poulakos (1993, 1994), Vitanza (1997), Welch (1990).

5. As John T. Kirby (1990) argues, the terms *bia, eros,* and *peitho* (or at least actions that can be characterized by them) often form dyadic relationships in various Greek discourses from archaic epics to Attic drama to Plato's dialogues. Kirby suggests that until Aristotle, all three notions are "treated under the discourse of power," so that even Plato "can find no exit from the ethical problems that beset his understanding of rhetoric" (226). Aristotle, on the other hand, aligns *peitho* with knowledge, rather than power, by redefining rhetoric "not as the *use of peitho* but as the *study of peitho*" (227).

6. See Consigny (2001) on the agonistic character of Gorgias's verbal artistry.

7. See Yunis (1996) and Ober (1998) on the response of Athenian intellectuals to rhetoric in the polis. See also Leff (1996) on Thucydides.

8. For a comparison between "liberty" and *eleutheria,* see Wood (1996).

9. For a reading that construes Gorgias as both an antifoundationalist and a responsible political agent, see Consigny (2001, 119–45).

10. The two modern English-language commentaries, by Cope (1970) and Grimaldi (1980, 1988), have attempted to resolve this puzzle by treating the *Rhetoric* as a theory that investigates and orders practice. For an incisive critique of this theory/practice approach, see Atwill (1998, 190–206). For a review of U.S. scholarship on the issue of *Rhetoric*'s place within Aristotle's system of arts and sciences, see Leff (1993).

11. *The Constitution of the Athenians* is not a theoretical treatise, like the bulk of Aristotle's other works. For a discussion of its style, see Rhodes (1981, 37–51).

12. It may be objected that Aristotle does consider the so-called summation argument according to which the many collectively may possess the virtue and wisdom comparable to that of the excellent few (*Politics* 1281a42–1281b6; cf. Miller 1995, 261–62). This consideration, however, leads Aristotle to question over what matters the authority of free men should extend. He concludes that the participation of the mass of the citizens should be confined to the deliberative and judicial functions (*Politics* 1281b22–32).

13. In the *Athenian Constitution,* Aristotle records that Pericles "urged the state very strongly in the direction of naval power, which resulted in emboldening the multitude" (27.1). In the *Politics,* however, Aristotle states that "it is not necessary for states to include the teeming population that grows up in connection with the sailor crowd, as there is no need for these to be citizens" (1327b8–10). This view is somewhat at odds with the statement regarding the constitutional government of the multitude (*politeia*) in book 3 of the *Politics,* where participation in the state is granted to the many who excel in military valor. The admission to citizenship in the latter case presupposes that military training teaches one to obey orders before one can give them, thus instilling the sense of legitimate hierarchy. See chapter 4 for the discussion of Aristotle's view of citizenly virtue.

14. Carnes Lord (1996), for instance, also defends a broad definition of classical *paideia:* "Where, as in Athens of the classical age, the common or public culture dominates society, where citizens are continuously exposed to powerful collective experiences in the law courts and the popular assembly, in religious gatherings and in the

theater, *paideia* in its broad and informal sense must be expected to dominate *paideia* in a narrowly institutional sense" (276). But Aristotle, referring to a systematic training of youths, says that "*paideia* comes to an end at some point" (*Politics* 1333b4).

15. Aristotle's own vocabulary disallows conflation of *phronēsis* as deliberative rationality and *technē* qua *dunamis*. For an elaboration of this point, see Gross (2000).

16. Indeed, Garver (1986) makes an explicit comparison of Aristotle's *Rhetoric* and speech-act theory: "Each is looking for a kind of action in which everything that could be accomplished *by* words is accomplished *in* words, and so each makes something like an illocutionary act into the central phenomenon covered in their inquiry" (6).

17. See, for instance, Too's "Brief Afterword" (1995, 233–34) and Livingstone (1998) on the antidemocratic tenor of Isocrates' "voice."

18. I borrow this designation of Isocrates' rhetoric from McGee (1985).

19. It must be noted, however, that the association of classical philology with dry pedantry does not accurately reflect some of the recent trends in Greek and Roman studies, such as, for example, the growing trend toward transforming classics into "classical cultural studies." See Cartledge (1998).

20. On the "invention" of the barbarian in the process of Greek self-definition, see Hall (1989). On the connection between the Athenian democracy and imperialism, see Raaflaub (1994). For an interpretation of Isocrates' anti-imperialism, see Davidson (1990).

21. For a discussion of changes of Isocrates' rhetorical strategy with respect to the discourse of Panhellenism, see Perlman (1976).

22. See my discussion of *Antidosis* and *Panathenaicus* in chapter 1 of this book.

23. For example, *On the Peace, Archidamus,* and *Panathenaicus*. Also of interest is Isocrates' use of strategic ambiguity as a way of addressing several audiences at once. On this aspect of composition in Isocrates, see Bons (1993).

24. Because in Isocrates the rhetor's linguistic prowess and leadership are always contingent upon the audience, I disagree with scholars like Samuel Ijsseling, who interprets Isocrates' *hēgemōn* as a metaphor for "complete control over the logos" (1976, 20).

Chapter 6—Classical Rhetorics and the Future of Democratic Education

1. The decline of public culture and the rise of the culture of marketing has been widely documented and lamented by critics. See, among others, Lasch (1979), Berman (2000), Lapham (1997), and Washburn and Thornton (1996). For the ascent of advertising to the position of the central institution, see Twitchell (1996).

2. For a criticism of representations of this ethos in contemporary fiction and film, see especially Goodnight (1995).

3. For a spirited polemic regarding the issue of cultural and ethnic diversity in the controversy over the literary "canon," see Gates (1992).

4. For a similar sentiment regarding contemporary debates over curriculum, see Graff (1992).

BIBLIOGRAPHY

Aeschylus. 1927. *Aeschylus.* Vol. 1. Translated by H. W. Smyth. Cambridge: Harvard University Press.
Althusser, Louis. 1971. *Lenin and Philosophy and Other Essays.* Translated by Ben Brewster. New York: Monthly Review.
Aristophanes. 1926. *Lysistrata.* Translated by Benjamin B. Rogers. London: William Heinemann.
Aristotle. 1935. *The Athenian Constitution. The Eudemian Ethics. On Virtues and Vices.* Translated by H. Rackham. Cambridge: Harvard University Press.
———. 1938. *Categories. On Interpretation. Prior Analytics.* Translated by H. P. Cooke and Hugh Tredennik. Cambridge: Harvard University Press.
———. 1960. *On the Heavens.* Translated by W. K. C. Guthrie. Cambridge: Harvard University Press.
———. 1968. *Nicomachean Ethics.* Translated by H. Rackham. Cambridge: Harvard University Press.
———. 1976. *Topics.* Translated by E. S. Forster. Cambridge: Harvard University Press.
———. 1977. *Politics.* Translated by H. Rackham. Cambridge: Harvard University Press.
———. 1980. *Metaphysics.* Translated by Hugh Tredennik. Cambridge: Harvard University Press.
———. 1982. *Poetics.* Translated by W. Hamilton Fyfe. Cambridge: Harvard University Press.
———. 1991. *The Art of Rhetoric.* Translated by J. H. Freese. Cambridge: Harvard University Press.
———. 1995. *Poetics.* Translated by Stephen Halliwell. Cambridge: Harvard University Press.
———. 1997. *The Politics of Aristotle.* Translated by Peter L. Phillips Simpson. Chapel Hill: University of North Carolina Press.
Armstrong, J. M. 1998. "Aristotle on the Philosophical Nature of Poetry." *Classical Quarterly* 48:447–55.
Atwill, Janet M. 1993. "Instituting the Art of Rhetoric: Theory, Practice, and Productive Knowledge in Interpretations of Aristotle's *Rhetoric*." In Poulakos, *Rethinking the History of Rhetoric,* 91–117.
———. 1998. *Rhetoric Reclaimed: Aristotle and the Liberal Arts Tradition.* Ithaca, N.Y.: Cornell University Press.

Auerbach, Eric. 1953. *Mimesis: The Representation of Reality in Western Literature.* Princeton, N.J.: Princeton University Press.
Austin, John L. 1962. *How to Do Things with Words.* Cambridge: Harvard University Press.
Bakhtin, Mikhail. 1981. *Dialogic Imagination.* Translated by Caryl Emerson and Michael Holquist. Edited by Michael Holquist. Austin: University of Texas Press.
———. 1986. *Speech Genres and Other Late Essays.* Translated by Vern W. McGee. Edited by Caryl Emerson and Michael Holquist. Austin: University of Texas Press.
Bakker, Egbert J. 1993. "Activation and Preservation: The Interdependence of Text and Performance in an Oral Tradition." *Oral Tradition* 8:5–20.
Barwick, Karl. 1963. "Das Problem der isokrateischen Techne." *Philologus* 107:43–60.
Bauman, Richard. 1986. *Story, Performance, and Event: Contextual Studies of Oral Narrative.* Cambridge: Cambridge University Press.
Bauman, Richard, and Charles L. Briggs. 1990. "Poetics and Performance as Critical Perspectives on Language and Social Life." *Annual Review of Anthropology* 19:59–88.
Beale, Walter H. 1978. "Rhetorical Performative Discourse: A New Theory of Epideictic." *Philosophy and Rhetoric* 11:221–46.
Beiner, Ronald. 1983. *Political Judgment.* Chicago: University of Chicago Press.
Belfiore, Elizabeth. 1984. "A Theory of Imitation in Plato's *Republic*." *TAPA* 114:121–46.
Bellah, Robert N. 1967. "Civil Religion in America." *Daedalus* 96:1–21.
Benoit, William. 1991. "Isocrates and Aristotle on Rhetoric." *Rhetoric Society Quarterly* 20:251–59.
Berkenkotter, Carol, and Thomas N. Huckin. 1995. "Rethinking Genre from a Sociocognitive Perspective." In *Genre Knowledge in Disciplinary Communication: Cognition/Culture/Power,* edited by Carol Berkenkotter and Thomas N. Huckin, 1–25. Hillsdale, N.J.: Lawrence Erlbaum.
Berman, Morris. 2000. *The Twilight of American Culture.* New York: Norton.
Bitzer, Lloyd F. 1959. "Aristotle's Enthymeme Revisited." *Quarterly Journal of Speech* 45:399–408.
———. 1968. "The Rhetorical Situation." *Philosophy and Rhetoric* 1:1–17.
Bonitz, Herman. 1955. *Index Aristotelicus.* 2d ed. Graz: Akademische Druck–U. Verlagsanstalt.
Bons, J. A. E. 1993. "ΑΜΦΙΒΟΛΙΑ: Isocrates and Written Composition." *Mnemosyne* 46:160–71.
Bowman, Alan K., and Greg Woolf, eds. 1994. *Literacy and Power in the Ancient World.* Cambridge: Cambridge University Press.
Brunschwig, Jacques. 1996. "Aristotle's Rhetoric as a 'Counterpart' to Dialectic." In Rorty, *Essays,* 34–55.

Bryant, Donald C. 1953. "Rhetoric: Its Function and Its Scope." *Quarterly Journal of Speech* 39:401–24.
Burgess, Theodore C. 1902. "Epideictic Literature." In *Studies in Classical Philology* 3:89–261. Chicago: University of Chicago Press.
Burke, Kenneth. 1952. *A Grammar of Motives*. New York: Prentice-Hall.
———. 1968. *Language as Symbolic Action*. Berkeley: University of California Press.
———. 1969. *A Rhetoric of Motives*. Berkeley: University of California Press.
———. 1973. *Philosophy of Literary Form*. Berkeley: University of California Press.
———. 1984. *Permanence and Change: An Anatomy of Purpose*. 3d ed. Berkeley: University of California Press.
Burnyeat, M. F. 1996. "Enthymeme: Aristotle on the Rationality of Rhetoric." In Rorty, *Essays,* 88–115.
Butler, Judith. 1997. *The Psychic Life of Power: Theories in Subjection*. Stanford, Calif.: Stanford University Press.
Buxton, R. G. A. 1982. *Persuasion in Greek Tragedy: A Study of Peitho*. Cambridge: Cambridge University Press.
———, ed. 1999. *From Myth to Reason? Studies in the Development of Greek Thought*. Oxford: Oxford University Press.
Cahn, Michael. 1989. "Reading Rhetoric Rhetorically: Isocrates and the Marketing of Insight." *Rhetorica* 7:121–44.
Calame, Claude. 1999. "The Rhetoric of *Muthos* and *Logos:* Forms of Figurative Discourse." In Buxton, *From Myth to Reason?* 119–43.
Campbell, John Angus. 1984. "A Rhetorical Interpretation of History." *Rhetorica* 2:227–66.
Carter, Michael F. 1991. "The Ritual Function of Epideictic Rhetoric: The Case of Socrates' Funeral Oration." *Rhetorica* 9:209–32.
Cartledge, Paul. 1998. "Classics: From Discipline in Crisis to (Multi-)cultural Capital." In Too and Livingstone, *Pedagogy and Power,* 16–28.
Chroust, Anton-Hermann. 1973. *Aristotle: New Light on His Life and on Some of His Lost Works*. Vol. 1. Notre Dame: University of Notre Dame Press.
Cicero. 1977. *De Oratore*. Book 3. Translated by. H. Rackham. Cambridge: Harvard University Press.
Clark, Norman. 1996. "The Critical Servant: An Isocratean Contribution to Critical Rhetoric." *Quarterly Journal of Speech* 82:111–24.
Cmiel, Kenneth. 1990. *Democratic Eloquence: The Fight over Popular Speech in Nineteenth-Century America*. New York: William Morrow.
Cole, Thomas. 1991. *The Origins of Rhetoric in Ancient Greece*. Baltimore: Johns Hopkins University Press.
Consigny, Scott. 2001. *Gorgias, Sophist and Artist*. Columbia: University of South Carolina Press.
Cope, Edward M. 1970. *The Rhetoric of Aristotle with a Commentary*. 3 vols. Edited and revised by J. E. Sandys. Hidesheim: Olms.

Crowley, Sharon. 1979. "Of Gorgias and Grammatology." *College Composition and Communication* 30:279–84.

Davidson, J. 1990. "Isocrates against Imperialism: An Analysis of the De Pace." *Historia* 39:20–36.

Depew, David J. 1991. "Politics, Music, and Contemplation in Aristotle's Ideal State." In *A Companion to Aristotle's Politics,* edited by David Keyt and Fred D. Miller, 346–80. Oxford: Blackwell.

———. 1995. "Humans and Other Political Animals in Aristotle's *History of Animals*." *Phronesis* 40:156–81.

———. N.d. "The Natural History of the *Polis*." Unpublished manuscript.

Depew, David J., and John Durham Peters. 2001. "Community and Communication: The Conceptual Background." In *Communication and Community,* edited by Gregory J. Shepherd and Eric W. Rothenbuler, 3–21. Mahwah, N.J.: Lawrence Erlbaum.

de Romilly, Jacqueline. 1958. "Eunoia in Isocrates or the Political Importance of Creating Good Will." *Journal of Hellenic Studies* 78:92–101.

———. 1975. *Magic and Rhetoric in Ancient Greece.* Cambridge: Harvard University Press.

———. 1992. *The Great Sophists in Periclean Athens.* Translated by Janet Lloyd. Oxford: Clarendon.

Derrida, Jacques. 1981. "Plato's Pharmacy." In *Dissemination,* translated by Barbara Johnson, 63–171. Chicago: University of Chicago Press.

Detienne, Marcel. 1996. *Masters of Truth in Archaic Greece.* Translated by Janet Lloyd. New York: Zone Books.

De Vries, G. J. 1953. "Isocrates' Reaction to the *Phaedrus*." *Mnemosyne* 6:39–45.

Diels, Hermann, and Walter Kranz. 1952. *Die Fragmente der Vorsokratiker.* 3 vols. Berlin: Weidmannsche Verlagsbuchhandlung.

Dionysius of Halicarnassus. 1974. *Dionysius of Halicarnassus: The Critical Essays.* 2 vols. Translated by Stephan Usher. Cambridge: Harvard University Press.

Dubois, Page. 1993. "Violence, Apathy, and the Rhetoric of Philosophy." In Poulakos, *Rethinking,* 119–34.

Eagleton, Terry. 1983. *Literary Theory: An Introduction.* Minneapolis: University of Minnesota Press.

Else, Gerald F. 1958. "'Imitation' in the Fifth Century." *Classical Philology* 53:73–90.

Enos, Richard Leo. 1993. *Greek Rhetoric before Aristotle.* Prospect Heights, Ill.: Waveland.

Euben, Peter J., John R. Wallach, and Josiah Ober. 1994. *Athenian Political Thought and the Reconstruction of American Democracy.* Ithaca, N.Y.: Cornell University Press.

Falkner, Thomas, Nancy Felson, and David Konstan, eds. 1999. *Contextualizing Classics: Ideology, Performance, Dialogue.* Lanham, Md.: Rowman and Littlefield.

Farrar, Cynthia. 1988. *The Origins of Democratic Thinking: The Invention of Politics in Classical Athens.* Cambridge: Cambridge University Press.

Farrell, Thomas B. 1976. "Knowledge, Consensus, and Rhetorical Theory." *Quarterly Journal of Speech* 62:1–14.
———. 1993. *Norms of Rhetorical Culture*. New Haven, Conn.: Yale University Press.
Finley, M. I. 1975. *The Use and Abuse of History*. New York: Penguin.
Foley, John M., ed. 1985. *Oral-Formulaic Theory and Research: An Introduction and Annotated Bibliography*. New York: Garland.
Ford, Andrew. 1993. "The Price of Art in Isocrates: Formalism and the Escape from Politics." In Poulakos, *Rethinking,* 31–52.
Foucault, Michel. 1972. *The Archaeology of Knowledge and the Discourse on Language*. Translated by A. M. Sheridan Smith and Rupert Swyer. New York: Pantheon.
Fuks, Alexander. 1972. "Isocrates and the Social-Economic Situation in Greece." *Ancient Society* 3:17–44.
Gagarin, Michael. 2001. "Did Sophists Aim to Persuade?" *Rhetorica* 19:275–91.
Gaines, Robert. 1990. "Isocrates, EP. 6.8." *Hermes* 118:165–70.
———. 2000. "Aristotle's *Rhetoric* and the Contemporary Arts of Practical Discourse." In Gross and Walzer, *Rereading Aristotle's* Rhetoric, 3–23.
Garver, Eugene. 1986. "Aristotle's *Rhetoric* as a Work of Philosophy." *Philosophy and Rhetoric* 19:1–22.
———. 1994. *Aristotle's* Rhetoric: *An Art of Character*. Chicago: University of Chicago Press.
Gates, Henry Louis, Jr. 1992. *Loose Canons: Notes on the Culture Wars*. Oxford and New York: Oxford University Press.
Golden, Leon. 1962. "Catharsis." *Transactions of American Philological Association* 93:51–60.
———. 1992. *Aristotle on Tragic and Comic Mimesis*. Atlanta: Scholars Press.
Goodnight, G. Thomas. 1995. "The Firm, the Park, and the University: Fear and Trembling on the Postmodern Trail." *Quarterly Journal of Speech* 81:267–90.
Gorgias. 1972. *Encomium of Helen*. In *The Older Sophists,* edited by Rosamond K. Sprague, 50–54. Columbia: University of South Carolina Press.
Graff, Gerald. 1992. *Beyond the Culture Wars: How Teaching the Conflicts Can Revitalize American Education*. New York: Norton.
Grimaldi, William. 1980. *Aristotle, Rhetoric I: A Commentary*. New York: Fordham University Press.
———. 1988. *Aristotle, Rhetoric II: A Commentary*. New York: Fordham University Press.
Gronbeck, Bruce. 1972. "Gorgias on Rhetoric and Poetic: A Rehabilitation." *Southern Speech Communication Journal* 38:27–38.
Gross, Alan G. 2000. "What Aristotle Meant by Rhetoric." In Gross and Walzer, *Rereading Aristotle's* Rhetoric, 24–37.
Gross, Alan G., and Arthur E. Walzer, eds. 2000. *Rereading Aristotle's* Rhetoric. Carbondale: Southern Illinois University Press.
Hall, Edith. 1989. *Inventing the Barbarian: Greek Self-Definition through Tragedy*. Oxford: Clarendon.

Halliwell, Stephen. 1990. "Aristotelian Mimesis Reevaluated." *Journal of the History of Philosophy* 28:487–510.

Halverson, John. 1992. "Havelock on Greek Orality and Literacy." *Journal of the History of Ideas* 53:148–63.

Hariman, Robert. 1995. "Status, Marginality, and Rhetorical Theory." *Quarterly Journal of Speech* 72:2–17.

Harris, William V. 1989. *Ancient Literacy*. Cambridge: Harvard University Press.

Haskins, Ekaterina V. 1999. "Orality, Literacy, and Isocrates' Political Aesthetics." In *Rhetoric, the Polis, and the Global Village: Selected Papers from the 1998 Rhetoric Society of America Conference,* edited by C. Jan Swearingen and Dave Pruett, 83–92. Mahwah, N.J.: Lawrence Erlbaum.

———. 2000. "*Mimesis* between Poetics and Rhetoric: Performance Culture and Civic Education in Plato, Isocrates, and Aristotle." *Rhetoric Society Quarterly* 30:7–33.

———. 2001. "Rhetoric between Orality and Literacy: Cultural Memory and Performance in Isocrates and Aristotle." *Quarterly Journal of Speech* 87:158–78.

———. 2002. "Paideia versus Techne: Isocrates's Performative Conception of Rhetorical Education." In *Professing Rhetoric: Selected Papers from the 2000 Rhetoric Society of America Conference,* edited by Frederick Antczak, Cinda Coggins, and Geoffrey Klinger, 199–206. Mahwah, N.J.: Lawrence Erlbaum.

Havelock, Eric A. 1963. *Preface to Plato*. New York: Grosset and Dunlap.

———. 1982. *The Literate Revolution in Greece and Its Cultural Consequences*. Princeton, N.J.: Princeton University Press.

———. 1983. "The Linguistic Task of the Presocratics." In *Language and Thought in Early Greek Philosophy,* edited by Kevin Robb, 7–82. La Salle, Ill.: Hegeler Institute.

———. 1986. *The Muse Learns to Write: Reflections on Orality and Literacy from Antiquity to the Present*. New Haven, Conn.: Yale University Press.

Heidlebaugh, Nola J. 2002. *Judgment, Rhetoric, and the Problem of Incommensurability: Recalling Practical Wisdom*. Columbia: University of South Carolina Press.

Heilbrunn, Gunter. 1975. "Isocrates on Rhetoric and Power." *Hermes* 103:154–78.

Herodotus. 1942. *The Persian Wars*. Translated by George Rawlinson. New York: Modern Library.

Howland, R. L. 1937. "The Attack on Isocrates in the *Phaedrus*." *Classical Quarterly* 31:151–59.

Hunt, Everett Lee. 1962. "Plato and Aristotle on Rhetoric and Rhetoricians." In *Studies in Rhetoric and Public Speaking in Honor of James Albert Winans, by Pupils and Colleagues,* edited by A. M. Drummond, 3–60. New York: Russell and Russell.

Ijsseling, Samuel. 1976. "Isocrates and the Power of Logos." In *Rhetoric and Philosophy in Conflict,* by Samuel Ijsseling, 18–25. The Hague: Martinus Nijhoff.

Isocrates. 1928, 1929, 1945. *Isocrates*. 3 vols. Translated by George Norlin (vols. 1–2) and LaRue Van Hook (vol. 3) Cambridge: Harvard University Press.

———. 2000. *Isocrates I*. Translated by David Mirhady and Yun Lee Too. Austin: University of Texas Press.

Jaeger, Werner. 1971. *Paideia: The Ideals of Greek Culture.* 3 vols. Translated by Gilbert Highet. New York: Oxford University Press.

Jameson, Frederic. 1979. "Reification and Utopia in Mass Culture." *Social Text* 1:130–49.

Jamieson, Kathleen Hall, and Karlyn Kohrs Campbell. 1982. "Rhetorical Hybrids: Fusions of Generic Elements." *Quarterly Journal of Speech* 68:146–57.

Jarratt, Susan. 1991. *Rereading the Sophists: Classical Rhetoric Refigured.* Carbondale: Southern Illinois University Press.

Johansen, Thomas K. 1999. "Myth and Logos in Aristotle." In Buxton, *From Myth to Reason?* 279–91.

Johnstone, Christopher L. 1996a. "Introduction: The Origins of the Rhetorical in Archaic Greece." In Johnstone, *Theory, Text, Context,* 1–18.

———, ed. 1996b. *Theory, Text, Context: Issues in Greek Rhetoric and Oratory.* Albany: State University of New York Press.

Kennedy, George A. 1963. *The Art of Persuasion in Greece.* Princeton, N.J.: Princeton University Press.

———. 1996. "The Composition and Influence of Aristotle's *Rhetoric.*" In Rorty, *Essays,* 416–24.

———. 1991. *Aristotle on Rhetoric: A Theory of Civic Discourse.* New York: Oxford University Press.

Kerferd, G. B. 1981. *The Sophistic Movement.* Cambridge: Cambridge University Press.

Kinneavy, James. 1986. "*Kairos:* A Neglected Concept in Classical Rhetoric." In *Rhetoric and Praxis: The Contribution of Classical Rhetoric to Practical Reasoning,* edited by Jean Dietz Moss, 79–105. Washington, D.C.: Catholic University of America Press.

Kirby, John T. 1990. "The 'Great Triangle' in Early Greek Rhetoric and Poetics." *Rhetorica* 8:213–28.

———. 1991. "Aristotle's *Poetics:* The Rhetorical Principle." *Arethusa* 24:197–217.

———. 1992. "Rhetoric and Poetics in Hesiod." *Ramus* 21:34–60.

Kroll, W. 1940. "Rhetorik." *Paulys Real-Encyclopadie der Classischen Altertumswissenschaft.* Supplementband 7:1039–1138.

Lapham, Lewis. 1997. *Waiting for the Barbarians.* London: Verso.

Lardinois, André, and Laura McClure. 2001. *Making Silence Speak: Women's Voices in Greek Literature and Society.* Princeton, N.J.: Princeton University Press.

Lasch, Christopher. 1979. *The Culture of Narcissism: American Life in an Age of Diminishing Expectations.* New York: Norton.

Leff, Michael C. 1986. "Genre and Paradigm in the 2nd Book of *De Oratore.*" *Southern States Communication Journal* 51:308–25.

———. 1993. "The Uses of Aristotle's Rhetoric in Contemporary American Scholarship." *Argumentation* 7:313–27.

———. 1996. "Agency, Performance, and Interpretation in Thucydides' Account of the Mytilene Debate." In Johnstone, *Theory, Text, Context,* 87–96.

Lentz, Tony M. 1989. *Orality and Literacy in Hellenic Greece.* Carbondale: Southern Illinois University Press.

Lincoln, Bruce. 1997. "Competing Discourses: Rethinking the Prehistory of *Mythos* and *Logos.*" *Arethusa* 30:341–67.

Livingstone, Niall. 1998. "The Voice of Isocrates and the Dissemination of Cultural Power." In Too and Livingstone, *Pedagogy and Power,* 263–81.

Lloyd, G. E. R. 1990. *Demystifying Mentalities.* Cambridge: Cambridge University Press.

———. 1996. *Aristotelian Explorations.* Cambridge: Cambridge University Press.

Loraux, Nicole. 1986. *The Invention of Athens: Funeral Oration in the Classical City.* Translated by Alan Sheridan. Cambridge: Harvard University Press.

Lord, Carnes. 1981. "The Intention of Aristotle's *Rhetoric.*" *Hermes* 109:326–39.

———. 1996. "Aristotle and the Idea of Liberal Education." In Ober and Hedrick, *Dēmokratia,* 271–88.

Lucaites, John Louis, and Celeste Michelle Condit. 1999. "Introduction." In *Contemporary Rhetorical Theory: A Reader,* edited by John Louis Lucaites, Celeste Michelle Condit, and Sally Caudill, 1–18. New York: Guilford Press.

Marrou, Henri I. [1956] 1964. *A History of Education in Antiquity.* Translated by George Lamb. New York: Sheed and Ward; reprint, New York: Mentor.

Martin, Richard. 1989. *The Language of Heroes: Speech and Performance in the Iliad.* Ithaca, N.Y.: Cornell University Press.

McGee, Michael Calvin. 1982. "A Materialist's Conception of Rhetoric." In *Explorations in Rhetoric: Essays in Honor of Douglas Ehninger,* edited by Raymie E. McKerrow, 23–48. Glenview, Ill.: Scott, Foresman.

———. 1985. "The Moral Problem of *Argumentum per Argumentum.*" In *Argument and Social Practice: Proceedings of the Fourth SCA/AFA Conference on Argumentation,* edited by Robert Cox, Malcolm Sillars, and Gregg Walker, 1–15. Annandale, Va.: SCA.

———. 1990. "Text, Context, and Fragmentation of Contemporary Culture." *Western Journal of Speech Communication* 54:274–89.

McKeon, Richard. 1936. "Literary Criticism and the Concept of Imitation in Antiquity." *Modern Philology* 34:1–35.

———. 1946. "Aristotle's Conception of Language and the Arts of Language." *Classical Philology* 41:193–206.

———. 1947. "Aristotle's Conception of Language and the Arts of Language." *Classical Philology* 42:21–50.

McKerrow, Raymie E. 1989. "Critical Rhetoric: Theory and Praxis." *Communication Monographs* 56:91–111.

Merlan, Philip. 1954–55. "Isocrates, Aristotle, and Alexander the Great." *Historia* 3:60–81.

Miller, Carolyn. 1984. "Genre as Social Action." *Quarterly Journal of Speech* 70: 151–67.

Miller, Fred D. 1995. *Nature, Justice, and Rights in Aristotle's* Politics. Oxford: Clarendon.

Morgan, Kathryn. 2003. "The Tyranny of the Audience in Plato and Isocrates." In Kathryn Morgan, *Popular Tyranny*. Austin: University of Texas Press.

———. Forthcoming. "The Education of Athens: Politics and Rhetoric in Isocrates (and Plato)." In Poulakos and Depew, *Isocrates*.

Most, Glenn W. 1994. "The Uses of *Endoxa*: Philosophy and Rhetoric in the *Rhetoric*." In *Aristotle's "Rhetoric": Philosophical Essays*, edited by David J. Furley and Alexander Nehamas, 167–99. Princeton, N.J.: Princeton University Press.

———. 1999. "From Logos to Mythos." In Buxton, *From Myth to Reason?* 25–47.

Munscher, Karl. 1916. "Isokrates." *Paulys Real-Encyclopadie der classischen Altertumswissenschaft* 9:2146–227.

Nagy, Gregory. 1996. *Poetry as Performance: Homer and Beyond*. Cambridge: Cambridge University Press.

Neel, Jasper. 1994. *Aristotle's Voice: Rhetoric, Theory, and Writing in America*. Carbondale: Southern Illinois University Press.

Nussbaum, Martha. 1986. *Fragility of Goodness: Luck and Ethics in Greek Tragedy and Philosophy*. New York: Cambridge University Press.

Ober, Josiah. 1989. *Mass and Elite in Democratic Athens: Rhetoric, Ideology, and the Power of the People*. Princeton, N.J.: Princeton University Press.

———. 1991. "Aristotle's Political Sociology: Class, Status, and Order in the Politics." In *Essays on the Foundations of Aristotelian Political Science*, edited by Carnes Lord and David K. O'Connor, 112–35. Berkeley: University of California Press.

———. 1998. *Political Dissent in Democratic Athens: Intellectual Critics of Popular Rule*. Princeton, N.J.: Princeton University Press.

Ober, Josiah, and Charles Hedrick, eds. 1996. *Dēmokratia: A Conversation on Democracies, Ancient and Modern*. Princeton, N.J.: Princeton University Press.

Ong, Walter. 1982. *Orality and Literacy*. London: Methuen.

Oravec, Christine. 1976. "'Observation' in Aristotle's Theory of Epideictic." *Philosophy and Rhetoric* 9:162–74.

Oravec, Christine, and Michael Salvador. 1993. "The Duality of Rhetoric: Theory as Discursive Practice." In Poulakos, *Rethinking*, 173–92.

O'Sullivan, Neil. 1996. "Written and Spoken in the First Sophistic." In Worthington, *Voice into Text*, 115–27.

Owen, G. E. L. 1986. *Logic, Science and Dialectic. Collected Papers in Greek Philosophy*. Edited by Martha Nussbaum. London: Duckworth.

Papillon, Terry. 1995. "Isocrates' *techne* and Rhetorical Pedagogy." *Rhetoric Society Quarterly* 25:149–59.

Parker, Andrew, and Eve Kosofsky Sedgwick, eds. 1995. *Performativity and Performance*. New York: Routledge.

Perelman, Chaim, and L. Olbrechts-Tyteca. 1969. *The New Rhetoric: A Treatise on Argumentation*. Translated by J. Wilkinson and P. Weaver. Notre Dame: University of Notre Dame Press.

Perlman, S. 1976. "Panhellenism, the Polis and Imperialism." *Historia* 25:1–30.

Photius. 1960. *Photius Biblioteque*. Edited by Rene Henry. Paris: Société d'Édition "Les Belles Lettres."

Plato. 1914. *Plato VII: Timaeus, Critias, Cleitophon, Menexenus, Epistles*. Translated by R. G. Bury. Cambridge: Harvard University Press.

———. 1967a. *Plato II: Laches, Protagoras, Meno, Euthydemus*. Translated by W. R. M. Lamb. Cambridge: Harvard University Press.

———. 1967b. *Plato III: Lysis, Gorgias, Symposium*. Translated by W. R. M. Lamb. Cambridge: Harvard University Press.

———. 1982. *Plato I: Euthyphro, Apology, Crito, Phaedo, Phaedrus*. Translated by H. N. Fowler. Cambridge: Harvard University Press.

———. 1986. *Ion, Hippias Minor, Laches, Protagoras*. Translated by R. E. Allen. New Haven, Conn.: Yale University Press.

———. 1994. *Plato V, VI: Republic Books 1–5 and Books 6–10*. Translated by Paul Shorey. Cambridge: Harvard University Press.

Poster, Carol. 1997. "Aristotle's *Rhetoric* against Rhetoric: Unitarian Readings and Esoteric Hermeneutics." *American Journal of Philology* 118:219–49.

———. 1998. "(Re)positioning Pedagogy: A Feminist Historiography of Aristotle's *Rhetorica*." In *Feminist Interpretations of Aristotle*, edited by Cynthia Freeland, 327–49. University Park: Pennsylvania State University Press.

Poulakos, John. 1983. "Toward a Sophistic Definition of Rhetoric." *Philosophy and Rhetoric* 16:35–48.

———. 1986. "Argument, Practicality, and Eloquence in Isocrates' *Helen*." *Rhetorica* 4:1–19.

———. 1990. "Interpreting Sophistical Rhetoric: A Response to Schiappa." *Philosophy and Rhetoric* 23:218–28.

———. 1995. *Sophistical Rhetoric in Classical Greece*. Columbia: University of South Carolina Press.

———. 1996. "Extending and Correcting the Rhetorical Tradition: Aristotle's Perception of the Sophists." In Johnstone, *Theory, Text, Context*, 45–63.

Poulakos, Takis. 1987. "Isocrates' Use of Narrative in the *Evagoras*: Epideictic Rhetoric and Moral Action." *Quarterly Journal of Speech* 73:317–28.

———. 1988. "Towards a Cultural Understanding of Classical Epideictic Oratory." *Pre/Text* 9:147–66.

———. 1994. "Human Agency in the History of Rhetoric: Gorgias' *Encomium of Helen*." In *Writing Histories of Rhetoric*, edited by Victor Vitanza, 59–80. Carbondale: Southern Illinois University Press.

———. 1997. *Speaking for the Polis: Isocrates' Rhetorical Education*. Columbia: University of South Carolina Press.

———, ed. 1993. *Rethinking the History of Rhetoric: Multidisciplinary Essays on the Rhetorical Tradition*. Boulder, Colo.: Westview.

Poulakos, Takis, and David J. Depew, eds. Forthcoming. *Isocrates and Civic Education*. Austin: University of Texas Press.

Press, Gerald A. 1995. "Plato's Dialogues as Enactments." In *The Third Way: New Directions in Platonic Studies,* edited by Francisco J. Gonzalez, 133–52. Lanham, Md.: Rowman and Littlefield.

———, ed. 1993. *Plato's Dialogues: New Studies and Interpretations.* Lanham: Rowman and Littlefield.

Raaflaub, Kurt A. 1994. "Democracy, Power, and Imperialism in Fifth-Century Athens." In Euben, Wallach, and Ober, *Athenian Political Thought,* 103–46.

Rademacher, Ludwig. 1951. *Artium Scriptores (Reste der Voraristotelischen Rhetorik).* Osterreichische Akademie de Wissenschaften, Philosophisch-historische Klasse, Sitzungsberichte, 227. Band 3 Abhandlung. Vienna: Rudolf M. Rohrer.

Reeve, C. D. C. 1996. "Philosophy, Politics, and Rhetoric in Aristotle." In Rorty, *Essays,* 191–205.

Rhodes, P. J. 1981. *A Commentary on the Aristotelian* Athenaion Politeia. Oxford: Clarendon.

Robb, Kevin. 1983. "The Linguistic Art of Heraclitus." In *Language and Thought in Early Greek Philosophy,* edited by Kevin Robb, 186–200. La Salle, Ill.: Hegeler Institute.

———. 1994. *Literacy and Paideia in Ancient Greece.* New York: Oxford University Press.

Robinson, T. M. 1979. *Contrasting Arguments: An Edition of the Dissoi Logoi.* New York: Arno Press.

Roochnik, David. 1996. *Of Art and Wisdom: Plato's Understanding of Techne.* University Park: Pennsylvania State University Press.

Rorty, Amelie Oksenberg, ed. 1996. *Essays on Aristotle's* Rhetoric. Berkeley: University of California Press.

Rorty, Richard. 1989. *Contingency, Irony, and Solidarity.* Cambridge: Cambridge University Press.

Rosenmeyer, Thomas. 1955. "Gorgias, Aeschylus, and *Apate.*" *American Journal of Philology* 76:225–60.

Roundtree, Clark. 2001. "The (Almost) Blameless Genre of Classical Greek Epideictic." *Rhetorica* 19:293–206.

Rummel, Erika. 1979. "Isocrates' Ideal of Rhetoric: Criteria of Evaluation." *Classical Journal* 75:25–35.

Schiappa, Edward. 1990a. "Did Plato Coin *Rhētorikē?*" *American Journal of Philology* 111:457–70.

———. 1990b. "History and Neo-Sophistic Criticism: A Reply to Poulakos." *Philosophy and Rhetoric* 23:307–15.

———. 1990c. "Neo-Sophistic Rhetorical Criticism or the Historical Reconstruction of Sophistic Doctrines." *Philosophy and Rhetoric* 23:192–217.

———. 1991. *Protagoras and Logos: A Study in Greek Philosophy and Rhetoric.* Columbia: University of South Carolina Press.

———. 1996. "Toward a Predisciplinary Analysis of Gorgias' *Helen.*" In Johnstone, *Theory, Text, Context,* 65–86.

———. 1999. *The Beginnings of Rhetorical Theory in Classical Greece.* New Haven, Conn.: Yale University Press.

Segal, Charles. 1962. "Gorgias and the Psychology of the Logos." *Harvard Studies in Classical Philology* 66:99–155.

Shklovsky, Viktor. 1965. "Art as Technique." In *Russian Formalist Criticism: Four Essays,* translated and edited by Lee T. Lemon and Marion J. Reis, 3–24. Lincoln: University of Nebraska Press.

Slater, Niall W. 1996. "Literacy and Old Comedy." In Worthington, *Voice into Text,* 99–112.

Snell, Bruno. 1953. *The Discovery of the Mind: The Greek Origins of European Thought.* Trans. by T. G. Rosenmeyer. Cambridge: Harvard University Press.

Solmsen, Friedrich. 1941. "The Aristotelian Tradition in Ancient Rhetoric." *American Journal of Philology* 62:35–50.

———. 1966. Review of Havelock, *Preface to Plato. American Journal of Philology* 87:99–105.

Sprague, Rosamond K., ed. 1972. *The Older Sophists.* Columbia: University of South Carolina Press.

Steiner, Deborah T. 1994. *The Tyrant's Writ: Myths and Images of Writing in Ancient Greece.* Princeton, N.J.: Princeton University Press.

Sullivan, Robert G. 2000. "Isocrates and the Forms of Rhetorical Discourse." Ph.D. diss., University of Maryland.

———. Forthcoming. "Classical Epistolary Theory and the Letters of Isocrates." In *Letter Writing Manuals from Antiquity to the Present,* edited by Carol Poster and Linda Mitchell. Columbia: University of South Carolina Press.

Sutton, Jane. 1993. "The Marginalization of Sophistical Rhetoric and the Loss of History." In Poulakos, *Rethinking,* 91–118.

Thomas, Rosalind. 1989. *Oral Tradition and Written Record in Classical Athens.* Cambridge: Cambridge University Press.

———. 1992. *Literacy and Orality in Ancient Greece.* Cambridge: Cambridge University Press.

Thompson, Wesley E. 1983. "Isocrates on the Peace Treaties." *Classical Quarterly* 33:75–80.

Thucydides. 1968. *History of the Peloponnesian War.* 4 vols. Translated by Charles Smith. London: William Heinemann.

Timmerman, David M. 1998. "Isocrates' Competing Conceptualization of Philosophy." *Philosophy and Rhetoric* 31:145–59.

Too, Yun Lee. 1995. *The Rhetoric of Identity in Isocrates: Text, Power, Pedagogy.* Cambridge: Cambridge University Press.

Too, Yun Lee, and Niall Livingstone, eds. 1998. *Pedagogy and Power: Rhetorics of Classical Learning.* Cambridge: Cambridge University Press.

Toulmin, Stephen E. 1958. *The Uses of Argument.* Cambridge: Cambridge University Press.

Trevett, J. C. 1996. "Aristotle's Knowledge of Athenian Oratory." *Classical Quarterly* 46:371–79.

Twitchell, James B. 1996. *Adcult USA: The Triumph of Advertising in American Culture.* New York: Columbia University Press.

Usher, Stephen. 1999. *Greek Oratory: Tradition and Originality.* Oxford: Oxford University Press.

Vernant, Jean-Pierre. 1983. *Myth and Thought among the Greeks.* London: Routledge.

Vickers, Brian. 1988. *In Defence of Rhetoric.* Oxford: Clarendon.

Vitanza, Victor. 1997. *Negation, Subjectivity, and the History of Rhetoric.* Albany: State University of New York.

Walker, Jeffrey. 1994. "The Body of Persuasion: A Theory of Enthymeme." *College English* 56:46–65.

———. 2000. *Rhetoric and Poetics in Antiquity.* Oxford: Oxford University Press.

Walzer, Arthur E. 2000. "Aristotle on Speaking 'Outside the Subject': The Special Topics and Rhetorical Forums." In Gross and Walzer, *Rereading Aristotle's Rhetoric,* 38–54.

Washburn, Katharine, and John Thornton, eds. 1996. *Dumbing Down: Essays on the Stripmining of American Culture.* New York: Norton.

Welch, Kathleen. 1990. *The Contemporary Reception of Classical Rhetoric: Appropriations of Ancient Discourse.* Hillsdale, N.J.: L. Erlbaum.

White, Eric Charles. 1987. *Kaironomia: On the Will-to-Invent.* Ithaca, N.Y.: Cornell University Press.

Wilcox, Stanley. 1943. "Isocrates' Genera of Prose." *American Journal of Philology* 64:427–31.

Wolf, Hieronymus. 1570. *Isocratis Scripta.* 2 vols. Edited by Hieronymous Wolf. Basel: Oporini.

Wood, Ellen Neiskins. 1996. "Demos Versus 'We the People': Freedom and Democracy Ancient and Modern." In Ober and Hedrick, *Dēmokratia,* 121–37.

Worthington, Ian. 1996a. "Greek Oratory and the Oral/Literate Division." In Worthington, *Voice into Text,* 165–77.

———, ed. 1996b. *Voice into Text: Orality and Literacy in Ancient Greece.* Leiden: E. J. Brill.

Yunis, Harvey. 1996. *Taming Democracy: Models of Political Rhetoric in Classical Athens.* Ithaca, N.Y.: Cornell University Press.

INDEX

Academy (Plato), 1, 2, 31, 35, 38, 39, 41, 43, 101, 131
Achilles, 12, 22, 35
acting: and speaking, 31
acting well (*eu prattein*), 41
activity (*energeia*), 113
actors, 34
actuality (*energeia*), 113
advantage (*pleonexia*), 43
advertising, 84, 132, 135
Aeschines, 17
Aeschylus, 92, 111, 125
Against the Sophists (Isocrates), 18, 41, 71
Agamemnon, 22
agency, 5, 109–12; human, 3, 5, 11, 16, 30, 31, 50; political, 29, 134
aido (respect), 88
akolasia (lack of restraint), 91
akroatēs (hearer), 59
alētheia (truth), 11–16, 16–22, 27, 110
Althusser, Louis, 85–86, 87, 90
amplification (*auxēsis*), 63, 65
anaisthesia (insensitivity), 91
Anaxagoras, 14
animals, 95, 97, 98, 113
anoia (senselessness), 91
Antidosis (Isocrates), 19, 21, 39–46, 78, 82, 87, 126, 129, 134
Antigone (Sophocles), 63
apodeixis (demonstration), 65, 79
Apology (Plato), 39
appearances (*phainomena*), 23, 24
apragmones (quietists), 16–17
Archidamus (Isocrates), 147n. 23

Areopagiticus (Isocrates), 91–95
aretē (virtue), 98–100, 104–7, 116–18, 128, 131, 132; and democracy, 130
aristocracy, 94, 98, 100, 111, 116, 131
Aristophanes, 82, 110, 139n. 13
"The Aristotelian Tradition in Ancient Rhetoric" (Solmsen), 2, 60
Aristotle's Rhetoric: An Art of Character (Garver), 113–14, 120, 133
The Art of Rhetoric (Aristotle), 1–2, 7, 26–29, 43, 44, 57–65, 70, 99, 112–19, 124, 133, 140n. 1, 143n. 5, 145n. 5; audience in, 8, 55, 81, 95, 101–7; education in, 48; Isocrates in, 65–66, 78–79; *mimēsis* in, 31–32, 47, 50; performance in, 80–81; style in, 34, 55
Aspasia, 75
Athens, 19, 60–61, 82, 111, 117, 118, 128; in *Areopagiticus,* 91–95; courts, 39, 44; democracy in, 7, 16–17, 22, 76, 77, 109–13, 121–22, 125, 130, 131, 134; in *Panegyricus,* 73–77; rhetoric in, 101
audience, 3, 13, 56, 70, 83–84, 108, 128–29, 129, 133; Aristotle and, 7, 27–29, 47, 49, 55, 58–60, 62–64, 66, 95–107, 99, 100–102, 116, 119, 133; as community, 87; corrupting influence of, 80; democratic, 99, 100–101, 131; emotion and, 115; Gorgias and, 15; identity and, 81, 87, 90, 125; Isocrates and, 2, 17, 19–21, 42, 74, 78, 87, 89, 91, 92–93, 95, 111, 127; participation, 83; *peithō*

164 INDEX

and, 82; performance and, 68; Plato and, 31, 33, 35–38, 87; as political agents, 90; rhetorical, 8, 81; rhetoric and, 68
Auerbach, Eric, 36–37
autarkeia (self-sufficiency), 97, 106, 116
authority, 130, 131
auxēsis (amplification), 63, 65

Bakhtin, Mikhail, 8, 58, 69–70, 133
Bakker, Egbert, 12, 13
barbarians, 125
Bauman, Richard, 68
Beiner, Ronald, 120–21
bia (force), 15, 109–12, 122, 126, 129
bios apolaustikos (life of enjoyment), 116
bios politikos (political life), 116
bios theoretikos (life of contemplation), 116
Birds (Aristophanes), 139n. 13
Bitzer, Lloyd, 102, 105
Brunschwig, Jacques, 28, 66
Burke, Kenneth, 8, 81, 83–84, 85, 108, 129, 135
Butler, Judith, 85–86

Callicles, 43
capacity (*dunamis*), 99, 107, 109, 122, 126; and instrumentality, 112–21
Capra, Frank, 111, 145n. 2
Cassandra, 12, 13
Categories (Aristotle), 26
catharsis, 52, 53
character (*ēthos*), 103, 132; Aristotle and, 43, 52–55, 66, 105, 114, 118; Isocrates and, 39, 45, 81, 95; Plato and, 44
Chroust, Anton-Hermann, 1
Cicero, 1, 84
citizenship, 94, 97, 100, 116, 127–28, 146n. 13
city, 91, 92

city-state (*polis*), 93, 96–100, 106
civilization, 126
classification: in Aristotle, 57, 61–62, 64, 66, 81
Cleisthenes, 128
Cleon, 142n. 4
Cmiel, Kenneth, 123
colorful (*poikilos*), 34, 44
commercialism, 132
community, 83, 90, 91, 97, 100, 105–6; audience as, 87; democratic, 136; language and, 126; political, 128, 134
community (*koinonia*), 88
The Constitution of the Athenians (Aristotle), 112–13, 146n. 13
constitution (*politeia*), 93, 94, 96, 98–101, 115, 116, 118, 126
consubstantiality, 84, 85, 106, 129
consumers, 132, 134, 136
contemplation, 31, 46, 49, 50, 52, 80, 90–91, 97, 116, 131
context, 68, 124, 127, 130, 136; Aristotle and, 8, 24–25, 26–28, 64, 66; cultural, 80, 135; discourse and, 61; of education, 134; Isocrates and, 121
Cope, Edward, 102
corrupt form (*parekbasis*), 118
corruptness (*mochthēria*), 115
cosmology, 13
courts, 39, 44, 103
Ctesippus, 72
cultural diversity, 135
culture, 4, 9, 80, 134; Aristotle and, 57, 112; democratic, 131; Isocrates and, 3, 87, 124; mass, 132, 135, 136; oral, 14, 16, 19, 27, 32, 34, 38; political, 81, 130, 131; public, 132, 133, 136; and race, 125
culture (*paideia*), 8, 118–19

deliberative (*symbouletikon*) genre, 58–66, 102, 133. *See also* rhetorical genres

Demeter, 76
democracy, 75, 102, 145n. 2; American, 111; Anglo-American, 123; Aristotle and, 8, 81, 99–102, 115–18, 121; Athenian, 7, 16–17, 72, 76, 77, 109–13, 121–22, 125, 130, 131, 134; discourse in, 126; Isocrates and, 40, 44, 91–95, 98, 121–23, 127–29; Plato and, 75, 76; speech and, 112; and virtue, 130
Democratic Eloquence (Cmiel), 123
Democritus, 35
dēmokratia (democracy), 117–18
Demonicus, 72–73
demonstration (*apodeixis*), 65, 79
demonstrative (*epideiktikon*) genre, 58–66. *See also* epideictic genre; rhetorical genres
Demosthenes, 17
Depew, David J., 49, 95, 96–97
Detienne, Marcel, 12–15
dianoia (thought), 52, 54, 55
diction (*lexis*), 52, 54, 55
dignified (*onkōdēs*), 44
dikaion (just), 59, 60
dikanikon (judicial, or forensic genre), 58–66, 102. *See also* rhetorical genres
dikē (justice), 88
Diodotus, 142n. 4
Dionysius, 79
discourse, 29, 30, 31, 69, 83, 85, 130, 135; Aristotle and, 57, 62, 64, 112, 113, 116–18, 121; audience and, 107; civic, 98, 99, 120, 122, 126, 133; Gorgias and, 112; Isocrates and, 11, 21, 43–44, 58, 71, 74, 78, 87, 89, 125–26, 127, 128, 134; and power, 108, 110; rhetorical, 99, 118; as versions of rhetoric, 80; and writing, 10, 20. *See also logos politikos* (political discourse)
disunity, 85

doxa (opinion), 8, 15, 40, 41, 110, 111–12, 119
doxa (reputation), 21, 22, 26, 80, 128
drama, 6, 7, 82, 124; Aristotle and, 31; Isocrates and, 93, 95; social, 69; tragic, 52, 57, 66, 80, 119
dunamis (capacity, or power), 99, 107, 109, 122, 126; and instrumentality, 112–21
dunastēs (ruler), 14–15, 109, 110, 129

Eagleton, Terry, 108
education (*paideia*), 4, 5, 7, 9, 36, 44–46, 51, 110, 119; Aristotle and, 46–49, 118; civic, 6–7, 31, 80, 118, 130; democratic, 9, 130–36; discursive (*logōn paideia*), 4, 41, 71, 78, 94, 114, 141n. 9; European, 122, 123; Homeric, 34, 35, 38; Isocrates and, 18, 19, 21, 30, 39–43, 56, 71, 107, 123, 133; liberal, 4; moral, 130; Plato and, 33, 39, 40, 116; poetic, 33, 43; and writing, 141n. 4. *See also mousikē* (poetic education)
eikota (probabilities), 61
Elements of Style (Strunk and White), 123
eleutheria (freedom), 111, 117, 125
emotions (*pathai*), 28–29, 50, 53–54, 55, 65, 66, 102, 103, 104–5, 115
Empedocles, 25
Encomium of Helen (Gorgias), 14–15, 20, 36, 67, 110, 111–12, 113, 139n. 16
end (*telos*), 58, 59, 61, 63
endoxa (received opinions), 6, 130; Aristotle and, 23–30
energeia (actuality, activity), 113
enthymeme, 8, 26, 27, 44, 83, 99, 101–5
epea (words), 68, 69, 70, 77–78; *epea pteroenta* (winged words), 69
epics, 14, 111

epideictic genre, 58–66, 73, 75, 119, 126, 133, 144n. 22. *See also* rhetorical genres
epideiktikon (demonstrative genre), 58–66. *See also* epideictic genre; rhetorical genres
epistēmē (scientific knowledge), 5–6, 114; *tōn logōn epistēmē* (science of speech), 18
epitaphios logos (funeral oration), 75, 86, 111
epos, 21, 68–69, 70, 77–78
ergon (function), 53, 54, 61
eros, 146n. 5
ethics, 24, 27, 98, 107, 120, 128, 132, 133
ethismos (habituation), 49
ēthos (character), 103, 132; Aristotle and, 43, 52–55, 66, 105, 114, 118; Isocrates and, 39, 45, 81, 95; Plato and, 44
eudaimonia (good life), 97, 106
Eudemian Ethics (Aristotle), 106
eugeneia (nobility of birth), 94
eu legein (speaking well), 19, 41, 43
eu prattein (acting well), 41
Euripides, 25, 47
Evagoras (Isocrates), 19–20, 20

Farrell, Thomas B., 105–6, 107, 127, 133
Feast of the Panathenaia, 22
Finley, M. I., 123, 124
flattery, 84, 128
forensic (*dikanikon*) genre, 58–66, 102, 103. *See also* rhetorical genres
formalism, 144n. 17
formalists, 70, 79
freedom (*eleutheria*), 111, 117, 125
friendship (*philia*), 81, 106, 107, 133
function (*ergon*), 53, 54, 61
funeral oration (*epitaphios logos*), 75, 86, 111

Gaines, Robert, 2, 79
Gaisford, Dean, 123
Garver, Eugene, 113–14, 118, 119, 120, 121, 133
genres. *See* rhetorical genres
Glaucon, 33, 34
good life (*eudaimonia*), 97, 106
Gorgias, 29, 47, 107, 109, 122, 126, 129, 138n. 8, 142n. 16. See also *Encomium of Helen* (Gorgias)
Gorgias (Plato), 17, 40–41, 43, 145n. 6
grammatikē, 45
Greek alphabet, 10
Greek culture, 6, 11–12, 30, 66–70, 76
Greek Enlightenment, 10
Greek gods, 11
Grimaldi, William, 27, 102–3
gumnastikē, 45, 47
gymnastics, 40, 45; mental, 42, 134

Habermas, Jürgen, 120
habituation (*ethismos*), 49
Halliwell, Stephen, 54
Halverson, John, 10
Havelock, Eric, 10, 13, 25, 32–38
hearer (*akroatēs*), 59
hēgemōn (leader), 87–95, 109; *tōn logōn hēgemōn* (leader of words), 22
hēgemonia (leadership), 73–74
hegemony, 121–29
Heilbrunn, Gunter, 17
Hellas, 44, 111
Hellenes, 125
Heraclitus, 13, 14
"The Heritage of Isocrates" (Finley), 123
Hermes, 12
Herodotus, 19, 63, 111, 125
Hesiod, 13, 25, 45
Hippocrates, 114
Histories (Thucydides), 110

Homer, 2, 10, 34, 35, 36, 38, 45, 68–69, 70; Aristotle and, 63; Isocrates and, 18, 19, 20, 21–22, 39, 77–78, 125
Homeric Hymn to Demeter, 76
homonoia (unity), 22
honorable conduct, 18
household (*oikos*), 93, 96, 97, 98
huparchonta pithana (existing means of persuasion), 82–83
"Hymn to Logos" (Isocrates), 8, 21, 82, 87, 88, 90, 91, 95, 126, 127, 129, 145n. 3

iatreumata (remedies), 104
identification, 8, 96, 97, 127; and *hēgemōn,* 87–95; and persuasion, 5, 80–107
identity, 5, 30, 37, 57; and *alētheia* (truth), 16–22; Aristotle and, 103, 117, 119; audience, 81, 87, 90, 125; citizen, 47; civic, 16, 31, 57, 119, 121, 130; constructed, 22; democratic, 118; Greek, 125; Isocrates and, 6, 29, 80, 90, 91, 94, 122, 125, 127–28, 134; language and, 126; and literacy, 16–22; of performer, 21–22; Plato and, 33, 87; political, 9, 11, 16, 39, 56, 116, 122, 128, 130, 132; and values, 135
ideology, 85–86
Iliad (Homer), 12, 22, 68
imitation, 70, 76; Aristotle and, 50, 51, 119; Isocrates and, 57, 78, 80; Plato and, 32–36
insensitivity (*anaisthesia*), 91
instrumentality, 112–21
interpellation, 85–86, 87, 90, 104
intertextuality, 21
Ion (Plato), 37, 38
ironist, 108–9, 135

Jaeger, Werner, 124–25
Jameson, Frederic, 136

Johansen, Thomas K., 27
judge (*kritēs*), 58, 61, 81, 104, 107
judicial (*dikanikon*) genre, 58–66, 102. *See also* rhetorical genres
jurors, 103, 104
justice, 60–61
justice (*dikē*), 88

kairos (opportune moment), 7, 8; defined, 67; and discursive knowledge, 71–79; and genre, 5, 57–78; and Isocrates, 71–79; and speech genres, 66–70
kalokagathia (nobleness), 42–43, 94
kanon (measuring instrument), 102
Kennedy, George, 101
knowledge, 56; and Aristotle, 4, 26–27, 42, 62, 131; cultural, 7, 9, 15, 16, 20, 135; discursive, 58, 70, 71–79, 81; extrarhetorical, 5–6, 58–66; hierarchy of, 29, 42; Isocrates and, 2, 18, 40, 71–72, 72; Plato and, 33, 34, 37, 38; political, 62, 143n. 9; rhetorical, 8; social, 57, 58, 105. *See also* scientific knowledge (*epistēmē*)
"Knowledge for What?" (Finley), 123
koinonia (community), 88
koinonia (partnership), 96, 100
kritēs (judge), 58, 61, 81, 104, 107

lack of restraint (*akolasia*), 91
language, 29–30, 70, 122, 123, 126, 144n. 16; Aristotle and, 63; and identification, 84; and power, 57, 85; and rhetoric, 83; social function of, 12, 14
language of praise (*logos epainos*), 63, 64
leader (*hēgemōn*), 87–95; leader of words (*tōn logōn hēgemōn*), 22
leadership (*hēgemonia*), 73–74
learning: tragic, 50, 52, 54

168 INDEX

learning (*mathēsis*), 35–36, 131, 140n. 1; Aristotle and, 48, 49, 50, 51, 54, 119; Isocrates and, 45, 72
legein (to speak), 114
legislation, 93–94, 115, 118
leisure, 46, 47, 49, 50, 97, 100, 117
lexis (style): Aristotle and, 28, 34, 47, 52, 54, 55, 66, 115; Plato and, 33, 36, 38, 44
"The Linguistic Task of the Presocratics" (Havelock), 6
literacy, 31, 38; and *alētheia* (truth), 16–22; and identity, 16–22; and orality, 5, 6, 10–30
The Literate Revolution in Greece (Havelock), 6
logography, 19, 42, 132
logōn paideia (discursive education), 4, 41, 71, 78, 94, 114, 141n. 9
logos and power: as title of book, 3, 109
logos epainos (language of praise), 64
logos politikos (political discourse), 3, 16, 19, 20, 44, 58, 62, 90, 121, 126, 131, 134, 140n. 21
Longinus, 83
Loraux, Nicole, 111
Lyceum (Aristotle), 1, 2, 4, 26, 78
Lysimachus, 41–42
Lysis, 72
Lysistrata, 82

marketing, 147n. 1
Martin, Richard, 12, 21, 68–69
Marxism, 87
mass media, 132
mathēsis (learning), 35–36, 131, 141n. 1; Aristotle and, 48, 49, 50, 51, 54, 119; Isocrates and, 45, 72
McGee, Michael, 125
Mead, G. H., 133
measuring instrument (*kanon*), 102
medicine, 101, 103

melopoiia (song making), 52, 54
Melos, 60
memorization, 35–36, 40, 41
Menexenus (Plato), 35, 63–64, 75–76
Meno (Plato), 44
mental gymnastics, 42, 134
metaphysics, 26
Metaphysics (Aristotle), 23, 25
mimēsis (imitation, representation), 6–7, 107, 132; in Aristotle, 31–32, 46–56, 57; in Homer, 22; in Isocrates, 39–46, 47, 76, 91; and performance, 56; in Plato, 20–21, 31, 32–38, 87
mochthēria (corruptness), 115
monarchy, 100, 127, 129
morality, 104–5, 119
Morgan, Kathryn, 127
mousikē (poetic education), 33, 40; Aristotle and, 47, 49, 119; Isocrates and, 41, 45, 46; Plato and, 49
Muses, 82
music: Aristotle and, 48–49, 119
muthos (plot), 11, 21, 52–53, 56, 68–69, 139n. 14
myth, 11, 13, 14, 16, 23, 24
Mytilene, 142n. 4

Nagy, Gregory, 22
nationalism, 125
Nazis, 84, 124, 125, 145n. 2
necessary signs (*tekmēria*), 61
Negation, Subjectivity, and the History of Rhetoric (Vitanza), 122
New Rhetoric (Perelman and Olbrechts-Tyteca), 102
Nicocles, 128, 145n. 4
Nicocles (Isocrates), 87–89, 92, 94, 95, 127–29, 128, 129
Nicomachean Ethics (Aristotle), 24, 113, 116, 118, 143n. 5
nobility of birth (*eugeneia*), 94
nobleness (*kalokagathia*), 42–43, 94

Norlin, George, 17–18, 74
Norms of Rhetorical Culture (Farrell), 106, 133
Nussbaum, Martha, 24, 139n. 18, 19

Ober, Josiah, 92, 94, 111–12, 128–29, 131
Odyssey (Homer), 22, 36–37
oikos (household), 93, 97, 98
Olbrechts-Tyteca, L., 102
oligarchy, 100, 116, 123, 125, 129
Ong, Walter, 6
On Interpretation (Aristotle), 140n. 25
onkōdēs (dignified), 44
On the Peace (Isocrates), 17, 18, 21, 147n. 23
opinion (*doxa*), 8, 15, 40, 41, 110, 111–12, 119
opsis (spectacle, spectacular effect), 52, 54, 55
oralistic impulse, 13
orality, 80; and literacy, 5, 6, 10–30
oral tradition, 6, 10, 14, 22
oratory, 6, 56, 57, 94, 128; Aristotle and, 7, 66; classification of, 60; forensic, 63, 103; Isocrates and, 2, 16, 44–45, 58, 74, 93, 130; judicial, 102; poetic style of, 29; and poetry, 57

paideia (culture), 8, 118–19
paideia (education). *See* education (*paideia*)
Paideia (Jaeger), 124
paidia (play), 47
paignion (plaything), 15, 112
Panathenaicus (Isocrates), 22, 78, 147n. 23
Panegyricus (Isocrates), 21, 73–76, 77–78
pan-Hellenism, 8, 81, 124, 125
parekbasis (corrupt form), 118
Parmenides, 14

partnership (*koinonia*), 96, 100
pathos, 103, 105
paying court (*therapeia*), 128–29
Peace of Antalkidas, 73, 75
Peithō (goddess), 82
peithō (persuasion), 82–87, 146n. 5
Peloponnesian War, 60, 74, 75, 77, 91, 122
Perelman, Chaim, 102
performance, 5, 10, 21, 57, 58, 80, 87; Aristotle and, 30, 48, 119, 130, 133; civic, 5, 49, 123; defined, 68; epic, 6, 35; Gorgias and, 14; Homer and, 69; Isocrates and, 16, 19, 22, 90; and *mimēsis,* 56; oral, 16, 17, 20; Plato and, 33; poetic, 13, 17, 29; political, 90, 121–29, 133, 135–36; rhetorical, 7, 64, 65, 114, 120, 129
performance culture, 31
performance skills, 119
Pericles, 75, 114, 128, 146n. 13
Persae (Aeschylus), 92, 111, 125
Persian Wars, 20, 77, 92, 111
persuasion, 2, 23–30, 120, 132; Aristotle and, 8, 62, 66, 71, 113–14, 118, 121, 131; Gorgias and, 14–16, 110, 112; and identification, 5, 80–107
persuasive euphony, 13
Peters, John Durham, 95
Phaedrus (Plato)*,* 35, 38, 141n. 9
phainomena (appearances), 23, 24
pharmakon, 142n. 16
philēkoia (love of listening), 70, 72
philia (friendship), 81, 106, 107, 133
Philoctetes, 1
philosophia, 3, 14, 31, 40, 42–46, 50, 56, 71, 141n. 10
philosophy, 1, 5, 14, 39–43, 57, 87–88, 134
phronein (prudential thinking), 19, 43, 114
phronēsis (practical rationality), 99, 106, 107, 114, 120

phronēsis (practical wisdom), 6, 104, 107, 116, 121, 130, 131, 143n. 5
pisteis (proofs), 27, 28, 55, 102–3, 121
Plato, 5, 16, 17, 41–42, 44, 47, 60, 77, 124, 131, 139n. 16, 145n. 6; Aristotle and, 60, 95–96, 106, 116; democracy and, 75; emotions and, 28; ethics and, 24, 128; flattery and, 84; identity and, 57; and *mimēsis,* 31, 32–38; *mousikē* and, 49; orality and, 20; *pharmakon* and, 142n. 16; *philēkoia* and, 72; and poetry, 7, 31, 32, 36, 45, 50, 55, 56, 80, 86, 138n. 6; and rhetoric, 4, 31, 89, 286–87
play (*paidia*), 47
plaything (*paignion*), 15, 112
pleonexia (advantage), 43
plot (*muthos*), 52–53, 54, 55, 80
poetics: and rhetoric, 5, 6, 31–56. *See also* poetry
Poetics (Aristotle), 31–32, 47, 50, 52, 53–54, 55, 57, 66, 101, 119, 141n. 5
poetry, 12, 19, 51–52, 66, 82, 95, 124; and Aristotle, 24, 55, 56, 80, 119; and Gorgias, 14, 67; and Isocrates, 50; and oratory, 57; and Plato, 7, 55, 56, 75, 80, 86–87, 138n. 6; and rhetoric, 80. *See also* poetics
poikilos (colorful), 34, 44
polis (city-state), 93, 96–100, 106
politeia (constitution), 93, 94, 96, 98–101, 115, 116, 118, 126
politeia (government), 44
politeia (polity), 92
political aesthetics, 122, 125
politics, 26, 50, 57, 62, 70, 84, 98, 107, 111, 117, 120, 126
Politics (Aristotle), 50, 98, 101, 125, 126; community in, 88, 100; democracy and, 81, 118; education and, 48, 53–54, 119; emotions and, 53–54; *endoxa* in, 25–26; logos and, 95–96; 99; performance and, 31, 47, 119; virtue in, 98, 104, 116–17
Poulakos, Takis, 19, 20, 71–72, 88, 89–90, 91, 111, 127–28
power: defined, 85
power and logos: as title of book, 3, 108
practical rationality (*phronēsis*), 99, 106, 107, 114, 120
practical wisdom (*phronēsis*), 6, 104, 107, 116, 121, 130, 131, 143n. 5
Preface to Plato (Havelock), 6
Presocratics, 13, 14, 15, 24
Principle of Non-Contradiction, 24
probabilities (*eikota*), 61
Prodicus, 138n. 8
proofs (*pisteis*), 27, 28, 55, 102–3, 121
propositions (*protaseis*), 61
Protagoras, 109
Protagoras (Plato), 88, 114, 119
protaseis (propositions), 61
Proteus, 37
prudential thinking (*phronein*), 19, 43, 114
psuchē (soul), 53, 93

quietists (*apragmones*), 16–17
Quintilian, 143n. 10

rationalism, 111
rationality, 11, 13, 23, 30, 51, 98, 100, 104, 105, 115, 134; deliberative, 120; practical, 95, 99, 106, 107, 114, 120; technical, 95
reality, 14, 15, 34
reason, 138n. 10
reasoning, 83
reflection, 11–16
relativism, 90
religious ritual, 12
remedies (*iatreumata*), 104
representation, 48, 51, 52, 56; *mimēsis* as, 31–32, 34, 38, 47, 52–53, 54, 55

Republic (Plato), 37, 39, 72, 117, 139n. 16, 145n. 6; poetry in, 32, 44, 49, 55; poets in, 17, 33, 34
reputation (*doxa*), 21, 22, 26, 80, 128
respect (*aido*), 88
rhapsodes (*rhapsodoi*), 8, 13, 20, 21, 22, 34, 35, 37, 86, 125, 144n. 15
rhetoric, 1, 4–6, 10, 57, 110, 118–20; Aristotle and, 23, 26–27, 28–30, 50, 57, 61, 66, 81, 82, 99, 101, 106, 107, 115–16, 132; audience and, 56, 105; as a civic art, 113–14; discourse as versions of, 80; in education and culture, 9; and ethics, 115, 133; Isocrates and, 17, 19, 78, 126; and language, 83; Plato and, 86–87; and poetics, 5, 31–56; and poetry, 80; and politics, 115–16
rhetorical genres, 2, 3, 7–8, 57, 80–81, 99, 104, 120; and *kairos*, 5, 57–78
rhetorical proofs, 104–5
rhetorical theory, 1–2, 4, 10–11, 142n. 2
rhētorikē, 3, 89, 141n. 10
Robb, Kevin, 13
role differentiation, 95–107
Rorty, Richard, 9, 108–9
ruler (*dunastēs*), 14–15, 109, 110, 129

Sardanapallus, 116
science of speech (*tōn logōn epistēmē*), 18
scientific knowledge (*epistēmē*), 5–6, 114
Segal, Charles, 15
self-governance, 94
self-sufficiency (*autarkeia*), 97, 106, 116
self-understanding, 81, 89–90, 91, 94, 95, 117
sēmeia (signs), 61
senselessness (*anoia*), 91
signs (*sēmeia*), 61
Sirens, 82

social change: and social permanence, 5, 9, 108–29
social order, 85, 110, 111, 126
social permanence: and social change, 5, 9, 108–29
social roles, 95, 97, 99, 104, 116
social theory, 85–87
Socrates, 28, 33, 34, 35, 37, 39–40, 63–64, 72, 75, 76, 114
Socratics, 17, 18
Solmsen, Friedrich, 2, 60, 79
Solon, 94, 128
song making (*melopoiia*), 52, 54
Sophist (Plato), 28
sophistry, 14, 75
Sophists, 14, 16, 34, 71, 73, 88, 109–10, 111, 114, 118, 121, 122, 140n. 1
Sophocles, 25
soul (*psuchē*), 53, 93
sovereignty, 100, 118
Sparta, 60, 77, 91, 118
speaking: and acting, 31
speaking well (*eu legein*), 19, 41, 43, 114
spectacular effect (*opsis*), 52, 54, 55
spectator (*theōros*), 58, 61, 143n. 5
speech, 8, 11–15, 18, 20–22, 30, 41, 47, 57, 59, 62, 68, 69, 78–79, 95–97, 110, 129, 142n. 16; Aristotle and, 58; and democracy, 112; Isocrates and, 42, 72–73, 75, 82, 88–89, 126; Peithō and, 82; as social control, 15; social impact of, 16
speech-acts, 59–60, 62, 68, 69
speech-act theory, 120, 142n. 2, 143n. 13
speeches, 29, 43, 44, 45, 60, 69; Aristotle and, 63, 66
speech genres, 8, 58, 78, 81, 136; Isocrates and, 58; and *kairos,* 66–70
Steiner, Deborah, 16–17
style (*lexis*): Aristotle and, 28, 34, 47, 52, 54, 55, 66, 115; Plato and, 33, 36, 38, 44

subject positions, 132, 134
sycophants, 19, 42
symbouletikon (deliberative genre), 58–66, 102, 103. *See also* rhetorical genres
Symposium (Plato), 38

technē (productive art), 2, 3, 7, 26, 27, 57, 79, 101–2, 113–14, 130, 132, 143n. 5; Isocrates and, 19, 79; *kairos* and, 34; *logos* and, 95; *paideia* and, 119; *phronēsis* and, 121; style and, 34; *tetagmenē*, 18, 79
technē rhētorikē, 30, 62, 112, 119
tekmēria (necessary signs), 61
telos (end), 58, 59, 61, 63
Thelxiepeia, 82
Thelxinoe, 82
Themistocles, 128
"Theogony" (Hesiod), 13
theōros (spectator), 58, 61, 143n. 5
therapeia (paying court), 128–29
Third Reich, 122, 124
thought (*dianoia*), 52, 54, 55
Thucydides, 19, 60–61, 110, 111, 117
Timotheus, 128
To Demonicus (Isocrates), 72, 73
To Nicocles (Isocrates), 19, 21
Too, Yun Lee, 16, 20, 131
To Philip (Isocrates), 17
Topics (Aristotle), 23, 27

topoi, 58, 62, 74, 143n. 10
Toulmin, Stephen, 102
tragedy, 52–55, 57, 87–88, 126
Trojans, 20
Trojan War, 125
truth (*alētheia*), 11–16, 16–22, 27, 110
Turner, Victor, 69
tyranny, 100, 127, 129
"The Tyranny of the Audience in Plato and Isocrates" (Morgan), 128

unity (*homonoia*), 22
Use and Abuse of History (Finley), 123
Uses of Argument (Toulmin), 102

values: and identity, 135
virtue (*aretē*), 98–100, 104–7, 116–18, 128, 131, 132; and democracy, 130
Vitanza, Victor, 122, 124–25

Walzer, Arthur, 62
White, Eric, 67–68
Why We Fight (Capra), 111, 145n. 2
wisdom, 23, 41, 70, 72; practical, 6, 104, 107, 116, 121, 130, 131, 143n. 5
words, 12, 14
writing, 6, 10, 14, 15, 38, 108, 142n. 16; Isocrates and, 16, 19–22, 80, 127

Xenophanes, 14
Xerxes, 92, 125

www.ingramcontent.com/pod-product-compliance
Lightning Source LLC
Chambersburg PA
CBHW032046150426
43194CB00006B/434